Endorsements

One of the best accident analysis books I have read. The authors' clinical expertise is effectively blended with an understanding of the psychological and organizational factors that create conditions for adverse events. Their first-hand experiences of the aftermath create a powerful account of the cultural shift that was achieved. Highly recommended reading for those striving to improve patient safety.

Rhona Flin PhD FBPsS FRSE, Professor of Industrial Psychology
Aberdeen Business School,
Robert Gordon University, Aberdeen

Jan Davies, Carmella Steinke & Ward Flemons describe the many facets of a tragedy and use it to tell the story of patient safety and illuminate the role that Just Culture plays in keeping patients safe and responding humanely when harm occurs. Stories, science and practice are seamlessly interwoven in a fascinating narrative.

Charles Vincent PhD, Professor of Psychology,
University of Oxford

One of the strengths of this book is to report clinical dramas in all their human dimension and to speak of a global story in which we understand the deep distress of all parties – patients, families, professionals and institutions. The book delivers to us, with the art of speaking simply of complex things, a series of keys to cognitive functioning. These are just as much the engine of success in most cases, thanks to brilliant heuristics, as they are the rare source of dramas. Suddenly, the question of blame, learning culture, transparency and saying sorry can be reread differently, not so as to evade the problem, but to remain coherent and useful for all parties.

René Amalberti MD PhD, Directeur & Professeur de Médecine
FONCSI, Toulouse, France

In this excellent book, the authors have made brilliant use of the stories of two patients to link everything together, and to illustrate the ground-breaking work done in Calgary. What a model for others to follow!

Dr. Rod Westhorpe OAM FRCA FANZCA, Past President,
Australian Society of Anaesthetists
Founding and Life Member,
Australian Patient Safety Foundation, Melbourne, Australia

Fatal Solution

Fatal Solution
How a Healthcare System Used
Tragedy to Transform Itself and
Redefine Just Culture

Jan M. Davies MSc MD FRCPC FRAeS,
Carmella Steinke RRT MPA, and
W. Ward Flemons MD FRCPC

Routledge
Taylor & Francis Group

A PRODUCTIVITY PRESS BOOK

First published 2022
by Routledge
605 Third Avenue, New York, NY 10158

and by Routledge
2 Park Square, Milton Park, Abingdon, Oxon, OX14 4RN

Routledge is an imprint of the Taylor & Francis Group, an informa business

ISBN: 9781032028132 (hbk)
ISBN: 9781032028088 (pbk)
ISBN: 9781003185307 (ebk)

DOI: 10.4324/9781003185307

Typeset in Garamond
by codeMantra

Dedication

This book is dedicated to the two families at the center of this tragedy and to all patients, their families and friends, who have been harmed in the course of receiving healthcare. We also dedicate this book to healthcare providers and leaders who have suffered psychological harm from their involvement in an event in which a patient was harmed.

Epigram

Systems awareness and systems design are important for health professionals, but are not enough. They are enabling mechanisms only. It is the ethical dimension of individuals that is essential to a system's success. Ultimately, the secret of quality is love.

Avedis Donabedian (1919–2000)

Donabedian A. 2001. Interview: A founder of Quality Assessment encounters a troubled system firsthand. *Fitzhugh Mullan Health Affairs* 2001; 20:1137–141. doi:10.1377/hlthaff.20.1.137.

Contents

Foreword

Medicine advances on the analysis of well-documented errors. Errors do not occur in isolation but have traceable systemic origins. We know that we cannot eliminate error entirely – it is deeply rooted in the human condition. We cannot change the human condition, but we can change the conditions under which health carers work. That means changing the culture of medical education and health care delivery. It also means removing known error traps and encouraging a climate of learning. Each investigated event in which a patient is harmed is an opportunity to improve our understanding and practice.

This excellent book provides just such an opportunity. A sequence of events in Calgary was set in motion when a box of potassium chloride bottles was mistaken for a similarly appearing box of sodium chloride. Once it was acknowledged that the chemical mix-up was not intentional and no violations had been made, the concept that errors should not be punished was followed. Safety was recognized as the priority of the Calgary Health Region. Comprehensive and significant changes were recommended and implemented.

I regard this book as essential reading for all health care professionals. I commend it most strongly because it brings the problem of human fallibility to a wider audience that needs to know and understand. I am delighted to be able to acknowledge my appreciation of the work of Jan Davies and her colleagues, Carm Steinke and Ward Flemons.

James Reason CBE PhD FRA FRAeS,
Emeritus Professor of Psychology, The University of Manchester

Acknowledgments

We are grateful to all those who shared their memories with us as we put together the story of what happened in the former Calgary Health Region in 2004 and from then into 2008. Any errors, either of omission or commission, in the telling of the story are ours alone. We thank the following individuals for their interviews and written contributions, as well as their personal documents from those years: Rob Abernethy MD FRCPC (Emergency Medicine), Paul J E Boiteau MD FRCPC, Jewel Buksa MBA, Kelley Charlebois, Jack Davis MSc, Chris Eagle MD MBA FRCPC, Greg Eberhart BSc Pharm, Sue Gudmundson BN MN, Nancy Guebert BScN, MCEd, Bob Holmes, Bruce MacLeod BSc MD FRCPC, Gary G Mar QC, Bruce McKenzie BSP, Richard Musto MD FRCPC, Sharon Nettleton BA MA, Deb Prowse QC, Joanne Stalinski MSW MBA, Nancy Thornton RN MScN CNN(C), Howard Waldner MBA CHE ICD.D, Tracy Wasylak BN MSc CHE, and Arlene Weidner BScN MSc (CHE).

Two other individuals should also be acknowledged. Bob Johnston MDCM CCFP (EM) and Steve Long BSc (Pharm) MBA were important and inspiring leaders in this story and others, and we owe both our thanks.

This book took a team to write it, and similarly, a team to produce it. We thank our Editor, Kristine Rynne Mednansky, Senior Editor Business Improvement – Healthcare Management. Taylor & Francis Group, LLC for her friendly and knowledgeable direction, help, and encouragement, as well as Guy Loft, Senior Editor at Routledge, who was our initial contact and advocate for this book at Routledge. W21C at the University of Calgary provided technical support, and we gratefully acknowledge Jill De Grood MA PMP, Leora Rabatch MSc, Zoha Khawaja BA, and Fillitsa Shillington for their assistance. We also thank Elena Novikova BSc at Postmedia for helping us acquire permission to quote articles from the Calgary Herald and the Calgary Sun.

We are also appreciative of our reviewers for their knowledge, expertise, and skills in helping to improve our manuscript. We thank the following individuals: Kim Audette PhD, Devon Currie MSc, Edie Heavin BSKin BEd MEd PhD,

Bronwyn Shumack BAppSci (Occupational Therapy) MPH, Sarah Simmons PhD, Rod Westhorpe OAM MB BS FRCA FANZCA, and Ron Westrum PhD.

We are especially appreciative of the support and contributions of Jack Davis MSc and Deb Prowse QC. We would not have started on this project without their enthusiastic agreement. As they both said: "This is a story that must be told!".

Finally, we could not have written this book without James Reason's original work, guiding and inspiring us, and we thank him.

Preface

Several years ago we decided to write a book about Just Culture. We had used James Reason's Just Culture theory as the basis of our plan to promote, influence, and build a safety culture in the former Calgary Health Region, and we were unaware of any other healthcare system that systematically had set out to accomplish that. We did not believe any attempts to define Reason's line between acceptable and unacceptable behaviors had managed to get it completely right. There were important considerations missing. Additionally, no one had described that the broader concept of Just Culture, in contradistinction to Reason's very focused one, applied to everyone involved in providing and receiving healthcare. Thus, we believed we had something to contribute.

We therefore started to write this book – with good intentions to complete it within a year or two. After numerous stops and starts over about five years, we completely changed our approach. The three of us were in Edmonton in February 2019, viewing a video shown as part of our teaching. Although we had watched the video many times before, we suddenly realized the story of what occurred in the former Calgary Health Region had to be told and the story would include our ideas about Just Culture. After that, our thoughts and concepts came together over the next year, although completion of the manuscript still took about another nine months.

A Little About Us

At the time of the deaths of the two patients in a Calgary hospital as described in this book, the three of us were all working in or for the former Calgary Health Region (the Region). Because of our backgrounds, our passions, and our positions, we then became involved and entangled in the events that followed.

Jan M Davies (JMD) is a Professor of Anesthesiology, Perioperative and Pain Medicine and an Adjunct Professor of Psychology at the University of Calgary. At the time she had consulting privileges as an anesthesiologist in the Region's hospitals and had spent the previous twenty years in safety and quality in healthcare and aviation. Away at the time of the deaths, on her return she joined the group that developed the Region's patient safety strategy. She became a safety advisor to the Region, a position that ended when the Region was amalgamated into the single provincial health authority, Alberta Health Services, in 2008.

Carmella Steinke (CS) currently works in Alberta Health Services in a leadership role. She trained as a Respiratory Therapist and worked mainly in adult and neonatal Intensive Care Units until becoming involved in Quality Improvement efforts in Neurosciences. Before the deaths, she was also Chair of the Health Advisory Committee and in that capacity was involved with the Board of the Calgary Health Region. After the deaths and with creation of the new safety teams, Carm was offered the position of Senior Clinical Safety Leader. She then went on to become the Manager of Clinical Safety Evaluation. She oversaw the creation of the new reporting system, the setting up of the Clinical Safety Committees, and the hiring of those who supported them. In 2008, she transitioned into a new role in Alberta Health Services as the Director of Safety Reporting.

Ward Flemons (WF) is an Academic Respirologist at the University of Calgary. He was the inaugural Quality Improvement Physician for the Department of Medicine in the former Calgary Health Region before he agreed to lead the Region's Quality Improvement and Health Information portfolio. Following the deaths, he accepted responsibility for leading the Region's patient safety strategy and was appointed Vice President – Quality, Safety, and Health Information. His position also ended in 2008.

A Little About the Book

Fatal Solution describes the journey of, and important lessons learned by, the former Calgary Health Region, its employees, and physicians as it struggled to define, promote, and put into operation Just Culture principles and practices. This was felt to be a central piece of its patient safety strategy, which was triggered by the tragic deaths of two patients. Our experiences during the events surrounding the deaths, the responses, and the work that followed led us to redefine what a truly Just Culture is and should be in healthcare. Just Culture is not simply an issue to be devolved to Human Resources (HR). Rather, it is an overall concept guiding the attitudes and behaviors of all those involved, directly and indirectly with providing healthcare, toward each other and especially toward patients and their families.

To describe the journey, this book does not start with Chapter 1 but with a Prologue, which tells the stories of the two patients who died and the personnel involved in the search to determine why they died and how. From there, each of the eight chapters starts with a narrative, with each installment of the narrative providing more of the story of what then happened in the Region. As with the Prologue, to write the narrative we relied on our memories, the memories of the many we interviewed, notes and documents, and articles from the newspapers. The latter proved invaluable – given the fallibility of our memories. These articles also provided a great reminder of and insight into the media and public responses to the deaths. The comments by and in the media all had an influence on establishing and developing our view of Just Culture, and we therefore quote from many news articles.

The second part of each chapter is a discussion – the academic component of the book, in which we elaborate on concepts featured in the newspaper articles, as related to events that occurred and our responses, and pertinent to the story. References are included at the end of each chapter. They were not selected from a systematic review of the literature. Rather, some references were selected for their historic importance. Others were picked for their relevance to a particular problem. We have included references from a wide range of topics and from domains outside healthcare, where appropriate.

We purposefully wrote both the Prologue and the narrative parts of each chapter in an informal style, to help convey the concept of the story. We then changed styles when writing about the more academic parts of the book, in the discussion sections, to a less informal style. Where medical or technical terms were required, we provided explanations, and hope our readers will find the book easy to read.

Because we chose to prioritize the narrative sections of the story with respect to how the chapters flow, some readers may find Just Culture concepts are introduced out-of-sequence. Then in the final chapter we bring all these concepts together and link them to show our thoughts about and our vision for what the Just Culture can mean.

Finally, we think *Fatal Solution* is more than a book about Just Culture, and more than a book about how an organization dealt with personnel involved in events in which patients were harmed. This is a book that describes how a large healthcare organization and its people coped with tragedy related to care and how they were all changed, as we were. Thus, as you read this book, we hope you will discover your own important insights from the story and lessons we recount, and apply and use them in your professional – and personal – lives.

Introduction

James Reason first put together his view of Just Culture and its components as part of thinking about a safety culture in the mid-1990s. These well-honed thoughts were then detailed in what was to be his 1997 authoritative and best-selling book, *Managing the Risks of Organizational Accidents.*[1]

In fact, Reason was not writing solely about Just Culture but about how to minimize the bad outcomes that can arise from hazardous technologies used by some organizations. His list of typical organizations included insurance companies and banks, institutions not often thought about as high-hazard organizations[2] at that time. What were included were organizations more traditionally associated with accidents and disasters: chemical processing and nuclear power generating plants, exploration and production of oil, and transport by air, rail, and sea. (Interestingly, healthcare organizations were not on the list, but this was rectified in Reason's book, *Organizational Accidents Revisited,*[3] two decades later.) His goal was to provide such organizations with some interdependent concepts that could be usefully adapted to help minimize bad outcomes or even close calls.

The concept of Just Culture was but one of these ideas. It was described as a prerequisite for developing a reporting culture, one of the four components of a safety culture. Of the book's 241 pages, only ten were devoted to Just Culture.

For those who are not familiar with the concept of Just Culture, Reason defined this as "an atmosphere of trust in which people are encouraged, even rewarded, for providing essential safety-related information – but in which they are also clear about where the line must be drawn between acceptable and unacceptable behaviour."[1] The expectation for members of the workforce was that they would voluntarily help the organization learn about problems they encountered. In return, the organization would not automatically blame workers when something went wrong nor punish them for making errors. However, organizations had to balance this with the principle that not everything would be allowed to pass without blame.

To have this concept function, trust was required – of the workers to report and of the organization not to behave arbitrarily. For Reason, trust was a requisite concept in an organization. This reinforced his point that "an atmosphere of trust"[1] – a Just Culture – was therefore the result of how an organization treated its staff.

Thus, from the small beginnings of ten pages in a book, the Just Culture concept has outgrown Reason's book, taking on its own importance, and becoming internationally recognized and incorporated into many organizations in different domains, including healthcare.[4–7] However, healthcare is not the same as aviation or nuclear power and the differences between healthcare and other industries have contributed to the Just Culture concept being more slowly adopted in some healthcare organizations. Despite differences between domains, certain healthcare organizations have established or are trying to establish a Just Culture. In this book, we tell the story of one such organization as it struggled to deal with a tragedy and to learn to do many things both differently and better.

A Just Culture cannot simply be bought off the shelf, for example, like a reporting system. To start with, an organization's concept of what Just Culture is must be defined. As we detail in the book, we began with Reason's statement that an organization must have an "agreed set of principles for drawing the line between acceptable and unacceptable actions".[1] We also concurred with the concept of not punishing errors but of systematically and systemically investigating events in which patients were harmed to determine the context and the contributing factors. Investigations then gave us the starting point for reviewing individuals' actions and behaviors to determine if any of these had crossed the line. In 2004, we chose to use the alternative term 'noncompliance' for violations, as well as 'intention to harm' instead of Reason's use of 'sabotage', based on feedback from other healthcare providers, leaders, and patients with whom we were working. Similarly, we have used the terms 'structure, process, and outcome-driven noncompliance', instead of Reason's necessary, routine, and optimizing violations. We made these changes in consultation with Reason. However, through the book we employ the terms interchangeably, using violations when we are referring directly to Reason's work and noncompliance when we are referring to our own.

We firmly believe a Just Culture must be developed and then maintained. Organizations should not wait until an untoward event occurs to reactively work out how to deal with tragedies – how to look after the patients and the staff involved in the event. Concepts such as responsibility and accountability must be clarified. Organizations and regulators must proactively share a common vocabulary and understanding to discuss and determine the behaviors. If this argument is accepted, and because the devil is in the details, then organizations and regulators also need to proactively adopt a procedure for reviewing individuals and a mechanism to tell people about the procedure before they have to use it.

Lastly, organizations are dynamic entities, as are their people and its culture. As part of this, an organization's thinking about its Just Culture must also be dynamic. Our thinking evolved from the concepts described by Reason to include a broader definition of Just Culture. We now consider that the 'just' in Just Culture should be defined as "consonant with principles of moral right or of equity; righteous; equitable; fair".[8] And this fairness applies to patients and families, in addition to healthcare workers.

Our initial work on Just Culture in the former Calgary Health Region started in 2004, and although we are close to two decades since then, we have come to accept that change takes time. We also anticipate more changes – in our thinking and in our organizations. For now, however, we invite you to read this part of the story.

References

1. Reason J. *Managing the Risks of Organizational Accidents*. Aldershot: Ashgate Publisher; 1997.
2. La Porte T, Roberts K, Rochlin G. Aircraft carrier operations at sea: The challenges of high reliability performance. Final report. Navy Manpower, Personnel, and Training R&D Program of the Office of Naval Research. Berkeley, California; 1998 Jul.
3. Reason J. *Organizational Accidents Revisited*. Aldershot: Ashgate Publishing; 2016.
4. Reason J. Human error: Models and management. *BMJ*. 2000 Mar 18;320(7237): 768–70.
5. Lowe A, Hayward B. Safety Culture Enhancement Project final report. A field study on approaches to enhancement of safety culture. Albert Park, Victoria; 2006 Aug.
6. Dekker S. *Just Culture: Balancing Safety & Accountability*. Aldershot: Ashgate; 2008.
7. Pellegrino F. *The Just Culture Principles in Aviation Law. Towards a Safety-Oriented Approach*. Cham: Springer International Publishing; 2019.
8. *OED Online*. Just, adj [Internet]. Oxford University Press; 2021 [cited 2022 Feb 9]. Available from: https://www.oed.com/

A Guide to the Book

James Reason popularized the notion of Just Culture and its importance to safety. He focused on trust and drawing the line, which in part was to encourage people to move away from focusing so much on blame. We have made three specific changes to take Just Culture concepts from being theoretical ideas to facilitating their actual application.

1. Better definition of the line. We name the behaviors that sit on either side of the line (the easy part) and provide pragmatic ways to think about and deal with the grey behaviors on either side of the line in the middle parts of the performance spectrum.
2. Emphasis on the importance of supporting healthcare workers who were involved in events leading to patients being harmed. In part, this involves applying the principles and practices of fair assessments, which in turn requires an assessment within the context of system factors. Also, healthcare workers must be supported through this challenging journey so there are opportunities for them to heal.
3. Expansion of Just Culture principles and practices to include how patients and families are treated and honoring their experiences following events that led to harm. Patients and families must also be provided with the care and support they deserve so they can heal.

An Overview of the Chapters

Chapter 1

If we expect healthcare providers to understand and adopt Just Culture principles, we need to help them to understand why in our societal culture we have a natural bias towards blame. This bias is conscious for some and unconscious for others, and was at the heart of Reason's description of Just Culture. We believe that once people understand blame and its origins, then they are more prepared to see Just Culture principles in a different light.

Chapter 2

We and others have made the case that, in a Just Culture, when people make errors we do not punish them for doing so. But why not? We take the opportunity in this chapter to explain how humans think – how they process information and what sets them up to make errors. We also briefly mention the issue of sabotage (willful intent to harm) because there is no debate about how unacceptable this is and how it clearly crosses the line. Finally, we introduce readers to the real challenge of how to deal with people who have been noncompliant (Reason's violations) with standard ways of doing things – following rules and procedures. We do this by providing operational descriptions of three different types of noncompliance that help to better define the line.

Chapter 3

We introduce readers to the ideas of expanding the Just Culture concepts to include patients and family members – because it is the right thing to do. The goal here is to approach those who experience harm with the respect and empathy they deserve and an understanding of how to meet their needs, which should allow them the best opportunity to heal.

Chapter 4

We build on Reason's ideas of linking Just Culture to the bigger concept of Safety Culture, focusing on the importance of reporting and safety information. We also draw attention to the interconnectedness between safety culture and organizational culture, and how both depend on trust and sharing of information. We do this by discussing the importance of organizations adopting the principles and practices of informing stakeholders.

Chapter 5

We discuss the original focus of Just Culture – those who work in the system. However, we go beyond expecting that if we simply provide a more precise definition of the line between acceptable and unacceptable behavior, then the result will be a workforce that has enough trust to participate actively in sharing important safety-related information. Similar to how we see the Just Culture supporting patients and families in the aftermath of events that harm, we describe approaches and mechanisms to support the healthcare providers who have been directly involved and also deeply affected.

Chapter 6

Underlying much of our view of the Just Culture, including the fair assessment of individuals, avoiding inappropriate blaming, and undertaking the conversations that must be held with patients and families, is the concept of gaining a system perspective of the events that unfolded. Therefore, in this chapter we look at what systems are and our approach for how to best obtain as unbiased as possible view of the system.

Chapter 7

In this chapter, we describe practical examples of how one large healthcare system worked to incorporate Just Culture principles and practices, and develop a safety strategy that intersected with organizational culture. The goal of these changes was to influence how decisions were made at the highest levels and things were done – at the front lines.

Chapter 8

We complete the story of how the tragic events that unfolded in our Region triggered and were translated into real changes. This story became embedded in the hearts and minds of the Region's leaders and helped point them in the direction the Region needed to take, highlighting the importance of the power of stories. We finish by bringing together the many strands in our Just Culture view and show how they can be woven together to support everyone involved in healthcare delivery.

Prologue: February 28th–March 5th, 2004

Saturday, February 28th, 2004

As the medical crew were loading Kathleen Prowse into the medivac jet at the Palm Springs Airport and destined for Calgary, the elderly woman was reassured to be traveling with one of her three daughters. Her daughter was also medically qualified, and although she was not *her* doctor, Kathleen felt better knowing her daughter was with her.

Kathleen had been visiting Palm Springs for a few weeks. The widowed 83-year-old hadn't been feeling well since Christmas and thought that the weather, warmer than back home in Calgary, might do her good. Her daughters had bought her the best healthcare travel insurance available, so she felt safe to make the journey south. But after a week or so there, she'd had a fall in the bathroom and didn't recover well. She needed to be hospitalized and was diagnosed with a *Staphylococcal* infection of her heart (endocarditis). Urgent, but not emergency, heart surgery was indicated – hence the air evacuation back to Alberta.

Once admitted to the Cardiac Intensive Care Unit (Cardiac ICU) on the tenth floor of the Foothills Medical Centre (FMC), her family gathered around her bed. This was a family with healthcare and legal backgrounds. Kathleen had been a nurse and married a lawyer who'd become a highly regarded Judge in Alberta's Court of Queen's Bench. Their daughters and grandchildren had all chosen similar careers. Those of the family present were reassured to see Kathleen joke with one of her daughters about a date she'd recently had with a lawyer, teasingly asking if marriage was "on the docket". But Kathleen was also very frightened about being back in hospital.

DOI: 10.4324/9781003185307-1

1

Thirteen months before, she'd undergone hip replacement surgery at another Calgary hospital. Postoperatively she'd nearly bled out, been taken back to the Operating Room (OR), and suffered a heart attack, spending 11 days in the ICU. Although told by her daughters what had happened, she fortunately had no memory of those events and had worked diligently at her rehabilitation – for her hip and her heart.

In the FMC, everyone was prepared for Kathleen to be taken to the OR that afternoon. But when the surgeon on-call arrived, the message delivered was not one they wanted to hear. The surgeon had been operating all day, was very tired, and thought it safer to postpone the operation until the Sunday morning.

Sunday, February 29th, 2004

While Kathleen was in the OR, the family spent the day in the Waiting Room on the ninth floor, not far from the cardiovascular (CV) ORs. Postoperatively, once Kathleen had been admitted to the CV ICU, her daughters were allowed to see her briefly and then left.

Monday, March 1st, 2004

One of the daughters arrived in the Family Waiting Room on the ninth floor, to find two other family members very concerned. Kathleen's vital signs were becoming unstable and they were convinced she was bleeding out. They'd been told by the nursing staff that, at most, Kathleen had a pneumothorax – a collection of air inside the chest but outside the lungs, which can occur after open-heart surgery. One of the family asked if an ultrasound examination of the chest and heart had been performed but was told that it had not been done. By late afternoon, concern had turned to agitation. Until the family could finally see Kathleen, they had spent their time taking searching looks through the window set high in the CV ICU doors. Only their own height had allowed them to see where their mother lay, at the back of the Unit. One of the daughters was at the window when she saw a commotion of staff around Kathleen's bed. She was apparently bleeding postoperatively – again, as in 2002. This time she also required another operation, during which the bleeding was controlled. Her heart stopped once preoperatively and then multiple times in the OR, but the team was able to resuscitate her. Six hours later she was readmitted to the CV ICU.

Tuesday, March 2nd–Thursday, March 4th, 2004

For the next 3 days, the family took turns visiting her and maintaining their vigil in the Family Waiting Room, a small, window-less space. As the days progressed, they were gladdened to see Kathleen regain consciousness and appear to be doing reasonably well. However, the ICU doctors determined her kidneys had failed.

As a result of the kidney failure and Kathleen's weakened heart, on the Thursday evening the CV ICU team had therefore instituted a special form of dialysis. Some ICU patients can undergo intermittent hemodialysis (IHD). But this can produce changes in blood pressure and heart rate that might not be tolerated by all patients. If so, continuous renal replacement therapy (CRRT) is used. With both IHD and CRRT, patients must be given a blood thinner, which can increase the possibility of more bleeding.

The solution used for CRRT was commercially available but only with one formulation of chemicals. However, the ICU specialists preferred the chemical make-up of the solution the Region had been mixing (compounding). Production of this solution was carried out in the newly opened Central Pharmacy, in batches of 36 bags. Each bag contained 3 litres (L) of sterile water to which specific chemicals were added in precise volumes by the Pharmacy Technicians who were responsible for the task.

One of Kathleen's daughters and a granddaughter were now at her bedside. While the first bag of Central Pharmacy prepared CRRT dialysis solution was being used, Kathleen's condition again worsened, prompting the granddaughter to spend the night at her grandmother's side. Although she still had the breathing tube in place and therefore couldn't speak, Kathleen was conscious and her granddaughter was able to interact with her. As the night progressed and the second bag was being used, Kathleen's condition became increasingly unstable. The nurse looking after her asked the granddaughter to leave, stating it was inconvenient to have family present at the bedside. Devastated, the granddaughter retreated to the Waiting Room.

Friday, March 5th, 2004

In the morning, one of Kathleen's daughters drove to the Courthouse in a nearby town, where she was to preside over Traffic Court. Pleased that conditions on the roads were their usual 'Friday lighter than normal', she didn't want any delays. She had a full docket, including a teenager whose sentencing she'd deferred until that day, to ensure one of his parents could attend Court with him. She then needed to get to the FMC, a minimum 30-minute drive back to Calgary, to spend the afternoon with her mother.

While the one daughter was in Court, the other daughters and the grand-daughter were in the Family Waiting Room, a space with which they'd grown all too familiar. That day, the room's lack of helpful fittings was even more apparent. There was only one telephone in the room and no adjacent toilet, which meant having to take the elevator to the Main Floor and possibly missing a phone call from the CV ICU. They stayed, taking turns straining to look through the CV ICU door's window. Later in the morning, one of the daughters was able to go back in to visit Kathleen, whose condition had become increasingly unstable. A sample of arterial blood had been drawn to check Kathleen's oxygen. To everyone's surprise, one of the results (automatically analyzed by the blood-gas machine) was tremendously elevated: the serum potassium was much higher than the normal of up to 5.2 mmol/L. The daughter was asking about the result when Kathleen's heart stopped. The daughter was asked to leave.

In the nearby town, the Judge had just finished delivering her sentence and Judge's Comments to the young man about driving at excessive speeds, when the Clerk of the Court passed her a note: "You're needed at FMC". She concluded the proceedings and drove to the hospital, all the while wanting to do so at the same speeds for which she had just admonished the young man. Once in the parking lot, she phoned one of her sisters. The CV ICU team had carried out cardiopulmonary resuscitation (CPR) but then had finally 'called the Code' and pronounced Kathleen dead.

The sisters met on the ninth floor of the FMC and then went in to the CV ICU to join their other sister and Kathleen's granddaughter. Viewing Kathleen's body, as it lay crookedly on the bed in a welter of tubing, one of the daughters could only think her mother looked violated. Another of the sisters didn't want to leave, but the CV ICU staff needed to talk with them. They moved to a small room, crowded now with the daughters, the granddaughter, the CV ICU specialist, the nurse, and a social worker. The specialist stated they'd done everything they could for Kathleen and that she'd died of surgical complications, in addition to being very ill when she was admitted a week ago. Despite their best efforts, they could not save Kathleen.

"What about the potassium", one of the daughters asked, "the K"? The ICU doctor replied that, while he could not currently explain the elevation, Kathleen had been extremely ill and had then died, despite their best efforts. He added, however, "We're going to test everything and will give you a phone call". The family then left the hospital.

In the CV ICU, the physician contemplated Kathleen's potassium result and considered what could have raised it that high. Kathleen had none of the usual problems, such as an overt breakdown of her muscles, nor was she receiving any medications that could have elevated the potassium. True, her kidneys had failed – but that was why she was undergoing CRRT. Without that therapy, her potassium would have been higher earlier, but not that high. The only other option was that, somehow, Kathleen had received additional potassium, although none was ordered. Her intravenous fluids were identical to those other patients were receiving – and they did not have elevated concentrations of potassium in their blood.

That left the CRRT. The physician examined the bag – its contents had been manufactured in the Calgary Health Region's recently opened and state-of-the-art Central Pharmacy. The CV ICU physician asked the Respiratory Therapist to take a sample of the CRRT bag of fluid and, using the blood-gas machine, test the dialysis liquid for potassium. Within minutes they knew – the result that should have been negative was not.

Kathleen's family had driven to the home of one of the daughters to plan the funeral and make other arrangements. While the others went to the funeral home, one daughter remained alone in the house. At about 3.00 p.m., the phone rang and she answered it, thinking it was one of her sisters. The voice on the other end of the phone said, "I was told to call and tell you that the dialysate was made with potassium chloride, and not sodium chloride". Later that evening, the sister who had asked the questions of the CV ICU doctor received a phone call from him. In that call, he confirmed the content of the message her sister had received.

At roughly the same time, once the problem with the CRRT and its relationship to Kathleen's death had been identified, several phone calls were made from the ICU. One of the first was to the ICU Department Head. In that call, the ICU Physician described Kathleen's death and also detailed the clinical events leading up to it. The two men discussed the dialysate's abnormal potassium content and then the possibility that, because this solution was made in batches, there could be other bags similarly affected. What they didn't know was how many bags were in a batch, if other patients had received any, and if there were more bags in any of the Region's three other ICUs. The Department Head directed that a call to the Region's Director of Pharmacy was imperative.

That call, made by the ICU Physician, was absorbed with surprise, shock, and great concern by the Regional Director of Pharmacy. He immediately phoned the Vice-President for the South-West Community Portfolio (VP-SW). She had responsibility for the Pharmacy and the Director gave her the few details he knew. The Pharmacy Director asked if she could inform the appropriate Executives, so he could then get on with "fixing things" to ensure no other patients were harmed.

The VP-SW then phoned her organizational dyad partner, the Executive Medical Director for the South-West Community Portfolio (EMD-SW). (The Region had successfully been using a dyad model of an operations lead and a medical lead for the previous few years. All the VPs were women who had trained and worked as nurses for many years, before taking on clinical leadership roles.) The VP-SW and the EMD-SW briefly discussed the problem. The EMD-SW called the Chief Medical Officer (CMO) and the VP-SW called the Chief Operating Officer (COO), to ensure the 'next level' of leadership was made aware.

Meanwhile, over at the recently opened Central Pharmacy and near the end of the day shift, the pharmacist who was the Regional Operations Manager for all Region pharmacies had received a similar call, but from the FMC ICU's Clinical Pharmacist. The Regional Manager – Operations was as equally as shocked and horrified as had been the Regional Pharmacy Director. The ICU Pharmacist asked him to check the Production Records against a particular batch-specific lot number. Each bag of dialysate was labeled with three specific things:

- The name of the type of the solution, e.g., "CPD High Sodium";
- The batch-specific lot number, devised by the Central Pharmacy. On close inspection, the first eight digits of this number represented the date of compounding, while the last two digits, e.g., 16, were for the bag number in the batch, e.g., 2004-02-20-16.
- The expiry date of the bag of solution, which was the more easily readable of the two numbers.

The ICU Pharmacist wanted to know what the Production Record showed for that particular batch lot number, as to which chemicals were recorded as being used in the compounding. The Regional Pharmacy Manager found the commercial lot number for what was supposed to be sodium chloride. He then went to the storage area but there was no sodium chloride on the shelf with that same lot number. He therefore had difficulty initially in identifying the product.

At that time, the Region purchased potassium chloride and sodium chloride from the same manufacturer. The Regional Pharmacy Manager immediately telephoned the local pharmaceutical products representative for the company supplying the potassium chloride and sodium chloride solutions to the Region. He asked, "What is this lot number for, please?". The answer came back quickly: "potassium chloride". The problem became very clear. The specific batch of dialysis solution, which Kathleen received, had inadvertently been prepared on February 20th with *potassium* chloride instead of *sodium* chloride.

After phoning the Regional Pharmacy Director with this dire news, the Pharmacy Manager then phoned all the Region's adult hospital pharmacies. He told each of the managers to pull all the CRRT dialysate bags from the Pharmacies and the ICUs immediately. When one manager wanted to assign an assistant, the Regional Pharmacy Manager's answer was direct: "This was the manager's job". All bags of dialysate were to be immediately sent back to the Central Pharmacy and quarantined. They were locked in the narcotics vault until the investigations were over and the bags were then destroyed.

While he was waiting for the bags to be returned and quarantined, the Regional Pharmacy Manager's next thought was to review the medication storage area, which was spacious and well-lit. All the pharmaceutical products were kept in their shipping boxes and placed on shelves in alphabetical order. By reason of alphabetical order, and the size and number of containers of each product, the potassium chloride and the sodium chloride were not only at the same height but also directly opposite each other. From a distance, the boxes were very difficult to distinguish from each other. Each box held 12 bottles of potassium chloride or 12 bottles of sodium chloride. In line with the company's branding, the cardboard boxes were very close in appearance, down to the color and printing on the labels. The largest word on the two boxes was the company's name, in the company's blue, and the second smallest sequence of words was "15% POTASSIUM CHLORIDE INJECTION, USP". The size of that type was about half that for the description "23.4% SODIUM CHLORIDE INJECTION, USP". If a technician turned to the right then sodium chloride would be selected, and if to the left, then potassium chloride. It was also possible that the boxes of potassium chloride and sodium chloride had been mixed up and stored on the wrong shelves.

Some bottles had been removed from their boxes, to provide ready access to working stock. It was easy to see the bottles of concentrated potassium chloride and concentrated sodium chloride were also difficult to distinguish. They were the same size (250 ml), shape, made of clear glass, and similarly labeled. There was one slight difference between the bottles in that the sodium chloride bottles had silver caps while the potassium chloride had black ones. Next in the sequence was for adequate numbers of bottles to be assembled on a cart, and, again, it was possible that the bottles had been mixed up as they were placed on the cart. Although the specific details were not clear, those factors helped explain the possible 'how' of the mix-up.

The Regional Pharmacy Manager had another important task to coordinate with his staff. Every formulation of potassium in the Central Pharmacy, no matter what size or preparation, was immediately moved to a locked cupboard. Again, the details of what was found, what was accomplished, and what was planned were then relayed to the Regional Director of Pharmacy.

By the end of the evening, 30 bags had been returned to the Central Pharmacy and consigned to the narcotics vault. From his review of the Production Record, the Regional Manager knew that 36 bags had been made in that batch, which was, as usual, prepared to order as the ICUs required new stock. However, one bag had been discarded because it had been spoiled during preparation. That meant 35 bags had been distributed to the three adult hospital pharmacy fridges, until a call was made by the ICU nurses to have more bags sent up to the appropriate unit. With 30 bags returned, and Kathleen having received three bags, two bags were therefore missing. No one seemed to know where those two other bags were.

Saturday, March 6th–Sunday, March 7th, 2004

That weekend was a busy one for many individuals, including ICU staff, a few members of the Administration Executive, the Regional Director of Pharmacy, and some of his staff.

In the ICUs, as well as providing critical care to their patients, the staff were detailing how they would ensure other patients were protected. The staff had already found their remaining unused bags of dialysate and returned them to the Central Pharmacy quarantine. Fortunately, no other patients appeared to require CRRT that weekend. But should a patient have needed CRRT, then the plan was to test the dialysate solution for potassium.

On the Saturday morning, the Executives involved met at Southport, the Region's headquarters. Those present included Jack Davis, the Chief Executive Officer (CEO) of the Region. The COO had already spoken with the CMO, who in turn had alerted Jack on Friday about the death. Jack had phoned the Chair of the Region's Board and the provincial Deputy Minister of Health and Wellness. The province's Minister of Health and Wellness had already been contacted by the CMO, who had an enviable list of contacts and little concern for chain-of-command proprieties when circumstances dictated.

The updated facts were detailed as the CMO described the patient who died, the circumstances, and what had been done since the death the day before. Normally, Jack would not be told about a patient who had died in the Region of natural causes. But this patient was different. There was nothing natural about Kathleen Prowse's cause of death.

The tone in the room was tense. Initial questions focused on "How could this happen?" Everyone was rightly concerned. The next questions related to what was to be done. The COO and the CEO were aligned in suggesting those involved be disciplined and perhaps even fired. This reaction certainly reflected the times and what was expected of them in their roles. Indeed, the CEO considered taking some sort of punitive action as his responsibility. In contrast, the clinically qualified Executives (doctors and nurses) were opposed to punishment. They felt sure the chemical mix-up was not an intentional act. They also knew, as clinicians, that things could go wrong when delivering care, without any one or more individuals being at fault. They recommended additional investigation be undertaken before any decisions were made. The meeting was adjourned, with plans to update the Board Chair and the Minister of Health and Wellness, and to continue the investigations, as well as the implementation of changes for the labeling and storage of potassium.

The Regional Director of Pharmacy had also questioned "How could this happen?", as well as being equally shocked and horrified when he learned of the patient's death and the link with Central Pharmacy. To say he felt an enormous sense of responsibility could only be an understatement. After fielding multiple phone calls, he had spent time over the weekend going over all the processes in the Central Pharmacy and the immediate changes made there, as well as planning other changes that would need to be made throughout the Region. He was determined to be involved in every change necessary to make improvements and to minimize the possibility of another patient being harmed in a similar way. This included searching for an alternate supplier of potassium chloride. It was important that in future there would be differences in labeling between the potassium chloride and sodium chloride boxes and bottles, and possibly in the bottle shape.

One of the immediate changes planned by the Regional Director of Pharmacy was for all potassium chloride stock in the Region to have the addition of a bright green label, stating "KCl". These green labels were to be applied to every box containing some form of potassium chloride product, as well as to any vials or bottles 20 mL in volume or larger. (Any vial less than 20 mL was too small to accommodate any additional green labeling, which would obscure the vitally necessary basic information of the original product label.) This plan was to be started immediately in the Central Pharmacy and completed first in all the Region's hospital pharmacies. Then all ward stock on the Nursing Units, in the Emergency Department and the Operating Rooms would be similarly addressed. There would be many bottles to find and to label. As for further factors leading to the death, it would take another, later review to determine the 'why' of the tragedy, and for which everyone would have to wait.

Monday, March 8th, 2004

On the morning of Monday, March 8th, the Director of Pharmacy was extremely busy. Before he did anything else, he phoned the Registrar of the Alberta College of Pharmacists (as it was then named) and spoke with him. The Director gave the Registrar as complete an account as he could of the events and then detailed the steps that had been undertaken to fix things, as well as those planned and either underway or not yet started. The Registrar thanked him for doing so and then the Director stated he was taking full responsibility for everything that had happened. The Pharmacy Technicians were not regulated by the College at that time. But the Director had designed the system in which they worked and how they worked. To the Director, there was no alternative to his being responsible – and therefore the one to be held accountable. He would accept whatever the College decided, no matter how strong the sanctions were.

At the same time, the Chief Medical Officer (CMO) for the Region met with his five EMDs, one for each of the quadrants of the city (NW, NE, SW, and SE), and one representing the overall Community. Also at the meeting was WF, who had been the Medical Director of Quality Improvement and Health Information (QIHI) since 2002.

For a few years, the Regional Executive team consisted of the CEO, a COO paired with a CMO, a Chief Financial Officer, a Chief of Planning & Capital Expenditure, and the Head of Communications. Reporting to specific members of this Regional Executive were five clinical VPs paired with five EMDs, forming the Region's Clinical Executives. They were responsible for different departments/programs and services. This structure helped ensure there was balanced medical and administrative leadership for the Region's day-to-day operations.

The CMO started to describe the death of a patient who had had *Staphylococcus aureus* endocarditis, had been taken to the OR, and had suffered complications. At this point, WF wondered why they were discussing an elderly patient who, preoperatively, would have been estimated to have had a very high probability of death. It was not immediately obvious to WF as to what needed to be done. But as he continued to listen, the CMO described the patient recovering consciousness postoperatively and interacting with her family. The patient needed dialysis, received the CRRT erroneously containing potassium, and then, suddenly arrested and died. WF had no idea the short account he had just heard of the last week of Kathleen's life and her death would completely change everything in the Calgary Health Region and his role in it.

WF learned further details, including the fact another 30 patients could possibly have died because of the number of bags made during the batch production of dialysate solution. Details became clearer as to how the mix-up had occurred and the role of the Pharmacy Technicians responsible for manufacturing the dialysate. Although the Region had been successfully compounding dialysate therapy for about a decade, what was new-to-Calgary in the protocol was the employment of several technicians to prepare the solution. Overseen by a Pharmacist, the protocol involved one technician checking another and was referred to as "Tech-Check-Tech".

After the meeting of the CMO and his medically qualified Executives, there were two other meetings of importance. First, the CMO met at the FMC with a group that included leadership from the ICU and Pharmacy, and the VP-NW who was responsible for the ICUs. Also present, and at the request of the CMO, was the (academic) Head of Family Medicine, who was about to copublish a landmark study on complications to, and harm suffered by, hospitalized patients in Canada. The discussion followed a pattern similar to the one earlier at Southport. Again, there was discussion of a "wait for more results" versus a "let someone go". But a decision was made to have the Region's Critical Incident Review Committee investigate the death.

The second meeting involved the VP-SW and the EMD-SW, who traveled to north-east Calgary, where the Central Pharmacy was located near the Airport. There they met with the Pharmacy leadership and the pharmacy technicians who had been involved in the preparation of the dialysate. The Executives had a detailed discussion with everyone. The technicians repeated what they had told the Regional Pharmacy Director and the Manager earlier that morning when they had first met: they had followed the protocol as it was written, believing they were working with sodium chloride. The two Executives were very clear. They told the technicians they would be given time off with full pay while everything was being investigated. More importantly, the VP-SW and EMD-SW told the technicians and the pharmacists that they had their backs.

Later that day, the VP-SW and the EMD-SW met with one of the members of the Regional Executive team. The Executive was insistent someone be let go. This time the duo suggested "letting people know we're investigating to understand what happened, to get to the bottom of this". "We shouldn't be making *any* decisions without the facts." "Decisions shouldn't be made on the basis of emotions." The Executive again insisted. The VP-SW's answer was simple: if the Executive wanted someone fired immediately, then she would be the one to be fired. The EMD-SW stood in alignment with the VP-SW and added if anyone was fired at that point, then he would resign. This was a clash of "What was the right thing to do?". The meeting ended in an impasse.

Back at the FMC and after the meeting there with the CMO and the others, the ICU Department Head also started to look into things. He was determined to learn if any other patient(s) in the ICUs had been affected by the February 20th batch of dialysate solution. This search was to answer the question of why all the bags of incorrectly prepared dialysate had not been found. The Department Head had learned at the meeting that morning that 36 bags had been prepared but one was spoiled during preparation and therefore discarded. But what about the other two bags, still not yet accounted for? Had any other patients received some of the dialysate and, if not, where were those other potentially lethal bags? Or could he determine only if two bags had been administered to one or more ICU patients, but not exactly to whom? The ICU Department Head was about to test his new Patient Care Information System.

The ICU Head decided to review the records of all patients admitted to all the Region's adult ICUs in the past weeks. Because of the conditions imposed by the information system, he was forced to look for patients who had had an elevated blood potassium and creatinine (a measure of kidney function). This search was to take several hours and complete confirmation would take a few days.

Some readers might ask why the Pharmacy did not have a record of which patient received which bag of dialysate. There were two answers to that question. The first was related to historical practice. That information had never been needed before. Historically, information needs were focused on documenting care and results for individual patients. Written notes in each patient's chart would capture that they had undergone CRRT but there would be no searchable database of all patients who had received CRRT. The second answer was that the ICU had just started using their locally designed and built information system, and it had not been designed to capture this degree of detail about specific patients' care. With the new system, the ICU staff had computerized access to patients' laboratory results. The new information system of 2004, therefore, did not collect data about which patients were dialyzed and which patients received which specific bag of dialysate. There was also no computerized record of the number of bags of a specific batch used for a patient, nor the location of the remaining bags in the batch. This was a classic example of how not thinking forward, the decision made in the past, became a system deficiency. As a result, the ICU Head had to be creative as he tried to determine if any other patients might have been dialyzed with the mistakenly mixed, February 20th dialysate solution.

While that search was underway, and having learned of Kathleen's death and the link with the dialysate solution, the Head of the Critical Incident Review Committee (CIRC) had notified the Head of the Medical Advisory Committee to whom he reported. They discussed the need and request for a review, which would be conducted as a Critical Incident Review. The Head of the CIRC was able to gain the assistance of the Regional Manager for Quality Improvement (QI), who reported to WF. She was a senior nurse clinician, with experience in investigating a tragic outcome in another healthcare jurisdiction.

One of the Regional staff who was not at any of the meetings up to that point was the (Acting) Head of Communications. This was not a reflection on the individual or the "Acting" position but rather typical of the time, to not have called anyone from communications. It was not in anyone's consciousness how to handle crisis communications, except by ignoring or denying the problem. The (Acting) Head had overheard a corridor conversation that day about the Region's involvement in the death of a patient. Joining the conversation, he learned that potentially 30 other patients could have died. From then on he was centrally involved in the discussions of going public: if this should be done, which he thought it should, then when and how.

Tuesday, March 9–Thursday, March 17th, 2004

The reviews of the Central Pharmacy and its planned changes, the search of the ICU patient records, and meetings of various members of the Executive continued. The VP-SW met regularly with the Central Pharmacy staff and her executive colleagues. She had collected two empty boxes from the Central Pharmacy, one of which had held potassium chloride and the other sodium chloride. She then showed these to various executives. One of the attendees at that meeting was struck by the dull brown cardboard boxes with the blue label of the pharmaceutical company's name. He also noted how large the company label was, in contrast to the other information on the box, including how difficult it was to read the names of the specific chemicals. Everyone at the meeting quickly realized how easy it could (still) be to confuse the two chemicals.

The VP-SW also met with Jack, saying she had put her job on the line. She suggested the Region should "let people know we're investigating to understand what happened, to get to the bottom of the problem". She repeated what she'd said to the Executive: "We shouldn't be making *any* decisions without the facts." "Decisions shouldn't be made on the basis of emotions." Again, she was clear and firm: if Jack wanted someone fired immediately, then he would have to fire her.

The VP-SW was not the only executive to say that to Jack. Others, including her physician dyad and some well-respected physician leaders, also put their jobs on the line. This was *still* a clash of "What was the right thing to do?" There were also ongoing, intermittent hallway discussions, among some members of Jack's Regional Executives and the EMDs, as well as WF. The impasse over "doing the right thing" continued.

In addition, several of the EMDS, again with WF, met together and with Jack, to talk about the latest concepts in safety management. Emphasis was placed on how easy it was to misread one label when focusing on another label on the same bottle or vial of medication or something else, and that this could happen to anyone.

In fact, the head of the CIRC had bought a can of cream of mushroom soup, the expiry date of which was stamped on the top lid. He had met with the CMO to talk about the chemical mix-up, the investigation, and the possible fates of the technicians. The Head of the CIRC handed the can to the CMO saying it was "cream of chicken" and asking him to check the expiry date. The CMO duly read off the expiry date. Retrieving the can, the Head of the CIRC then asked the CMO what kind of soup it was. Somewhat bemused, the CMO answered back quickly, "Why, it's cream of chicken soup". Pointing to where on the label the type of soup was described, about two inches down from the expiry date's location, the Head of the CIRC asked the CMO to take another look at the label. Duly impressed with the demonstration, the CMO borrowed the can of soup and asked Jack the same questions. The point of the exercise, that misreading the label on the can of soup was no different from the technicians misreading the label on the potassium chloride bottles, was not lost on Jack. The protocol the technicians followed had asked them to confirm *lot numbers* and not *content labels*, which were similarly placed at a distance from the numbers. Jack was clearly able to see that the problem in the Central Pharmacy was not so straightforward.

The discussion among the various EMDs, WF, and Jack then moved from these concepts to the idea that problems designed into the system needed system-oriented investigations to find them and to provide system-based recommendations for changes. This was a major shift from the traditional focusing on the individuals – who had not intended to harm anyone. Also discussed was how the Region could do things differently – and better, including more often talking openly with patients and their families when a patient had been harmed. Over the past few decades, this process, known as *disclosure*, had been intermittently carried out in the Region. In fact, the FMC Department of Anesthesia had started doing this in the mid-1980s. While the protocol for disclosure, coupled with investigating and fixing problems, had spread throughout the hospital, there was no Region-wide protocol for doing so. Additionally, the concept of going public with news of what had occurred was described and debated.

The ICU Head had finally been able to complete his search using the new computer system. Two patients, other than Kathleen, had had laboratory results showing an elevated blood potassium and creatinine – and both patients had undergone dialysis. One patient's medical diagnosis provided a clear answer to the elevated potassium, and a different medical diagnosis related to the cause of death – unrelated to potassium. However, the other patient seemed to fit the picture. A middle-aged man, he had been rushed to the FMC soon after being admitted with stomach pains to a smaller regional hospital. Postoperatively, and over the following week in the Medical-Surgical ICU, the man's kidneys had shut down, requiring CRRT. He died a week before Kathleen, on February 29th, not long after being visited by his family. Because of his diagnosis and overall condition, his death was expected at that time.

In 2004, the standard process in the ICU did not include noting in the patient's record details such as the batch-specific lot number (devised by the Central Pharmacy for the CRRT). It was therefore not possible to tell if that patient had received any of the tainted dialysate solution. However, the man had received two bags of CRRT, and with each bag, his potassium had increased. At the time, the increase was thought to be congruent with his diagnosis. Now, with the benefit of hindsight, the elevation also suggested an additional diagnosis. After discussion with colleagues, including the Head of the CIRC, the fate of the two missing bags of dialysate seemed clear. The safety of other patients who might have needed CRRT was confirmed. All 35 bags of dialysate were accounted for. Some had been used and the rest had been found and locked away. Thus, there had been, not just one, but *two deaths*, related to the dialysate solution.

This finding was greeted with mixed feelings. There was surprise and sadness that another patient's death was related to the chemical mix-up. But there was also relief in the Region and particularly in the Central Pharmacy, where a wave of emotion had overcome all those who worked there. The Regional QI Manager undertaking the internal review was certainly mindful of the emotional strain those involved were undergoing, as well as the emotional toll shared by their colleagues. At the Central Pharmacy, she interviewed a number of individuals and gathered some preliminary information, as well as developed an investigative Process Map. This Map showed each of the steps undertaken in the preparation of the dialysate. The investigation was conducted under Section 9 of the Alberta Evidence Act,[1] protecting information collected during such an investigation from subpoena for release either verbally or in written form. That meant that she was one of the few who even knew the identities of the technicians or what each of them had done, and she would defend that information with her job. The technicians could trust her with what they said, without fear of reprisal related to the investigation. Information about the no-longer missing bags of dialysate also helped everyone focus the review more on the Central Pharmacy production system for dialysate, and not as directly on the actions of the technicians.

All eyes were on Jack, who was effectively "sitting in the hot seat". While the situation was quite different from an industry-related disaster, it was still an emergency for the Region, requiring careful assessment of the situation, clear decision-making, and decisive undertaking (or delegating) of action.[2] Jack had agreed with the medically qualified Executives to defer any decision to punish the technicians – and no one else. The first part of the decision was initially riding on the internal review. Problems had definitely been found in part of the protocol, related to four safety checks. A second decision then rested on whether or not there had been any intention to harm. Once it was confirmed there was none, that the mix-up was unintentional and from a combination of errors triggered and compounded by problems in the system, the question became: should the Region discipline the technicians for making errors? If there were to be voting, then the results were likely to be split. A few of the Executives were likely to say "Yes". Jack seemed to have moved from disciplining to willing to think about not disciplining, but he had not committed, one way or another at that point. The EMDs, VPs, CMO, and a few others were all likely to give a very firm "No". In fact, WF and the Head of the CIRC had joined the EMD-SW, the VP-SW, and the CMO in putting their jobs on the line over the issue of punishing *anyone* from the Central Pharmacy.

The decision not to pursue punishment for the technicians was seemingly on hold – at least for the moment. Discussions among the EMDs, VPs, the Head of the CIRC, and WF then led to an agreement that the families had to be told what had happened and what had been found. The families needed *disclosure* of the details of the dialysate and that there were two deaths.

Kathleen's family had received an initial disclosure conversation when they spoke with the ICU doctor immediately after Kathleen's death. The daughters had also learned from the two phone calls that the source of Kathleen's high blood potassium was thought to be the dialysate solution. Then, a few days after Kathleen's funeral, two of Kathleen's daughters met at the FMC with some of the Executives, to discuss the events of what had happened to their mother. The Executives were able to provide more details, including the fact a second patient had died. Both daughters were shocked, particularly when they learned their mother was the second patient to die. Thoughts of "what if" crossed everyone's minds.

Back at the Region's headquarters, the same Executives, as well as the (Acting) Head of Communications, all continued to speak strongly for *informing* the public about the deaths and the details. With the concept of going public on the table, discussion moved to "how would we manage informing the public?". The Region had no experience in doing so. Over the previous few years, the Region had on several occasions featured negatively in the press, with stories of patients with poor outcomes and questions about their care. Initially, it had not been the Region's intention to notify the public through the media about these latest two cases and there was little appetite for further attention. Jack's initial response had been to ask what they thought they were going to accomplish in telling everyone. But the CMO, WF, and other executives were very clear from the beginning that the Region had to inform the public. Their argument was that mistaking the bottles of potassium chloride for sodium chloride could be made anywhere, by anyone. The safety of other patients, elsewhere in Canada or even internationally, was what needed to be the focus. The cost to others from withholding this information was much higher than any cost the Region would pay, for example, in loss of reputation. This was a price the Region should be prepared to pay.

The other motivation was for the Region to lay the groundwork to regain trust with the public the Region served, as well as other stakeholders, by being transparent about the events. In the short-term, the Region knew that trust was 'going to take a hit'. But over the longer term, the Region could not afford to lose even more trust if there was even a hint it was trying to hide something.

The Region had to be trusted to maintain responsibility for its patients' care and to be accountable for that care. Transparency was essential and the Region needed to be seen to be transparent. To accomplish that, several individuals, including the Region's (Acting) Head of Communications, suggested it was important the Region proactively inform the public before the news leaked out and the media took control of the agenda. If that happened, the Region would be forced to respond. That had occurred in the past, when the Region's previous strategy for at least one other tragic event had not included transparency or openness. The public had not been informed until a Fatality Inquiry had forced the release of some information. The resulting publicity was very negative. Things had not gone well for the Region and its staff.

Discussions continued among the Executive. Two other points were raised. First, the family of the man who died in the other ICU had finally received disclosure. His widow had been told her husband's death was linked to the dialysate. She had also been told there was a second patient who had died. Second, if the Region were to inform the public, then both families again had to be notified and told of the impending Press Conference, as well as the fact that their identities could soon be discovered. The CMO emphasized the importance of keeping the patients' identities concealed in any descriptions given to the media about what had happened. However, obituaries for the two deceased had already been published in the newspapers and it might not take long before a reporter found them. Having that occur would not be fair to the families, after everything else. Part of the counterargument ran that, in *not* going public, there would be no media exposure. And again, a further counter: the families could prepare for any calls before the news conference. And at least then, any publicity would not be as much of a further shock.

Not all the Executives or the Legal Department were as fully supportive of informing the public. The reputation of the Region had been, at times, in tatters over the past few years. Going public, it was argued, would only dredge up the previous problems.

But another important discussion took place, independent of most of the Executives, which helped tip the balance of opinions. The Region's insurers, who were responsible for making payments to families should there be litigation or other financial arrangements, were told the Region accepted all responsibility for the two deaths. With that statement made, the insurers replied they would indeed "pay up". And that response removed the last formal barrier to the Region being open and transparent about what had happened to the two patients.

On Thursday, March 11th, the Regional Executives gathered for their regularly scheduled, weekly Executive Management Meeting with Jack. He started the meeting by reviewing what had occurred to the two patients, what had been found, and what he had learned during the discussions of the previous few days. He had obviously weighed the options, drawing on his many years in the public service. He looked around the table and thanked everyone for their opinions.

The Region would proactively inform the public by holding a news conference. For a few individuals, Jack's decision was a shock: it was as though he had woken up that morning with his mind made up. And he did not waver from that position, although he was to be misunderstood a few days later.

The date chosen for the Press Conference was Thursday, March 18th. With that decision made, the two families were again contacted and asked if a representative from the Region could meet with them for a second time. The families were told about the impending news conference. They had been assured their privacy would be respected, and they, and the Region's Executives, could only hope reporters would also respect their privacy. But that hope would soon be dashed.

References

1. Alberta Evidence Act. Revised Statutes of Alberta 2000. Chapter A-18. Current as of September 1, 2019. Edmonton, Alberta: Alberta Queen's Printer. 2019. [cited 2021 Oct 8]. Available from: https://www.qp.alberta.ca/documents/Acts/A18.pdf
2. Flin R. *Sitting in the Hot Seat. Leaders and Teams for Critical Incident Management.* Chichester, West Sussex, England: John Wiley & Sons Ltd. 1996.

Chapter 1

"Two Patients Are Dead and Foothills Hospital Staff Are to Blame."

For most Calgarians, March 18th had started as a typical late winter day. The temperature was about −3°C (27°F), the wind was gusting, and there'd been no fresh snow. It seemed like it would not be a bad day. But for the many Calgarians and especially the staff and employees of the Calgary Health Region (the Region), things would not be the same.

The morning of the proposed news conference and before any notification had been sent out to the media, the Region's Executives were all at Southport. Jack called a meeting, to check if everyone still believed going public was the right thing to do.

Jack, of course, had been in contact with the Region's Board Chair and indirectly with the provincial Minister of Health and Wellness. Both agreed to letting the public know what had occurred. March 18th also happened to be the day on which the Premier of Alberta was to hold his long-planned, annual Premier's Dinner in Calgary.

Rumor had it that the Premier's staff were not at all pleased. The date and time of the announcement had apparently provoked some "angry words"[1] spoken by the staff in Edmonton, followed by a flurry of phone calls south to Calgary. The Press Conference appeared very badly timed. Although the first death had occurred nearly three weeks previously, the media release would coincide with

DOI: 10.4324/9781003185307-2

the Premier's dinner, with attention on the deaths and not on the Premier's speech. But Jack refuted this, saying that the Region had made a commitment to the families not to release any of the details of what had happened until they gave their permission. That permission had not been granted until the 17th of March.

Despite the reaction from Edmonton, Jack voiced his now-unwavering opinion: "This is the right thing to do". If the Press Conference were to be delayed because of the Premier's Dinner, then that would look as though politics were more important than the safety of patients in Calgary and elsewhere. Everyone agreed. The (Acting) Head of Communications also provided a voice of reason with his calm approach to the multitude of arrangements for what was going to be a challenging event. A small team of communications experts was assembled, including a former reporter who would be responsible for Media Relations. Those who were to speak at the news conference were selected, their order determined, and then prepared. One of the Executive Medical Directors and WF were to be the point people in the news conference, which was scheduled for 2:00 p.m.

Jack also played an important role in the decision to inform the Region's staff at the same time as the Press Conference. From his experience he knew it was not good for an organization's staff to learn from external sources, such as the media, about problems within the organization. The Region's personnel and physicians needed to be informed as quickly as possible and a Region-wide email was the best way to disseminate the news. A few minutes after 2:00 pm, therefore, the Region's Media Advisor sent out an email announcing the same details that were being released at the Press Conference.

The tagline read: "Error contributing to deaths is the subject of a Critical Review". The email went on to state the Region was announcing the news of the tragic deaths of two patients who had been in Intensive Care Units (ICUs) at the Foothills Medical Centre. After extending the Region's sympathies and apologies to the patients' families, the email explained that the deaths had undergone review by the Critical Incident Review Committee. Meetings had been held with the families and they had been told that lessons from what had been discovered were being used to make changes, to minimize the probability of the event recurring. Today the media were being told what the families were told yesterday. No details would be released apart from the facts of the two patients being a middle-aged man and an elderly woman.

The Press Conference was held in the Boardroom and was quickly filled to overflowing, such was the interest. The Board Chair spoke first, followed by the Head of Legal. He echoed the statement in the email sent to all Region staff about limiting some of the information that could be released, such as the patients' identities. Next to speak was the Chief Medical Officer, who apologized on behalf of the Region. At one point, he was almost overcome with the sadness of these two patients' deaths and struggled to control his emotions. He spoke as a clinician who had been involved in patient care for many years, stating the Region's staff felt a "deep sense of loss and pain", adding this was something that would affect them for the rest of their lives.[2] At this point, one of the reporters asked what others in the room considered an inappropriately aggressive question but was quickly told off by colleagues. Then, the Executive Medical Director, and WF, the Medical Director of QIHI, detailed the facts of what had occurred and answered questions.

They announced the death of two critically ill patients in two ICUs at the FMC. They explained that both patients had been undergoing a special type of dialysis (CRRT). They were careful to stress that CRRT was used only in ICUs and was not the type of dialysis most kidney failure patients underwent. The ICU patients had been dialyzed with a solution inadvertently containing potassium chloride rather than sodium chloride. The two chemicals had been substituted when the dialysis fluid was prepared in the Central Pharmacy.

During the Press Conference, Jack was in his office, about fifty feet from the Boardroom where the press was gathered. He knew the CMO and the others would perform well. He also strongly held the belief never to get in the way of those doing a good job. He would wait to see how the media dealt with the admissions and explanations.

The only resulting media coverage later that day was on the local television channels. Despite the press conference team's statements and explanations of the substitution error, and the email with similar statements, the supper-time television news shocked viewers and set the tone for what was to come.

The opening statement, that two dialysis patients were dead, following a "chemical mix-up in a Calgary Hospital", was only the starter.[3] The reporter then stated that staff at the FMC were to blame. He added that the "improperly mixed dialysis solution" contained "potassium chloride, the toxic agent used in lethal injections to induce cardiac arrest".[3]

The day after the press conference, on what was considered 'Day Zero' of press coverage, the newspapers ran front-page stories. As well as headlines, one featured Kathleen's obituary photo, part of the death announcement, and the date on which those had been published in the same newspaper. Reporters had apparently reviewed all the obituaries published over the past few weeks and then telephoned families to inquire if their relative was one of the two newsworthy patients. The Region's promises of confidentiality and privacy had been foiled by the journalists' inquisitiveness.

The headlines in both papers were striking. On one paper, a one-inch tall black headline read, "Two patients dead in tragic error at Foothills Hospital",[4] while the other paper's headline was twice that size: "DEADLY ERROR. Two killed in tragic dialysis blunder at Foothills".[5] The blame continued as a reporter described how he had asked what "was happening to those who foul(ed) up in pharmacy". He stated he and others were "not informed of the fate of those who didn't do their job because that's the business of Human Resources and HR stuff is secret. Anyway, we don't want to blame anyone. Oh no".[2]

The following day, blame mixed with anger continued. One writer of a Letter to the Editor of one of the newspapers asked how "four competent people" could overlook such an obvious error? "Don't they even read the labels on the bottles?"[6] Another wrote, "This isn't like screwing up the order and forgetting the ketchup on the burger".[6] There were as yet no media comments asking to have those who made the errors named, as part of the blaming.

At the Press Conference, WF had emphasized patient safety was of the utmost importance. "We need to build a safer system. That's our ultimate goal here", he said, adding one individual should not be blamed for the deaths.[4] Others echoed WF's recommendation not to blame, including the Minister of Health and Wellness. He was "not interested in finding blame".[7]

However, three days after the Press Conference there seemed to be a call for punishment. And it came from an unlikely source – Jack Davis, the President and CEO of the Region, who had supported going public. He had given an interview to a well-known newspaper columnist, with the interview held in private, except for the presence of the (Acting) Head of Communications. The next day, much of the newspaper's front page was taken up with news of the election of a new leader for the national Conservative party, whose home riding was Calgary. But this was not enough to distract readers from another top of the front-page headline: "EXCLUSIVE. Pharmacy staff to answer for deaths. Health region boss Jack Davis vows those responsible will be held accountable".[8]

The text of the article went on to quote him as an "absolute believer in a very high level of accountability for those in healthcare". He had said, "Yes, there (would) be accountability". His statement was followed by three more separately presented quotations, which we have paraphrased as "We need to determine how much of a problem is related to what one or two people did and problems buried in the system". "We want to make our healthcare system better and ensure our healthcare providers feel confident". "But we must emphasize the importance of each individual being accountable for their work – and I know everyone in the Region would agree with that statement".[8]

Jack had then tempered what seemed to be a blame-oriented statement. Possibly he was influenced by the discussions he'd had with various executives about different options for the technicians. Another influencing voice was that of the Minister of Health and Wellness, who from the outset had been clear that the era of *naming, blaming and shaming* needed to come to an end.

Jack emphasized that the Region's going public about the two deaths was thanks to the Region's professionals being on the cutting edge of the concept of disclosure of harm to patients and informing others outside the Region. He added there was no intent to keep the details hidden. The team at the Region's headquarters were aware the press conference would result in a strong response from both newspaper and television journalists who would have some difficult questions. But the team who faced the media at the first press conference were experts in and devoted to healthcare safety. Their beliefs in what they did to promote and improve safety were greater than any reaction they would face.[8] They had decided to do what they thought was the right thing – for everyone involved. After that, everyone – the Region's staff and doctors – agreed the most important driving factor was the need to carry on making improvements to the care patients received.

But the next day, March 22nd, another columnist focused on Jack's making some remarkably candid statements about the Region's acceptance of responsibility and liability, related to the deaths. The interpretation was that one or perhaps all the pharmacy technicians working with the CRRT solution on February 20th would be found accountable. Jack had not specified any level of accountability, although the columnist did. "A head or heads have to roll. It's simply a matter of justice, of public safety and public confidence". Because two people died, the pharmacy technicians would need to seek employment outside healthcare, where they could no longer work. The columnist also suggested that charges of criminal negligence causing death could be brought, under the Criminal Code of Canada. He likened the technicians' actions to someone who was driving, and while distracted, had hit two pedestrians crossing at a marked intersection on a road with a reduced speed limit.[9] Another article repeated a politician's calls to fire the CEO,[10] as part of the *naming, blaming and shaming*. The news of what seemed like impending punishments spread quickly throughout the Region.

Did the headlines overreach what the columnists had written? Was Jack misinterpreted? Or was he still wavering about what should be done with the technicians? Jack had started his career as a Master's degree psychologist working in the Federal Justice Department at a correctional center. That background had indeed shaped his first opinion, that the individuals responsible should be fired. He was also under a lot of pressure to out the *guilty ones* and *fire them*. One columnist had suggested it made no difference if the events were clues as to an overall lack of competence in the job or if someone had been not as careful as possible. Two patients were dead.[9]

The pressure did not relent. Two days later, a newspaper article appeared without an author's byline. The nature of the two patients' deaths, from the erroneous administration of potassium chloride, was likened to use of the chemical in judicial executions, such as those of Timothy McVeigh, the Oklahoma bomber, and serial killer Aileen Wuornos. Dr. Jack Kevorkian, also known as "Dr. Death", was mentioned for his use of the chemical in his device for physician-assisted suicide. Finally, readers were told that, because of difficulties in detecting potassium in the body after death, some healthcare workers called potassium chloride "the perfect poison". Apparently, many healthcare personnel had used potassium for "surreptitious mercy killings" elsewhere and in Canada.[11]

The day before publication of the mercy killing comments, the Board Chair had provided a statement that was printed in the newspaper. His statement was positioned directly next to those about the anonymous mercy killing comments.[12]

The purpose of the Board Chair's statement was to do several things. Officially, it was intended to tell the public of the Region's commitment. Physicians and employees were doing "everything possible" to ensure the system was as safe as possible. People were working to remove "the frailties of human error out of the system". The Board Chair also defined 'accountability', speaking about the Press Conference the previous week and that the goal in doing so was to ensure they were "accountable to those who use our services". He added "with that professionalism (came) a responsibility to be accountable. To admit when we've done harm through a mistake. To care for the needs and wishes of the families affected by this tragedy and to learn from what we did wrong".[12]

Even the columnist who had interviewed Jack appeared to agree, although he didn't refer to the Board Chair's remarks, but referenced Jack. "Medical staff are trained to help people, not hurt them and cover up". He added any healthcare system that "spawns and hides"[13] hazards and harm would be offensive to healthcare providers' basic beliefs.

Additionally, on March 26th, the Minister of Health and Wellness repeated his belief that it was inappropriate to blame the workers for what happened and issued a request, which the reporter described as "Stop (the) health-care blame game". The Minister said the healthcare system had to eliminate the "culture of name, blame and shame" to help decrease the number of errors made and improve safety. He was quoted as saying "If you ignore the error and bury it, all you do is make your system less safe because the error can then be repeated". The Minister went on to describe the lack of perfection of any healthcare system in the world. He also pointed out that humans were the ones who made decisions and carried out activities. So the healthcare system would always be "subject to human frailties and their capacity to make errors".[14]

Despite the Region's having gone public, and these positive comments from the Board Chair and the Minister, Jack continued to feel the media's pressure. It was not until the arrival in Calgary of the Head of the External Review Team, and a very Canadian *walk in the snow*, that Jack would clearly make up his mind about what to do.

Blame

Life is not without its hazards and dangers, and things can go wrong, sometimes badly, whether any of us are at home, on our way to work, on vacation, or while seeking and obtaining healthcare. Frequently, when we hear of the problem, after learning the extent of the injuries and damage and who were involved, we ask "Who's to blame?". We then link that question with "How did they cause the accident?". In this chapter we therefore describe blame – including why we blame, contributing psychological concepts, blame and the media, and the Person Model and the Blame Cycle.

The Human Tendency to Blame

Why do we blame? The basic answer to that question is – because we're human, because we can think and make judgments. Indeed, much of what is described in this chapter relates to thinking, making judgments and decisions, and coming to conclusions – in general, rather than specifically about blame. These methods and patterns of thinking influence much more than our blaming others. For example, they contribute to our decisions to buy certain products at a certain price, and to facilitate making diagnoses of our patients. These will be further described in Chapter 2.

Some of the judgments and decisions we make are about moral concepts, about what is right and what is wrong. Most of us are brought up to believe that it is right to help those less fortunate than ourselves and those beset by terrible events, such as tsunamis or blizzards, and that it is wrong to steal and to kill. These and similar moral concepts constitute a set of "behavior-guiding norms".[15] Regulation of morality has existed for many thousands of years, enabling us to belong to a family or larger group, to be accepted and to share the necessities of life. These are some of the "social benefits" that come from adhering to the family or group's norms.[16] And if we do not adhere to these norms, then we are likely to be shunned and then blamed.

In English, use of the term, 'to blame', as an action, originated around the 1100s, when it meant to "find fault with". A century later, the action included laying "responsibility on (someone) for something deemed wrong". At about the same time, a term for blame as a concept came into use, when it meant "an act or expression of disapproval, rebuke, etc., for something deemed wrong".[17] Those definitions have differed very little since their origin a thousand or so years ago, reflecting their deep roots in our culture. Additionally, the terms and their meanings relate to the actions of humans – and not to objects or natural forces. Catastrophic deaths and damage resulting from the latter are sometimes referred to as 'Acts of God', a phrase which, interestingly, is still used by the insurance industry. Some would say use of that term is now often incorrect, as many natural disasters would be less horrific if their effects had not been magnified by the actions of some individuals, often in positions of power.

This response could well be based on the perhaps hopeful thinking that, if those involved were to be found guilty, blamed, and then punished, then the disaster, whatever it was, would never – ever – happen again! And then our safety would not be threatened. Yet we know this is not true. Changing the actors in the play, while leaving untouched the script, the settings, and the props means that the play will come to the same conclusions as before, not necessarily every time, but certainly at some time.

Our focus is therefore on the humans involved, which brings us back to the making of moral judgments about transgressions of social mores. In the psychology literature, humans may be considered "agents". As "agents", each of us has a set of 'norms', helping us "coordinate social interaction" and thus "regulate social behavior". These are the functions of moral judgments[15] or how we judge others actions and behaviors.

These judgments form the basis of blaming, which some experts have considered to be socially necessary. Without "social blaming", interpersonal regulation of behaviors changes. For example, over the past several decades, we have seen the rates of marriage decreasing in many societies. Unmarried couples now live together, perhaps for their full lifetimes, and raise children, without blame for the social transgression of not being married. In addition, their children are no longer labeled as 'illegitimate' or 'bastards', those being the terms previously applied to babies born 'out of wedlock'. Such changes in socially regulated behaviors can also lead to certain cultural values not being passed on to the next generation,[15] as well as the possibility of new values being adopted.

Also embedded in the tendency to blame lies the ever-feared concern about intention to harm or to create havoc. Hippocrates stated that physicians must either *do good* or *do no harm*. As we will describe in Chapter 6, it is the extremely rare healthcare provider who comes to work to intentionally harm patients. The resulting media response, describing the shock and horror of such a person's actions can, unfortunately, lead some to think that these actions are commonplace. Indeed, this response has been seen after reporting of deaths related to, for example, a general practitioner in the UK in the late 1980s, a nurse in Germany in the mid-1990s–early 2000s, and a nurse in Ontario, Canada, for a decade up to 2016. The true numbers of such individuals are extremely low. But the names and faces of these killers are often recalled with a degree of clarity that preferably should be awarded to those who do their best to provide comfort and care.

Psychological Concepts Underlying Blame

Even if we had never heard about serial killers in healthcare, the great majority of us still blame others when we learn of harm. Why do we choose this blame-oriented reaction and various associated terms? The answer lies in some of the many methods of problem solving and patterns of thinking that influence our reactions, our decision-making, and our ultimate responses to all situations in life, not only those which might lead us down the path to blaming others. These methods and patterns, known as heuristics, have been studied and explained over the last several decades and are now recognized as specific psychological concepts that can contribute to the rush to blame.

Heuristics have probably arisen as a result of our evolution,[18] with our brains having become very strong and capable of amazing feats of thinking or cognition. Consider, for example, the lunar landing in 1969 and the development of the SARS-CoV-2 (Coronavirus) vaccine in less than a year in 2020–2021. With this strength has also come increased energy requirements, with the average adult brain, which represents about 2% of body weight, requiring about 20% of the body's glucose-derived energy[19] (about 300 calories of glucose each day).

What we know about our thinking has also greatly changed. Starting in the middle of the last century, the new field of social psychology emerged.[20] This was defined as the study of how our thoughts, feelings, and behaviors are influenced by others (real or imaginary).[21]

Social psychology was 'followed' by the field of social cognition. Simply put, cognition is our ability to understand based on our thoughts, perceptions, and sensations. Starting in the 1940s, much of the early work in this area came from developments in computing. Other contributors to this new field were the ideas and methods from cognitive psychology, which developed from the 1950s onwards.[22] Social cognition is thus how we process information in a social setting or situation,[23] and encompasses the many ways by which we work to and succeed in making sense of ourselves and of other people.

The amalgamation of social factors with 'thinking about thinking' contributed to many new concepts and advances, one of which was the human as a processor of information.[24] A second important concept had been described earlier. In 1955, Herbert Simon had described the important concept of our "bounded" or limited rationality or reasoning abilities when we make decisions. These limitations arise from how difficult a decision might be to make, how well we can think (especially at that specific time under specific circumstances), and how much time we have available. This concept is also applicable to blame if one considers the role of strongly experienced emotions in temporarily distorting our abilities to make rational decisions. Such emotions can be triggered by actions committed by others, which then affect our wanted goal, and for which we then blame them.[25]

Yet another concept was that the brain was a "cognitive miser".[26] Previously, as humans, we were all considered to be *rational thinkers*, working our way through problems, thoroughly and carefully. But studies describing *how we actually think* versus *how we are presumed to think* helped modify the rational thinker concept. In fact, we are often *irrational* thinkers, because of our susceptibility to biases as we process all types of information, even that from our social lives. Some of this understanding has stemmed from recognizing *how* we actually decide: we do not seek perfection but adequacy.[27] The concept of the cognitive miser suggests that in some situations, such as when we have large amounts of information to process or if we are stressed, we must be efficient – by taking mental shortcuts. This we do through the use of heuristics, which are further described below.

The concept of the cognitive miser was built on Kahneman's and Tversky's thinking that heuristics reduced cognitive strain.[28] From there, the extension to heuristics potentially saving energy was a logical step. One suggestion is that glycogen, rather than glucose, is what is depleted when we undertake 'heavy thinking'. Glycogen is a form of glucose stored in the astrocytes of the brain, and when depleted, these stores are then replenished when we rest, sleep and when anesthetized. The authors of the study also suggested that mental fatigue was not a sign that the brain's energy source had been depleted. Rather, this was a warning signal that stores were decreasing and would be depleted if the current rate and intensity of activity continued.[29] However, whether or not the brain actually uses less measurable energy when employing heuristics has not yet been shown. Until such studies are successful, we can only continue to think and theorize about cognitive economy.

Sometimes our cognitively economic heuristics work well, for example, when we need to solve a diagnostic problem in a hurry or make a rapid decision about the best way to transport a trauma patient to the hospital in a white-out snowstorm. However, a number of different factors can incorrectly influence – or bias – our thinking to the point where we make cognitive errors or errors in our thinking. These cognitive biases can therefore lead us to making the wrong judgments or decisions, about individuals, events, and outcomes. This concept, linking heuristics, biases, and errors in judgment, was first described by Amos Tversky and Daniel Kahneman in 1973.[28] They were able to show that relying on various heuristics could lead to biased judgments of the probabilities of unique events,[30] and that some of these heuristics could affect both those with scientific and statistical training and those without.[31] For example, when we learn of an adverse but rare event affecting a patient, we start to apply our own statistical probabilities to all we learn about the event. But each probability is based on our own order of how likely the event and its antecedents might be. That is, if our choice(s) seem to represent the event, then we will increase its likelihood of occurrence. This representativeness heuristic can lead us to associating concepts that should not be linked, on the basis of our considerations of their likelihood.[28]

Such patterns of thinking thus influence our decision-making and our responses, including our attributions of blame, and we now describe several of these heuristics and biases that do so.

Illusion of Free Will

The idea of free will, and whether or not we have it, comes to us originally from the concept of fate, with one or more gods determining what would happen to us. Fate was the driver of the plot of Oedipus Rex, by Sophocles. Plato then gave us rational judgments that rule our passions, followed by Epicurus, who described (but in different words) the ideas of *free will* versus *determinism*. John Wesley, the Methodist preacher, then rejected Augustine's earlier predestination as it was contrary to free will. Another contributor to this conceptual evolution was Thomas Hobbes, the English philosopher, for whom free will was choosing to act but not to will, as that was related to things we desire, our passions.[32] By 1770, the concept was summed up by Paul-Henri Thiry, Baron d'Holbach, a French philosopher of the late 1700s. "...in spite of the shackles by which he is bound, it is pretended he is a free agent, or that independent of the causes by which he is moved, he determines his own will, and regulates his own condition....".[33]

Current thinking about the Illusion of Free Will was greatly contributed to by Ellen Langer, an American psychologist. She conducted studies on what she termed the "illusion of control".[34] Langer defined this as our anticipating the likelihood of personal success to be disproportionately greater than suggested by any objective evidence. She distinguished between activities in which skill was involved, and those where chance was the major factor, e.g., buying a winning lottery ticket. Despite this clarifying distinction, we tend to behave as though situations that are dependent only on chance can actually be controlled. Combining this tendency with our wanting to control our environment as much as possible can help us avoid the negative emotions that come with not being in control, or at least, not perceiving that we are.[34]

In 1990, Reason summed up Langer's work as our tendency to think that we have greater control over future events than in reality.[35] If we are brought up in Western societies, then we are likely to value the sense of being in control of what we do. We are considered to have a strong *internal* locus of control, over our actions, behaviors, and choices, as one of our characteristics. Alternatively, an *external* locus of control exists when we think an event was not predictable or resulting from others' control or even from good or bad luck.[36]

In practical terms, what the Illusion of Free Will means is that theoretically we are free to take care, not to work in haste, to pay adequate attention and not behave in a *negligent* manner, that is, free to be *perfect*. Of course, being human, we should know this is not ever possible. We may be tired, hungry, or feeling unwell; rushing because there is an even greater medical or surgical emergency arriving; or struggling to pay attention when distracted by alarms, conversations, or music. Additionally, distraction may come from the arrival of *strangers*, a concept that has been recognized as contributing to the evolution of things going wrong, through activation or initiation. (Strangers may also contribute to dealing with or escaping from the ensuing catastrophe.[37]) At work or at home, we are usually trying hard to do things as well as we can. And when reminded or rebuked, we can try even harder to be perfect – but to no avail. Events may turn for the worse. Thus, when things do go wrong and others are involved, we often rush to ascribe the 'should have been free to be perfect' illusion on them, and blame their involvement for the outcome.[38]

One final comment in this section describing the Illusion of Free Will concerns blaming the victims. Four of the earliest studies applicable to understanding this target of blame were carried out in the 1960s and detail how we tend to blame victims of a bad outcome. The first, by Melvin Lerner, an American social psychologist, described the concept that we work to feel we are not responsible for our wrongdoings. This helps us to minimize or negate personal feelings of shame or guilt. Lerner's study showed that we use an event's outcome to make sense of what we observe, even if luck was considered to play a part in the actions of those involved. This was paraphrased as "people deserve what happens to them".[39]

The second study, by Lerner and psychologist colleague, Carolyn Simmons, also recounted our tendency to blame the victims. We need to continue to believe that "people get what they deserve or, conversely, deserve what they get".[40] This is actually an ages-old concept, mentioned in Judeo-Christian and Islamic teachings – as you sow, you shall reap and do unto others as you would have done to yourself.

The third study was by Elaine Walster, an American social psychologist. She described the important concept that reflecting on a serious accident can lead us to think the victim might have had a role in it and was somehow at fault. Our thinking thusly – and falsely – reassures us that we will not be so affected in the future, because we are both different as a person and in our actions. We are therefore protected from similar calamities. Walster also observed that the worse the outcome, the more we tend to require victims to have been more careful than if the outcome had been less severe.[41] This paper tied in well with another of Walster's – that of second guessing important events,[42] which actually predated Fischhoff's work. (See below: Hindsight.)

Interestingly, the fourth study, by Kelly Shaver, then a PhD student at Duke University, was unable to replicate Walster's findings of "increased assignment of responsibility with increased severity of outcome". While "severity-dependent attribution" appeared consistent with "legal and moral tradition, as well as self-protection", Shaver suggested Walster's findings were possibly due to a lack of the subject matter's "relevance" of the situations posed to the studies' participants. He went on to determine that avoiding blame for an "accidental occurrence" was "more important than avoidance of the outcome itself". Responsibility for the accident was therefore *not attributed* to the individual who might be at fault, but rather to *chance*. Shaver characterized our self-protective tendencies as "defensive attribution" against the randomness of accidents. These could represent threats to our "characters", because of potentially being blamed, and to our "physical safety",[43] thus giving us seemingly greater control over our world.

The studies by Lerner and Simmons in 1966, and then Lerner and Miller in 1978, were the start of Lerner's work describing the Just World Hypothesis[44] (or Just World Fallacy). In the Just World, if we are *good people* and perform *good actions* then we should have *good outcomes* and we attribute the same to others. Conversely, those who are not good or do not do good things deserve bad consequences.

These concepts, while demonstrating what does happen, do not apply to the two patients who died in Calgary in 2004, nor to the other patients mentioned elsewhere. None of them had any control over the events that affected them. But the Just World concept does exist in healthcare and is sometimes misapplied to patients, for example, the intoxicated driver involved in a single-car rollover and now suffering catastrophically life-altering injuries. Healthcare providers may invoke the Just World Hypothesis as a way of coping. We may also apply it when we learn that an individual has been subject to discipline for involvement in the care of a patient when things did not go well.

Fundamental Attribution Error

If adding the *less than perfect* label to someone involved in an adverse event was not enough, we often also describe our colleagues as having certain negative personal characteristics responsible for their problems. However, if we were involved, then we would look outside ourselves for some excuse, some external factors, such as where we work, or the equipment with which we work. The old saying, a *bad workman blames his tools*, describes this reasoning and is an example of the Fundamental Attribution Error or Attribution Effect.

Although the experiments contributing to the description of the Fundamental Attribution Error (FAE) were reported by Jones and Harris in 1967,[45] the name FAE was actually applied a decade later. Ross described the attribution theory as being about ordinary people's attempts to comprehend how witnessed events came to unfold, including what caused them and what might come of them. This was the man-on-the-street psychologically examining his behaviors and those of others.[46] What Ross made clear was our tendency to over-attribute personal characteristics and under-attribute those related to the situation. In particular, the FAE describes our tendency to attribute an individual's error or specific action, for example, exceeding the speed limit, to some aspect of that person's personality or defect in their character, such as being a speed demon or not caring about others. However, if we were to do the same, then we would recognize and describe the context of the situation, for example, we were on call and rushing to the hospital to save a life. Thus, we blame the other person and not ourselves.

Availability Heuristic

The FAE is also related to the Availability Heuristic,[30] which describes our tendency to make judgments based on any immediate examples that come to mind, or are *available*, even if the examples are not closely related. Memories made or concepts learned more recently, and/or associated with strong emotions, are more readily connected to our understanding of a current event. The Availability Heuristic is based on our brain's associating concepts and memories, with the bond between these memories strengthened by repetition, in the same way as when we strengthen our muscles. The link with blame or negligence may come about in cases where increased publicity (especially in the media) may lead us into thinking that certain events occur more often than they really do. In addition, causal relationships between certain concepts, events, and outcomes[47] may be strengthened. This is possible even though our previous knowledge of the event or associated information related to the event was limited. It is the current availability of information in our minds – stimulated and triggered by that provided by the media – which then triggers our associations and reactions as we process the information.

Confirmation Bias

Once we have made our decision about the individual(s) involved, then we may be prey to Confirmation Bias, which describes our tendency to look for, remember and act on information that supports our knowledge or our chosen point of view. This bias is embedded is in our thinking, our values, and even our culture.

We discount or ignore what does not fit with or support what we believe, or refutes our way of thinking. Issues related to deeply held beliefs, or again, those that evoke a strong emotional response are more likely to trigger this specific bias than are their opposites. This bias is credited to Peter Wason, an English psychologist.[48,49] We often make decisions based on our bias very quickly, instead of summing up all the evidence and then coming to a *reasonable* conclusion. These *fast* versus *slow* types of thinking were also first specifically described by Wason and his colleague, Jonathan Evans, who applied the terms "Type 1 and Type 2 processes", and labelling that concept the Dual Process Theory. This theory differentiates between the rapid thinking and decision-making activities, which are unconscious and prone to errors, and the slower thinking and decision-making, which are conscious and much more deliberative.[50] (This fast versus slow thinking is further discussed in Chapter 2 with respect to decision-making.)

Hindsight Bias

Another type of bias related to blaming is perhaps more generally recognized. Hindsight Bias, known by colloquial terms, such as Monday morning quarterbacking and second guessing[42] or anyone could have seen that one coming…, flourishes in hospital and clinic coffee rooms, as well as at case discussions. However, as with many events, it is easy to see a problem coming, to see something happening, once it has happened. This psychological phenomenon was first formally described by Baruch Fischhoff over four decades ago, in his paper describing hindsight and foresight,[51] published at about the same time he gained his PhD. As well as distinguishing hindsight and foresight, Fischhoff showed that possessing knowledge about a past event leads us to judge the event and its outcome differently than if we had no knowledge of that outcome.

The relevance to blame, as well as to investigation, as we shall describe in Chapter 6, is so clear that it is worth detailing more of Fischhoff's paper, as well as some modern practical examples. He started by delineating the different types of information required for both foresight and hindsight. With foresight, there is no knowledge of the outcome, in contrast to hindsight. While this seems an obvious contrast, it led Fischhoff to answer two questions about judgment. These were "How does knowledge of what occurred influence judgment?" and "Are individuals aware of the effect on their judgment in knowing what occurred?"

Fischhoff coined the term "creeping determinism" to describe the concept that even thinking about how something happened renders that outcome more or less a given. He provided three examples. The first of these was how the "law of small numbers" (or "Gamblers' fallacy") describes our belief that small samples of a population must represent the larger, complete population.[52] The second described how normal people volunteered to be admitted to psychiatric hospitals. The paper detailed how the life stories of these *pseudopatients* in psychiatric institutes could be interpreted to show their backgrounds matched their so-called diagnoses.[53] The third example described how individuals, when considering serious outcomes, put together antecedent causes and effects and came to believe that the outcome was more predictable than if they had not spent time in considering it.[42]

Each of these three examples could help foster blame. For example, we link the errors related to potassium made by two technicians to the more numerous and purposeful actions of a nurse giving her patients an overdose of insulin. We then interpret an individual's background to reinforce our developing idea that the individual intended to do something wrong. And the possibility of intended actions contributing to unexpected deaths starts to loom larger in our minds.

One factor that can moderate the effect of Hindsight Bias is that of the consistency between observers' expectations and the outcome. This was shown in 1991 by Schkade and Kilbourne. They studied subjects evaluating employees' decisions related to good and bad outcomes, identifying consistency between expectations and outcomes. When there was a mismatch between what was expected of the employees and their outcomes, then the effect of Hindsight Bias was greater. The effect was magnified if a *good* employee was associated with a *bad* outcome, which Schkade and Kilbourne labeled the "disappointment effect".[54] This concept was partly based on previous findings that bad outcomes were given more weight than were positive ones. This disappointment effect could well help to explain part of the blaming seen in Calgary, with pharmacy technicians who were all considered good workers but involved with such bad outcomes.

Schkade and Kilbourne also cited Karl Weick's earlier work on "sensemaking"[55] to help explain the disappointment effect. In 1969, Weick, then a Professor of Psychology at the University of Minnesota, described sensemaking as our desire to understand events in our lives. We do this by looking back to *make sense* of things, by assimilating what we experienced and what we know. This process occurs automatically and immediately – we almost *can't not do so*. Such assimilation might also contribute to our seeming inability to forget what we learned about the outcome, even if instructed to do so.[51] Retention of the information then has implications for post-event investigators, of the system and of the individuals, as well as our tendency to blame.

Often linked to the Hindsight Bias is the concept of *prevention* – of events and outcomes. The word 'prevent' is derived from the Latin 'praevenire' which means both to anticipate and to hinder or make impossible.[56] Biased thinking can lead to a belief that both errors and death can be prevented, which, of course, is not possible. As will be described in Chapter 2, because errors are part of the human condition, we are unable to prevent them. Similarly, the phrase 'preventable deaths' is illogical because no death is truly preventable. Rather, some deaths are untimely and their too early occurrence might be avoided in some cases, given what was known at the time. (See also Chapter 6 in which avoiding use of the term *prevention* is discussed with respect to writing recommendations after investigations.) With respect to blame, we review the problem, declare it preventable, and then blame those involved in the patient's care for not seeing the problem coming, for not hindering the outcome. Again, it is easy to see the problem coming...after the fact...

Symmetry Bias

We also have an innate drive for symmetry – in what we see and perceive. This bias can be recognized when comparing beautiful and handsome faces – or not. Those at the *yes* end of the scale tend to be remarkably symmetrical, as often exemplified by the publicity photos of film and TV stars. This bias was first described by Theodore Newcomb, one of the earliest American social psychologists. In 1953 he showed that the stronger a subject's attitude toward another then the greater the likelihood of "cognitive distortion toward symmetry".[57] This seeking of symmetry applies also when we learn of a terrible outcome for a patient, such as a rapid death from the inadvertent administration of potassium. We innately feel that the shock and horror of the outcome must be matched by (or be symmetrical with) equally shocking and horrible actions on the part of those either directly or indirectly providing care. We have difficulty understanding that the death could occur partly because of a simple, unconscious substitution of one clear liquid, such as potassium chloride, for another clear liquid, i.e., sodium chloride. Surely the situation could not be that simple...

Negativity Bias

The final bias in this list is the Negativity Bias, first described in 2001.[58] This bias means that negative events are noticed, thought about, and remembered more often than positive events. And while there are many more positive events than negative, the latter have a greater effect than do the positive – even if they are of a similar strength.

All of this might be related to an underlying part of the Negativity Bias – "contagion and contamination", as in, exposure to or contact with substances, objects, or people with a negative effect ("contagion") leading to "contamination".[58] The Negativity Bias includes the principle that a *negative* body delivers *greater contagion* than a *positive* one can reduce contagion. (In real-world terms, adding pure water to dirty does not make the water safe to drink.[59]) The theoretical basis of the Negativity Bias suggests we have learned it is safer to be cautious in the face of threats, offering as an example, taste bud thresholds. While sweetness can be detected at one in two hundred parts, bitterness has a much lower threshold at one in two million parts, helping us detect poisons, which tend to be bitter rather than sweet. Additionally, the emotional response to a positive or safe taste is not as strong as the response to the negative or dangerous taste.[60] Thus, the evolutionary link of the Negativity Bias with dirty water is indeed possible, and this bias is therefore deeply engrained. Additionally, some further partial support for this theory comes from research related to Hindsight Bias.

The Path Model of Blame

Another way of looking at blame extends past moral judgments and heuristics. As Malle and colleagues detailed in their "Path Model of Blame" in 2014,[16] blaming also requires us to be able to think through five ideas. First, we need to understand our "behavior guiding norms" and observe another person not following those norms. Next, we must deduce that person's mental state, which requires our thinking about the "event or outcome". There must be a link between either of these and the person, allowing "causation" to be determined. Then we have to judge if the person had "intentionality" in deciding not to follow the norms. Fourth, we must question if the person had "justification" – or not – in acting as they did and if they had an "obligation" to minimize the probability of the event occurring, as in, they "should have…". Finally, we should learn if the person had the "capacity" to minimize the probability of the event occurring, or "could have…". Putting together all the answers to those points allows calculation of the degree of blame.[16] Thus, blaming has both social and cognitive aspects.

Two aspects of the Path Model of Blame, intentionality and the "should have known" concept, including its link to negligence, require further description and discussion.

Intentionality

Humans have the ability to recognize social behavior that is intentional. This ability starts in infancy and progressively evolves into the adult-level skills, where little cognitive effort is required to recognize someone's intentions. (Of course, some of the perception of intention could also be related to the Illusion of Free Will.) Generally, unintentional social norm violations are less badly perceived than intentional ones. In Malle and colleagues' model,[16] the basis for blame is the making of a retrospective decision about intention, which was linked to retribution. If there was no intention, the question arises of whether or not the individual had an "obligation" to *prevent* the action, that is, *should have done so.*

If this was not possible, then the next step would be to consider if the individual had "capacity" to *prevent* or avoid the event or outcome, that is, *could have done so*. These two concepts were linked to reformation[15] or restoration.

For example, in Jack Davis' interview in 2004, in which he said he believed strongly in healthcare workers' accountability, it could be that he was at the stage of determining causality. The Region had determined that there had been no intentionality on the part of the technicians, but obligation and capacity had yet to be determined.

Should Have Known

Readers with legal knowledge or experience will recognize this phrase as part of the definition of negligence. We raise this point for two reasons. First, in 1997, in his discussions of Just Culture, Reason described negligence as either a circumstance a *reasonable and prudent* individual would have anticipated and avoided, or a circumstance resulting from actions. At about that time, the term negligence was frequently bandied about by healthcare providers when discussing cases that had gone badly. The phrase, 'that's so negligent', was meant to imply the care provider *should have seen the problem coming*, with foreseeability being one of the four requirements for negligence. A Judge might pronounce the harm a patient suffered as *reasonably foreseeable*, followed by, "Doctor, you should have known". Interestingly, this phrase is the hallmark of Hindsight Bias, which can befall anyone, including judges and juries.[61–63]

Second, after the two deaths in the Region, the Press raised the concepts of blame and (criminal) negligence, although only the Courts can deliver a verdict of negligence. To be clear, we are not saying any blame-worthy act means the individual committing the act (or omitting to do something) is also negligent.

Essentially, we disagree with the concept of including a description of negligence in safety investigations. Indeed, we think negligence should not feature in any healthcare tools associated with Just Culture, because this concept belongs to the legal domain and not to healthcare. We do not dispute the rights of patients and their families to sue and to seek legal redress in the case of harm suffered during healthcare. However, litigation and possible findings of negligence are and should remain separate from the Just Culture, which is part of safety management for an organization.

Blame and the Media

Having described an individual's response to others' possibly blameworthy acts, and given one example of the media taking a specific point of view with respect to negligence, we now consider how the response of the media in general differs from that of individuals. One of most obvious differences is in the size of the audience. The media's reaction can be seen by more than just a few individuals, as might normally occur in a pre-newspaper/pre-internet society, and sometimes even in a pre-social media society. Today, media reports and opinions can be almost instantaneously transmitted to millions, the results of which can be either positive or negative if individuals are influenced, which they frequently are. For example, transmitting information about a truly blameworthy event that threatens the nation can result in individuals activating their own opinions, and possibly actions, for the good.

But the opposite can also occur. The media may not only play a role in transmitting information about situations in which blame was laid by others, it may take on a role in casting blame. While individuals who work for various media outlets have a right to express their opinions about an event, problems can arise when the media institution does so deliberately, making and forming opinions to encourage their adoption by the audience. About a decade ago, research looking at the prevalence and nature of blame in the top American news stories of 2010 determined that "blame in the news" had become "ritualized".[64] This term was adapted from the idea of "ritualized opposition" to concepts and events in the media, as well as in politics and the law. While opposition to reports can be considered essential and helpful in encouraging discussion and progressive change, problems arise when some reactions are automatically oppositional, occasionally to the point where they can be destructive.[65]

Blame can be part of that automatic negative reaction from the media, with the question or statement of "Who is to blame?" sometimes leading the response. This was seen in the first media announcement of news of the two deaths at the Foothills Medical Centre, where the staff were blamed. But the blame did not stop there. It was picked up and repeated by the newspaper reports, even after the lack of blameworthiness of the Central Pharmacy technicians was asserted in a published statement to the press by the Board Chair. Applying Malle and colleague's Path Model of Blame,[16] we can see that the technicians, who lacked intentionality, might have had some degree of obligation to try to stop the event during the phase of the dialysate preparation – if they had recognized it, which they had not. Moreover, they certainly had no capacity to do so once the dialysate had been put into the CRRT bags for use.

Furthermore, some in the media continued to wave the flag of blame, not on the basis of the incorrect preparation of the solution but on the basis of the deaths, the outcome. Comparisons were drawn with a driver whose unintentional but negligent actions led to a fatal outcome. This was described as a situation in which blame would officially be laid. Even individuals who made "errors" (but broke no rules) were to be similarly treated.[66] What the motivation might be for this approach is unknown. It could possibly be related to crafting specific headlines and editorials to increase sales of papers, a concept that is a slightly distant cousin to *clickbaity headlines.* (These are articles or other types of internet content that is specifically designed to entice readers to *click* on that item or webpage.)

Another motivation could be linked to the Negativity Bias. Thus, when we learn of bad news from the media, our innate bias is to pay greater attention to it than to good news, whether this is the report of two tragic deaths or an institution's report. We pay greater attention to the news of poor performance over good.[67] This in turn has us pay more attention to the media reports. Then, the more we notice negative events, the more we suspect that the institution or organization is faulty, regardless of the number of positive events that occur. This could also explain some of the media's reaction.

Blaming an organization is not helpful as it sets up a barrier to open discussions about improvements, with some institutions becoming averse to things going badly.[68] This may also help to explain why certain of the Region's Executives were not enthusiastic about informing the public of the two potassium-related deaths. They were part of the organization during previous events when the Region's reputation was at an all-time low. There was no interest to be part of something similar, with the prospect of calls to name, shame and blame – and potentially to punish – those who were considered to be at fault. This concept of punishment, therefore, brings us to the Blame Cycle and its associated Person Model.

The Blame Cycle

As described above, all of the cognitive biases contribute to our blaming and they also contribute to our wishing to or actually invoking punishment. The Blame Cycle starts with our judging an individual who made errors. Because of the Illusion of Free Will, we think these actions were not automatic but voluntary and deliberate. Management invokes warnings, cautions, and threats, but people continue to make errors. Management becomes angry because helpful advice is being ignored and therefore increases in number, frequency, and strength of exhortations and eventually punishment.[69] Certain punishments can have an effect on specific individuals. For example, if fired, then individuals can no longer make errors in that particular job.

That was what some individuals in the Region and some in the media in Calgary were calling for, in March 2004. Indeed, the CEO had initially thought the technicians should be fired but then changed his mind. Of course, firing individuals is not the only possible form of professional punishment. There are also personal forms of punishment that individuals mete out, which include reproach and rebuke. These terms are quite similar, but to reproach is considered a milder version of rebuke. Both express concerns with one or more individuals and attitudes expressed or actions undertaken. Use of either of these terms is intended to encourage the individual(s) to cease and desist whatever they are doing, without resorting to formal resources.

The Blame Cycle is associated with the Person Model, and, before 2004, the Region had unwittingly leaned heavily toward using this Model in its dealings with employees. The Person Model was one of three, described in 1989 by Dr. Deborah Lucas, a Human Factors specialist, with the other two models being the Engineering Model and the System Model.[70] She also aligned the models with thinking about and dealing with human error. The Person Model, the *classical* model, was aligned with occupational safety management. The model emphasized selection and training to deal with personal actions, as in "unsafe acts",[71] and personal characteristics such as carelessness and accident proneness. The Engineering Model was a part of risk management, focusing on the man-machine interface. Some of its associated problems were operators' errors and violations of procedures, with Human Reliability Assessment, fault and event trees, and databases featured as ways of dealing with the problems. The System Model was described as having system-induced errors related to latent failures in the system, while corrective action plans and a safety system were each suggested as improvement techniques.[70]

Lucas' three-part model was cited and described by Reason.[69] Thereafter, he simplified the concept to the first and third components. (See, for example, Reason, 2000.[72]) He described the Person versus the System Model in various presentations and further publications. This led to the popular reception and adoption of these two contrasting models, in aviation and healthcare, where the System Model has gained traction, particularly in aviation. Unfortunately, the Person Model continues to hold sway in some parts of the world in aviation and in much of healthcare, as well as in the eyes of the media and the public.

With respect to blame, the Person Model describes how we have traditionally viewed the role of individuals involved in events that either actually or nearly led to harm. In this model, individuals are considered agents who are free to choose what they do and how they do it. They are therefore free to choose to do things *carefully*. And when a patient is harmed or nearly harmed, then the individual is deemed to have acted – by choice – in an unsafe way. In addition, we – the recipients or the audience of these events – choose to project our own explanations of the actions onto the agent. We say the individual was careless, hasty or not paying *enough* attention. Sometimes we even deem the individual negligent, with the phrase, "That's so negligent", bandied about in corridor conversations.

In general, we can therefore see that blame in these situations is not a useful concept. As the late Professor John Senders, of the Faculty of Engineering, the University of Toronto, pithily observed in 1994, "Blaming people for making errors is like blaming them for breathing. They will do both willy-nilly".[73] Similarly, Dr. Todd Conklin, at the USA Los Alamos National Laboratory, questioned, "Does blame have any value at all in understanding this event?"[74] Thus, avoiding blame is generally to be encouraged.

In summary, in this chapter we have dissected and discussed blame and reasons why we blame, and determined the underlying psychological concepts, and the Path Model, as well as the role of the media and the Blame Cycle with its associated Person Model. Although blame might still be useful in some social circumstances because it helps to set social norms, blaming individuals for what they experienced or what they did is generally counterproductive. In the next chapter, we look at how and why we do some of the things that can result in us being blamed: how we remember, how we think, and why we make different types of errors and break rules.

References

1. Olsen T. Hospital tragedies boost CHR critics. *Calgary Herald: Inside Politics.* 2004;A6 (col. 5).
2. Bell R. Spin doctors. *The Calgary Sun.* 2004 Mar 19;5.
3. *CBC Calgary News.* Canada: CBC News. 2004.
4. Toneguzzi M. Two patients dead in tragic error at Foothills Hospital. *Calgary Herald.* 2004 Mar 19;A1 (col. 6) & A4 (col. 3).
5. Deadly error. Two killed in tragic dialysis blunder at Foothills. *The Calgary Sun.* 2004 Mar 18;1.
6. Cooper S, Wade JS. Saying sorry isn't good enough. *Calgary Herald: Opinion.* 2004 Mar 20;A20 (col. 2& 5).
7. Ward J, Mark M. Mar not interested in looking for blame. *The Calgary Sun.* 2004 Mar 19;5.
8. Braid D. Pharmacy staff to answer for deaths, Health region boss Jack Davis vows those responsible will be held accountable. *Calgary Herald: Exclusive.* 2004 Mar 21;A1 (col. 1).
9. Gradon J. Facing up to double jeopardy. *Calgary Herald: City & Region.* 2004 Mar 22;B1 (col. 2)–B4 (col. 4).
10. Richards G. Grit wants Klein to fire CHR boss. *Calgary Herald.* 2004 Mar 23;B5.
11. Potassium chloride a "perfect poison". *Calgary Herald: Top News.* 2004 Mar 24;A3 (col. 2).
12. Tuer D. It is vital we learn from these mistakes. *Calgary Herald.* 2004 Mar 24;A3 (col. 4).
13. Braid D. Reform for the patients. *Calgary Herald: City & Region.* 2004 Mar 26;B1 (col. 4) & B6 (col. 2).
14. Toneguzzi M. Stop health-care blame game. *Calgary Herald.* 2004 Mar 27;A1 (col. 1) & A16 (col. 2).

15. Malle BF, Guglielmo S, Monroe AE. Moral, cognitive and social: The nature of blame. In: Forgas J, Fiedler K, Sedikides C, editors. *The Sydney Symposium of Social Psychology (2012) Social Thinking and Interpersonal Behavior.* 1st ed. Philadelphia: Psychology Press; 2017. pp. 311–29.

16. Malle BF, Guglielmo S, Monroe AE. A theory of blame. *Psychol Inq.* 2014 Apr 3;25(2):147–86.

17. Blame [Internet]. Online Etymology Dictionary; 2021 [cited 2022 Feb 9]. Available from: https://www.etymonline.com/word/blame

18. Stevens J. The evolutionary biology of decision making. In: Engel C, Wolf S, editors. *Better than Conscious? Decision Making, the Human Mind, and Implications for Institutions.* Cambridge: The MIT Press; 2008. pp. 285–304.

19. Mergenthaler P, Lindauer U, Dienel GA, Meisel A. Sugar for the brain: The role of glucose in physiological and pathological brain function. *Trends Neurosci.* 2013 Oct;36(10):587–97.

20. Sewell WH. Some reflections on the golden age of interdisciplinary social psychology. *Annu Rev Sociol.* 1989 Aug;15(1):1–16.

21. Allport GW. *The Nature of Prejudice: 25th Anniversary ed.* Reading: Addison-Wesley; 1954.

22. Hilton D. The emergence of cognitive social psychology: A historical analysis. In: Kruglanski A, Stroebe W, editors. *Handbook of the History of Social Psychology.* Hove, England: Psychology Press; 2012. pp. 45–79.

23. Frith CD. Social cognition. *Philos Trans R Soc B Biol Sci.* 2008 Jun 12;363(1499): 2033–9.

24. North M, Fiske S. A history of social cognition. In: Kruglanski AW, Stroebe AW, editors. *Handbook of the History of Social Psychology.* Hove, England: Routledge; 2011. pp. 81–99.

25. Simon HA. A behavioral model of rational choice. *Q J Econ.* 1955 Feb 1;69(1): 99–118.

26. Fiske S, Taylor S. *Social Cognition.* 1st ed. New York: McGraw-Hill; 1984.

27. Herbert S, Simon HA, Herbert S. Rational decision making in business organizations. *Am Econ Rev.* 1979;69(4):293–513.

28. Kahneman D, Tversky A. Subjective probability: A judgment of representativeness. *Cogn Psychol.* 1972 Jul;3(3):430–54.

29. Christie ST, Schrater P. Cognitive cost as dynamic allocation of energetic resources. *Front Neurosci.* 2015 Aug 24;9: 1–15.

30. Tversky A, Kahneman D. Availability: A heuristic for judging frequency and probability. *Cogn Psychol.* 1973 Sep;5(2):207–32.

31. Tversky A, Kahneman D. Judgment under uncertainty: Heuristics and biases. *Science.* 1974 Sep 27;185(4157):1124–31.

32. Cary P. A brief history of the concept of free will: Issues that are and are not germane to legal reasoning. *Behav Sci Law.* 2007 Mar 28;25(2):165–81.

33. Holbach BP. The illusion of free will. In: Kolak D, Martin R, editors. *Experience of Philosophy.* 5th ed. Oxford: Oxford University Press; 2002. pp. 176–81.

34. Langer EJ. The illusion of control. *J Pers Soc Psychol.* 1975;32(2):311–28.

35. Reason J. *Human Error.* Cambridge: Cambridge University Press; 1990.

36. Rotter JB. Generalized expectancies for internal versus external control of reinforcement. *Psychol Monogr Gen Appl.* 1966;80(1):1–28.
37. Turner B, Pidgeon N. *Man-Made Disasters.* 2nd ed. Oxford: Butterworth-Heinemann; 1997.
38. Reason J. Foreword. In: Bogner M, editor. *Human Error in Medicine.* Hillsdale: Lawrence Erlbaum Associates Inc.; 1994. pp. vii–xv.
39. Lerner MJ. Evaluation of performance as a function of performer's reward and attractiveness. *J Pers Soc Psychol.* 1965 Apr;1(4):355–60.
40. Lerner MJ, Simmons CH. Observer's reaction to the "innocent victim": Compassion or rejection? *J Pers Soc Psychol.* 1966;4(2):203–10.
41. Walster E. Assignment of responsibility for an accident. *J Pers Soc Psychol.* 1966;3(1):73–9.
42. Walster E. Second guessing important events. *Hum Relations.* 1967 Aug;20(3): 239–49.
43. Shaver KG. Defensive attribution: Effects of severity and relevance on the responsibility assigned for an accident. *J Pers Soc Psychol.* 1970 Feb;14(2):101–13.
44. Lerner MJ, Miller DT. Just world research and the attribution process: Looking back and ahead. *Psychol Bull.* 1978;85(5):1030–51.
45. Jones EE, Harris VA. The attribution of attitudes. *J Exp Soc Psychol.* 1967 Jan;3(1):1–24.
46. Ross L. The intuitive psychologist and his shortcomings: Distortions in the attribution process. In: Berkowitz L, editor. *Advances in Experimental Social Psychology.* New York: Academic Press; 1977. pp. 173–220.
47. Perry A. Guilt by saturation: Media liability for third-part violence and the availability heuristic. *Northwest Univ Law Rev.* 2003;97(2):1045–73.
48. Wason P. On the failure to eliminate hypotheses in a conceptual task. *Q J Exp Psychol.* 1960 Jul 1;12(3):129–40.
49. Wason P. Reasoning about a rule. *Q J Exp Psychol.* 1968 Aug 1;20(3):273–81.
50. Wason PPC, Evans JSBT. Dual processes in reasoning? *Cognition.* 1974 Jan;3(2): 141–54.
51. Fischhoff B. Hindsight is not equal to foresight: The effect of outcome knowledge on judgment under uncertainty. *J Exp Psychol Hum Percept Perform.* 1975; 1(3):288–9.
52. Tversky A, Kahneman D. Belief in the law of small numbers. *Psychol Bull.* 1971; 76(2):105–10.
53. Rosenhan DL. On being sane in insane places. *Science.* 1973 Jan 19;179(4070): 250–8.
54. Schkade DA, Kilbourne LM. Expectation-outcome consistency and hindsight bias. *Organ Behav Hum Decis Process.* 1991 Jun;49(1):105–23.
55. Weick K. *The Social Psychology of Organizing.* 1st ed. Reading: Addison-Wesley; 1969.
56. Prevention [Internet]. Online Etymology Dictionary; 2021 [cited 2022 Feb 9]. Available from: https://www.etymonline.com/word/prevention
57. Newcomb T. An approach to the study of communicative acts. *Psychol Rev.* 1953; 60(6):393–404.

58. Rozin P, Royzman E. Negativity bias, negativity dominance, and contagion. *Personal Soc Psychol Rev.* 2001 Nov 1;5(4):296–320.

59. Angelakis AN, Antoniou GP, Yapijakis C, Tchobanoglous G. History of hygiene focusing on the crucial role of water in the Hellenic asclepieia (i.e., ancient hospitals). *Water.* 2020 Mar 9;12(3): 754–70.

60. Cacioppo JT, Cacioppo S, Gollan JK. The negativity bias: Conceptualization, quantification, and individual differences. *Behav Brain Sci.* 2014 Jun 27;37(3):309–10.

61. Guthrie C, Rachlinski J, Wistrich A. Inside the judicial mind. *Cornell Law Fac Publ.* 2001;86:777–830.

62. LaBine SJ, LaBine G. Determinations of negligence and the hindsight bias. *Law Hum Behav.* 1996;20(5):505–16.

63. Hastie R, Schkade DA, Payne JW. Juror judgments in civil cases: Hindsight effects on judgments of liability for punitive damages. *Law Hum Behav.* 1999 Oct;23(5):445–70.

64. Wyatt WN. Blame narratives and the news. *J Commun Monogr.* 2012 Sep 22; 14(3):153–208.

65. Tannen D. Agonism in academic discourse. *J Pragmat.* 2002 Oct; 34(10–11):1651–69.

66. Generous to a fault. *Calgary Herald: Opinion.* 2004 Jul 1;A10 (col.1).

67. Yang K, Holzer M. The performance-trust link: Implications for performance measurement. *Public Adm Rev.* 2006 Jan 9;66(1):114–26.

68. Charbonneau E, Bellavance F. Blame avoidance in public reporting. *Public Perform Manag Rev.* 2012 Mar 1;35(3):399–421.

69. Reason J. *Managing the Risks of Organizational Accidents.* Aldershot: Ashgate Publisher; 1997.

70. Lucas DA. Wise men learn by others' harms, fools by their own: Organisational barriers to learning the lessons from major accidents. In: Walter M, Cox R, editors. *Safety and Conference Proceedings Safety and Reliability in the 90s: Will Past Experience or Prediction Meet Our Needs?* 1st ed. Boca Raton: CRC Press; 1990. p. 20.

71. Williams S. The causes of automobile accidents. *Am Bar Assoc Sect Insur Neglig Compens Law Proc.* 1935:55–9.

72. Reason J. Human error: Models and management. *BMJ.* 2000 Mar 18;320 (7237):768–70.

73. Senders J. Medical devices, medical errors, and medical accidents. In: Bogner M, editor. *Human Error in Medicine.* 1st ed. Hillsdale: Lawrence Erlbaum; 1994. pp. 159–177.

74. Conklin T. *Pre-Accident Investigations. An Introduction to Organizational Safety.* Aldershot: Ashgate; 2012.

Chapter 2

"And She Died Because of One of the Most Dreadful Medical Mistakes Ever Revealed in Alberta, or All of Canada."[1]

News of the events leading to the two deaths triggered memories in other patients or family members of patients, who had also suffered mix-ups with medications. Some of the patients or family members contacted the newspapers, which ran larger font front-page headlines: "Medical mix-up occurred before". This was followed by a graphic account of one patient's experience, as she screamed at the nurse, "My heart's on fire. My heart's on fire.[2]"

The woman in question had, in error, been given a solution of potassium chloride rather than sodium chloride, to flush her IV line clear. Despite the patient's cries, the nurse apparently administered a second injection, before observing "something wasn't right" and alerting the doctors and the cardiac arrest team.[2]

DOI: 10.4324/9781003185307-3

A second patient recalled a frighteningly similar event. A man had been given an intravenous injection by a nurse, two months after the first event – and at the same hospital. He described feeling "an incredible burning sensation" that moved from head to toes and back again. He thought his "heart was going to burst out of (his) chest". Despite his cries he'd been given the wrong drug, he said the nurse argued with him. When he demanded that the doctor come, the nurse apparently turned, saw the vial, and called for help.[3]

Because of the press reports of other patients who had previously suffered harm related to potassium, the Region held another Press Conference on March 21st, with the CMO, the EMD-SW, and the Director of Pharmacy Services being the spokesmen. This was a more hastily arranged event, with one of the speakers called in from home without his being able to change from the sweat-shirt he was wearing.

The purpose of this second Press Conference was to clarify the difference between previous events and those that led to the recent deaths. In fact, the patients' stories in the paper were related to nurses erroneously using potassium chloride (from a 10 mL vial that was partly purple in color) instead of sodium chloride (from a 10 mL vial that was partly yellow in color). The liquid was used to flush the patients' intravenous lines in their arms. This was very different from the mix-up between twelve 250 mL bottles of potassium chloride instead of sodium chloride used in the Central Pharmacy for compounding the dialysate solution. The chemical, potassium chloride, was the only link between the events of 2000 and 2004.[4]

Not all the press accounts were about potassium. Another headline read: "Antibiotic dosage errors strike fear in mothers".[5] The previous month, two new mothers had received phone calls from a hospital in Edmonton, Alberta. The women had been told their newly discharged babies had been given an inadvertent overdose – of antibiotics. The report described the concerns felt by the mothers as they received the news and when their babies were readmitted for observation. Although nothing abnormal was found, the events were not to be forgotten by the families. And it didn't matter to these women that the medications were different from the ones substituted in the CRRT. What mattered to them was the fact that one medication or dose had been administered instead of another, the harm they had suffered (whether physical and/or psychological), and the fear this latest report had triggered.[5]

After all, dispensing the correct medication in the correct dose didn't sound that difficult. And the descriptions provided at the Press Conference seemed to confirm that. The procedure for CRRT required the technician to get the list of the three ingredients: sterile water, magnesium, and sodium chloride. After collecting each of the ingredients, the technician passed them to another technician who again verified the short list. A third technician then put together the mixture, working in a special sterile section of the Pharmacy. A fourth check of the ingredients was made and the CRRT sent to the distribution area.[6]

However, another healthcare provider was not so charitable when describing the problem. During his 30-year career, he had apparently given "thousands of safe doses" of potassium chloride. He was quoted as saying an individual would have to be "blind and illiterate" to confuse potassium chloride and sodium chloride. He described the label for potassium chloride as "purple" and that for sodium chloride as "yellow" and that the labels had been like that "from time immemorial". He added, that mixing up the labels was a "very, very hard mistake" to make, because the bottles' written labels were as distinct as their colors. He added a worker would have to "both not see and not read" to mix the two up. Any Regional employee who mixed up the drugs had to be "so stressed, overworked or distracted" that they just weren't paying any attention to what they were doing.[7] In fact, the colors of the vials described by this individual were for 10 mL vials of potassium and sodium chloride, and not the colors of the 250 mL bottles used in the Central Pharmacy to mix the CRRT, which were quite different and not so distinct from each other.

Another reporter succinctly summed up the problem. Two patients at the FMC had died. The deaths had apparently occurred after a series of errors led to a chemical mix-up. One chemical was "life-sustaining", the other was "life-destroying". And the latter was injected slowly "into the veins of two unsuspecting victims".[8]

By way of a partial explanation, the CMO tried to get at the fact that making errors was not from want of trying. "Despite our best efforts, errors do occur".[9] Another reporter added his own understanding, writing that the action of mixing chemicals had "probably been repeated correctly hundreds of times, or even thousands. But the odds were increasingly in favor of a mistake".[10] From elsewhere in Canada, a patient safety advisor and internal medicine specialist offered the explanatory concept of errors occurring during a slip in concentration, when an individual could "write down the wrong dose of a medication, or calculate the dose incorrectly", or could grab a "bottle they thought was something else".[11]

Three other statements were reported in the press. The first was about errors being made "daily" at the specifically designed and newly opened Central Pharmacy. These errors were reported to the President of the Pharmacists Association by other pharmacists who "deluged" him with calls after the facility was opened. No other details about reported problems were given in the article.[12] The two other statements arose from the release on March 25 of a Region-wide culture survey, which asked employees various questions, including those about working conditions and errors. Slightly more than three-quarters of survey respondents thought mistakes were truly hazardous to their patients' safety. And just over one-quarter of respondents said in the past year they'd observed a coworker trying to save some time and thus doing something risky.[13]

Similarly, a safety expert was clear that a nurse who gave potassium chloride directly from a vial and into a vein was demonstrating a "dereliction of duty".[7] (This had not happened at the FMC but at the Peter Lougheed Centre, one of the three other acute care adult hospitals in Calgary.)

Countering this expert's statement, however, was the Minister of Health and Wellness, who tabled a letter in the Legislature from the Canadian Society of Hospital Pharmacists. Received on March 23, the letter stated most errors in healthcare were from what were termed "system errors", as appeared to be the case in Calgary, and "not the negligence of individual providers".[14]

Additionally, in hoping to allay fears, the EMD-COM called the incident an "inadvertent error". He added that officials were "100 per cent sure this was not a deliberate event".[9]

From Memory and Information Processing to Errors, Noncompliance and Willful Intent to Harm

As humans, we all make errors; in fact, each of us makes many errors every day. For example, we may ask for salt instead of sugar, forget our lunch at home, or plan the wrong route to drive to work. As we explain shortly, each of these examples is a different type of error and each can contribute to a problem: coffee with a salty taste, hunger mid-afternoon, or an hour's delay in getting to work.

We also appreciate that making errors is how we learn to do things better or more correctly. In fact, Reason has suggested that, depending on the context, errors and violations are neither good nor bad but depend on evaluation of the performance and the outcome achieved.[15] However, in this chapter we consider the negative effect of errors (and noncompliance) in how they contribute to problems. As Rasmussen observed in 1982, "Human errors can in a way be considered as unsuccessful experiments with unacceptable consequences".[16]

Why do we make these errors? Essentially, the problem is related to information. We lack it or misunderstand it, misinterpret it, or misuse it. And sometimes we forget it. In this chapter we will therefore describe how we use and store information, starting with an explanation of memory and some problems with it. We follow this description with how the brain processes information (actually the brain's sole task), a description of two information processing frameworks and their associated types of errors, and how and why we make errors. We also discuss rule-breaking, which sometimes looks similar to making an error, for example, if we drive slowly past a stop sign that is hidden by overgrown bushes. At other times, albeit rarely, rule-breaking is completely different, as in sabotage, also known as intent to harm, which we describe at the end of this chapter.

Memory

Memory is used in all aspects of information processing and consists of three stages – sensory (or sensory buffer memory), short-term memory (sometimes called working memory), and long-term memory.[17]

Sensory Memory

Information rests here only briefly while it is being processed. This is the memory storage site and gateway of all sensory information to the brain. The capacity of this site to hold discrete items is not very large, except for those items relating to visual information. The important question, "What can be seen in one brief exposure?", was answered by a newly minted PhD, Dr. George Sperling. During his doctoral research at Harvard, he determined that "more is seen than can be remembered" by showing there was a limit on the number of items that could be remembered (and reported). This was 9.1 letters or 40.1 "bits of information", after the visual stimulus was shown for 50 ms. That we "see more than is remembered" related to the fact that a visual image persisted for a fraction of a second after the stimulus was removed, but also depended on a "persisting visual image of the stimulus".[18]

Short-Term Memory

Another temporary storage site is the short-term memory, which we use when actively processing new information, either for short-term use or for transfer and transformation into long-term memory. Short-term memory is composed of auditory information, visual-spatial information, and an attentional control system.[19] We retain information in short-term memory, while we transform it, through rehearsal, to create or consolidate a memory. This task uses cognitive resources, which are in limited supply in this part of the brain, and if we try to do something else at the same time, then the rehearsal comes to a halt. As a result, the memory fades more quickly. Retention in short-term memory is of limited duration, allowing us to immediately use the information, as in dialing a telephone number we read or heard spoken.

In 1959, Professor Lloyd Peterson, and his wife, Margaret Jean Peterson, psychologists at the University of Minnesota, contributed to what is now known as the forgetting curve. (This is also recognized as a landmark study of the duration of short-term memory.) Students were shown meaningless combinations of three letters (trigrams) and then prevented from rehearsing to consolidate the memories before being tested. The forgetting curve showed that, after three seconds, students correctly recalled 80% of the trigrams, but only 50% after six seconds and fewer than 10% after 18 seconds. Additionally, the results of this study became the basis for the general acceptance that we have perhaps 20 seconds at the most[20] to use information in the short-term memory, unless we reactivate the memory. We can do this, for example, by repeating the number verbally – that is, rehearsing it.

Our short-term memory's capacity is also limited. Most adults can recall seven, plus or minus two, pieces, items, or chunks of information,[21] with a chunk representing "recoding of smaller units of information into larger, familiar units".[22] Chunk pieces or items are bound together by two different types of properties. A physical property, for example, is represented by the white spaces between the three groupings of a typical North American phone number including an area code: 555 123 4567. A cognitive property would be the personal familiarity of the 555 area code, which renders the three numbers into one chunk. Our brains chunk things by "grouping or organizing a sequence of inputs and recoding it with a concise name".[22] Chunking therefore changes these ten numbers (5551234567) plus the white spaces (555 123 4567) into three chunks or meaningful groupings, which are now much more easily remembered. We can retain up to ten chunks, but the more chunks we try to retain, the shorter the period for recall, with up to 70 seconds for one chunk and only seven seconds for three. This concept of our being best able to remember *seven plus or minus two* chunks of information was determined by Dr. George Miller in the early 1950s, when he was at the MIT Lincoln Laboratory. He referred to seven as the "Magical Number", in a fascinating and wonderfully written article.[21]

Long-Term Memory

After information is used in short-term memory, it is either discarded or stored more permanently in long-term memory in the form of encoded memories. It is in long-term memory we keep things we care deeply about – memories of events, knowledge, and skills we use to advance in the world – and some we would rather not recall, such as the ear-worms from annoying pop songs or jingles. These memories are organized around a topic, such as different work tasks. Specific information, for example, preparation of solutions for intravenous use, is kept in "schemas",[23] the term coined by Cambridge psychologist, Frederick Bartlett, or in knowledge packages. Details of schematic knowledge structures for typical situations, particularly anything with a sequential list to be followed, are contained in a "script",[24] as in "How to prepare 'CRRT'". This concept was advanced by two Yale Professors, an Artificial Intelligence researcher, Roger Schank, and Robert Abelson, a psychologist.

When we remember a specific event or fact, we also remember associated sensations, including smells, sounds, and sights. Thinking about where we were or what was happening while we learned or did something new helps us to better retrieve the memory. Importantly, there is no such thing as a true or correct memory. Our brains are constantly rewriting our pasts each time we recall a memory.[25]

There are two main types of long-term memory – explicit and implicit. These were described and named by Drs. Peter Graf and Daniel L Schachter, behavioral and cognitive psychologists at the University of Toronto. Explicit (or declarative) memory refers to information we can intentionally recall, described by Graf and Schachter as the "conscious recollection of previous experiences".[26] When we search for a memory, our quests are strongly influenced by *feelings of knowing*. We don't strive to retrieve things we know that we don't know. Explicit memory can be divided into semantic memory, or all the facts that we've ever learned, and episodic memory, that describes all the episodes or events in our lives, for example, what you might have been doing when you decided to read this book.

In contrast, implicit memory is "revealed when performance on a task is facilitated in the absence of conscious recollection".[26] These memories provide us with the information about and skills for various things in life, including some *how-tos* when moving the body, such as automatically skipping with a single versus a double jump-rope. This type of recall does not require any intention or conscious effort.

The effect of sleep on memory has been known for long enough that the concept has entered the domain of folk-sayings, about early to bed. This saying was first recorded in 1486 by Dame Juliana Berners, an English writer on field sports and Prioress of Sopwell Nunnery. The shortened version of her description was "Who so will rise early, shall be holy, healthy and happy".[27]

More recently, Klinzing, Niethard, and Born reviewed the "memory-promoting effect of sleep". Long-term memories are formed during sleep, with a replay of memories, necessary for consolidation, starting in the hippocampus and leading to representation in neocortical networks. This formation occurs during slow-wave sleep and "quiet wakefulness", with replay detectable for longer periods for new events and/or those associated with positive or negative rewards.[28]

Problems with Memory

As described at the beginning of this chapter, memory plays a basic role in information processing and decision-making. We use our memory to make sense of stimuli that we perceive through our senses and to make decisions, by retrieving information in our memory stores and matching patterns of what we find with what we perceive. Our memories are surprisingly good in some situations and surprisingly poor in others. Simply put, the opposite of remembering is forgetting. And we are all prone to that!

The mistakes we make with short-term memory differ from those made in long-term memory. Short-term memory errors tend to be more about being distracted when performing a task and to be acoustic rather than visual. These errors are not based on the *image*[29] but on the *sound* of the information, with auditory memory being systematically less good than visual memory.[30] Errors of long-term memory are more about distorted meanings and tend to be *semantic*. For example, these can be things such as not being able to identify the source of information, as in a *source monitoring error* or our expertise preventing us from seeing something in a new way (also known as *functional fixedness*).

Our consciousness has no direct access to our long-term memory, only to its products (ideas, action, images, words, and the like). We retrieve our memories through recall, recognition, recollection, and relearning. Individuals demonstrate differences in ability to retrieve information from their long-term memory, which is also a predictor of intelligence. These differences in retrieval are believed to be related to our abilities for both encoding and retrieving information. Encoding abilities are affected by many factors, including attention-priming stimuli, sleep, and emotions such as stress, while retrieval is determined by the effectiveness of search strategies, search efficiency, and retrieval monitoring abilities.[31]

Our memory changes as we age. During our childhood years, our memory span and ability to use different cognitive strategies dramatically increase. However, over the age of about 65, many of us observe problems with our memory and start to worry about degeneration in our brains.

Our brains do degenerate, with Alzheimer's disease being the most common, but not the only, disease state associated with memory loss and senility. Additionally, psychologists have identified a number of factors that influence the effectiveness of our memory function, including vigilance and attentiveness, interest and motivation, and emotion. When we are vigilant, we are in a state of being alert and watchful. When we pay attention, we focus our thinking on a single object, maintaining our cognitive interest in a specific idea or task, while avoiding distraction. Thus, our vigilance and attention help to etch information into our long-term memory.[32] When we are interested in an idea, topic, or task, we are more likely to be motivated in the discovering, learning, or doing. We are motivated to concentrate and to apply conscious effort to ensure we understand and then repeat the information. This will help integrate the information into our memory. We are also more likely to retain information on topics that are of greater personal interest, for example, sports scores and players' statistics by sports fans.

One generality we can apply to these examples is that the more distinct an event, the more memorable, whether the distinction is related to emotion or to something entirely new. This helps explain why our memories from early adolescence and young adulthood are more explicit than those from later in life. As we age, we tend to have *seen that* and *been there* and therefore the memories created are not as distinct. Those wanting to *age well* might therefore choose to take up new hobbies and continue or adopt life-long learning.

For many of us, the most vivid and long-lasting memories are those related to an emotional event, for example, a birth, a marriage, or a death of a loved one. Emotions, however, can impair our memory, as well as increase our susceptibility to false memories. This is related to a tendency to focus on information most relevant to the current goals and the central information, the information that is central to the meaning of the emotional stimuli. For example, with severe emotional arousal or stress, focus is almost entirely on survival or endurance, resulting in extremely narrow attentional focus, a phenomenon called "emotional memory narrowing".[33]

Elizabeth Loftus' work at the University of California at Irvine, from the 1970s onward, really exposed how fallible and malleable our memories are.[25,34] As mentioned above, we are all prone to forgetting, and when we have a gap in a memory we *actively reconstruct* our memories. That is, we fill in the blanks from similar situations, using cues or information available to us, sometimes including somewhat understood policies and procedures. For example, in recalling the events that contributed to the Prologue and Narrative of this book, each of the three of us had varyingly different memories of certain specific events, which required careful cross-checking. Loftus, a cognitive psychologist and an expert in eyewitness testimony, has shown that we are all prone to *false memories*, especially under the right conditions. Memories can be changed by what we have been told after an event. Additionally, suggestive memory techniques, such as *suggestive questioning*, can create recollections that were never present to begin with. With this misleading information, we then create false memories that, when fully embraced, are expressed with confidence and detail.[35]

Processing Information

Before we undertake any action, except perhaps for automatic ones, like breathing, we process information. This occurs in three main stages, which are not carried out in a linear manner but in a dynamic and ongoing sequence. These stages are the perception of sensory stimuli or information from our environment (also known as Perceptual Encoding), the transformation of information (or Central Processing), and our response(s) (or Responding[17,36]), to the initial stimulus.

Perceptual Encoding

Processing information begins first with seeking and receiving sensory information, using our senses. We appreciate that in addition to the classic five senses of touch, sight, hearing, smell, and taste, there are other sensory modalities, not all of which are completely understood. These include sensations from different receptors in and on the head, body, and limbs, including the skin. These provide information such as proprioception or where the body is in space, balance and head tilt, and muscle stretch. All of these senses contribute to information received and processed.

Processing of sensory stimuli is through a combination of sensory perception, short-term memory, and long-term memory,[36,37] which help us to make sense of the stimuli. Sensory information briefly rests in sensory memory, in what was first described as a "buffer between an unordered environment and an informational processing system of fixed capacity",[38] thus allowing our brain extra time to process this incoming information. Each sense has its own form and functioning of sensory memory, but none of the banks hold information for very long. For example, auditory sensory or echoic memory remains for several seconds, while iconic or visual sensory memory stays less than one second. This sensory information then flows to short-term memory, a site with a smaller capacity but longer retention than that of sensory memory.

Central Processing

This is the stage where we think and make decisions, the latter involving different types of cognition, depending on the issue or problem being tackled and the complexity of the tasks required to address the issue. As with the working memory, the part of the brain involved in central processing regards complex decision-making as hard work, requiring attentional resources. As a result, we often resort to mental shortcuts, matching incoming information with known patterns of information or heuristics that are stored in long-term memory. Our minds are preprogramed to make sense of any new information that is presented. The easiest and most efficient way of accomplishing this is to relate new information to something already known, hence Reason's comments about humans as being "furious pattern matchers".[39]

Decisions are then required about what the information is and what it represents, as well as for formulating a plan to address these results. Exactly how we do that is explained by psychology's dual process theory, which was briefly mentioned in Chapter 1. Dual process theory started with the work of William James, an American physician who never practiced but followed his interests into psychology. More than a century ago, he described two kinds of thoughts that we have. The first was of recognition without remembering, as in seeing someone in the street but having no retrievable memory of the individual's name. The second was recollection/recall, where we have retained a remembered fact and from where we have been able to retrieve the wanted thought.[40]

Fast forward to the early 1970s, when English psychologist Peter Wason developed his thinking about reasoning when making a selection from two choices. He "coined the terms Type 1 and Type 2 processes to distinguish between rapid error-prone unconscious processes and slower deliberative ones".[41] At the end of 1974, he and his colleague, Johnathan Evans, published their experiments on their Dual Process Hypothesis, postulating that "performance and introspection" represented different underlying cognitive processes.[42]

This concept was then tested, expanded upon, and popularized by two psychologists also mentioned in Chapter 1 – Daniel Kahneman and Amos Tversky. They started working together in the late 1960s, when they were both at the Hebrew University of Jerusalem. Kahneman, a psychologist, and Tversky, an economist, were interested in intuitive judgments, which they thought sat between perception, which is considered automatic, and reasoning, a more deliberate operation. They used the term "Two System" view of cognition,[43] which Keith Stanovich, a developmental psychologist at the University of Toronto, and his long-time colleague, Richard West, a psychologist at James Madison University, Virginia, named System 1 and System 2 in 2000. They described the former as "automatic, largely unconscious, and relatively undemanding of computational resources", while characterizing the latter as invoked, conscious, and quite demanding of cognitive capacity.[44]

These two types of thinking, which Kahneman renamed "Thinking Fast and Slow" (also the title of his 2011 book[45]), describe two types of cognition. Type I, or *Thinking Fast*, involves processing information in an unconscious and automatic way, using heuristics or *rules of thumb*. When we invoke Type I thinking we are in a state of knowing what to do and continue without stopping to question if the problem has been correctly formulated and our actions are appropriate. This way of thinking is fast, efficient, and intuitive, and as humans, we depend on it to simplify tasks of handling complex information. But with this automatic mode of control and use of heuristics we are prone to predictable forms of error. (More on this later.)

Type II cognition is more controlled and conscious, requiring us to slow our mental processing and think carefully through a problem or issue. We question if the problem has been properly understood, if there are alternative explanations for the phenomenon being observed, and then calculate the potential effectiveness of any planned actions. However, rather than staying strictly with Type I or Type II, we may go back and forth between the two problem-solving cognitive methods.

Response Execution

Once a response has been chosen, we usually (choose to) carry it out. We then dynamically monitor the response, with a feedback loop reflecting the initial stimulus back into sensory reception and perception. Additionally, feedback feeds the results of *how* we conducted the response, and its results, into our memory bank in short-term memory and long-term memory. This last stage can also restart the processing.[46]

Human Information Processing Frameworks and Errors

As mentioned at the beginning of this chapter, making errors is part of the human condition. Errors occur because of problems in our memory and information processing. Two highly esteemed academics, Jens Rasmussen and James

Reason, each developed frameworks for information processing and types of related errors.

Rasmussen's Framework

In 1962, Jens Rasmussen was appointed Head of the Electronics Department at the Atomic Research Establishment Risø, Denmark, where he concentrated on technical and reliability aspects of the control room. He saw in this work, however, the importance of the human operators and how they interacted with the control room displays and instrumentation, including how the control staff reacted to abnormal conditions.[47] He started to focus on "mental procedures in real-life tasks", including troubleshooting when experts made repairs to electronics equipment.[48] Rasmussen then extended his thinking to include the human as a component of the system, as well as starting to develop a model for this.[47]

At about the same time, James Reason held the posts of Lecturer and then Reader at the University of Leicester, from where he had obtained his PhD in Psychology. After many years of interest in motion sickness, absent-mindedness and other related problems in human behavior started to claim his attention. (This was perhaps partly triggered by the horrific accidents at Tenerife Airport and the Moorgate, London tube station.[49]) In his first paper on absent-mindedness, Reason provided details of eleven aviation close calls and accidents involving UK aircraft, with the pilots' actions "resembling absent-minded behavior".[50] A second publication described instances of absent-mindedness as "trivial lapses". But Reason followed this statement with a description of how the careful study of rail and aviation accidents could show that "horrific consequences" evolved from the "environment" in which errors were made. Studying these "non-planned actions", he suggested, could help us better understand human error.[51]

Reason then tackled slips, which Don Norman had also studied. Norman had a Master's degree in engineering with a PhD in Psychology, founding the Institute for Cognitive Science, University of California San Diego. His interest in aberrant actions was triggered when he took a photo without intending to, while attempting to turn off the light exposure meter. This apparent *slip* caught his attention and he went on to collect examples of slips, developing an "outline for a theory of action". Norman proposed that "skilled actions – or actions whose components are themselves all highly skilled – are carried out by subconscious mechanisms".[52] Reason used Norman's "action theory", differentiating "failures and mistakes". Reason also started to incorporate Rasmussen's "generic model of cognition", which Rasmussen had initiated developing in the 1970s, when he turned his attention to quantifying human performance.[53]

Rasmussen's background as a master's degree electronics engineer helped him appreciate "what" a subject was doing, and perhaps giving a nod to Reason, stated having a "background in psychology" could explain "why" the subject had chosen a certain approach to problem solving. Rasmussen also thought it important to "consider the human role in rare events", such as those in the nuclear power plant where he worked.[48]

Rasmussen's model showed how different cognitive concepts controlled actions and behaviors. To explain this, he used a triad of skill, rule, and knowledge (SRK) based information processing.[16] He also connected each of the three levels to differing sensed information from the environment,[54] (signs, signals, and symbols, respectively), which could activate or initiate changes in behavior.

Rasmussen's Performance Types

Skill-Based Performance   This represents "sensory-motor performance during acts or activities". Because these are automated or subconscious[16] actions, skill-based (SB) performance has been dubbed *Auto-Pilot Mode*. After setting a goal or intention, SB behavior occurs without our attention,[54] giving us the ability to conduct movements in prepackaged and stored sequences or patterns of behavior, such as steering a car. These are procedural memories, an implicit component of long-term memory. SB activity is also the basis of *habits*, for example, always shoulder-checking when changing lanes. Habits are actions repeated so often they have become automatic in our lives. As William James aptly commented in 1890, "habit diminishes the conscious attention with which our acts are performed".[40]

Rule-Based Performance   Rule-based (RB) activity arises when we need to move up from the conceptually lower SB performance level of habitual activity. (However, Rasmussen admitted that the SB-RB boundary was "not very distinct" and could be influenced by both the degree of training and the degree of attention paid by the worker.[54]) What the shift from SB to RB usually means is that we need to deal with some kind of problem not covered in our *manual* of automatic tasks and then modify our virtually automatic behaviors to accommodate a change of circumstances, hence the term *If-Then Response Mode*. Simply put, RB behavior is directed by a stored rule or procedure and works best when we are in familiar settings or circumstances. As humans, we develop *prepackaged solutions* through our training and experience, and sometimes from written procedures, which can then be applied to different situations. Again, we use the example of driving. In Canada, if we are attempting to make a left turn

when faced with a solid green light, we must yield to oncoming traffic. This is an example of where the automaticity of driving is interrupted and overridden by the rules of the road.

Knowledge-Based (KB) Performance

Knowledge-based (KB) activity is the highest level of performance known colloquially as the *Not Enough Knowledge Mode*. We shift to KB in "unique, unfamiliar situations",[16] such as when RB behavior does not work. KB requires the slow, laborious, and limited application of conscious attention, with our thought processes relying heavily on images or words to guide our actions. Thus, in this "Figuring It Out Mode", we attempt to analyze the problem, determine and formulate our goal, and develop and select a plan by reviewing options.[54] While this type of performance is computationally powerful, it requires much effort, is extremely restricted in scope, and is cognitively tiring.

Rasmussen considered that each of these levels was prone to errors, with each error of a different type. He also confessed that it was "very difficult to give a satisfactory definition of human errors", suggesting they be considered "instances of man-machine or man-task misfits", with some problems related to errors in design.[16]

Rasmussen's Different Error Types

SB actions are "controlled by stored patterns of behavior in a time-space domain". We therefore make errors related to variability in coordination of "force, space or time".[16] SB automatization also has the potential to facilitate our occasional absent-mindedness. For example, while distracted by the latest news headlines, we might erroneously add salt to our cup of coffee instead of sugar.

Because RB actions direct "performance in familiar situations controlled by stored rules for subroutine coordination", we make RB errors when we wrongly recognize or classify situations, or when we make erroneous associations with certain tasks. Also, because it is a higher level of performance, RB behavior controls subroutines for SB activities. Consequently, mechanisms of error remain active for these SB routines,[16] for example, memory slips when recalling parts of procedures. RB errors are generally associated with whether or not we recalled the relevant rules or followed them correctly. These can include applying a bad rule (which we were taught or we learned the wrong response to a particular situation), misapplying a normally good rule (because we did not notice a contraindication), and/or failing to apply a normally good rule (because we thought that to do so was preferable).

KB performance is also very error-prone, as the cognitive mechanisms used in the task are both person and situation dependent, with task details, and knowledge type and availability all varying according to the worker and context. When we try to work out the problem, we often start by doing what we know. Further problems can arise if we continue to try what we know, with the same failed response. We can guess or we can use a trial and error approach. Alternatively, we can seek the missing knowledge as soon as possible. For all these reasons, as humans, we do not like KB performance very much.

Reason's Framework

Reason, meanwhile, was advancing his own concepts, for example, with a definition of error.[55] He defined error as a "generic term to encompass all those occasions in which a planned sequence of mental or physical activities fails to achieve its intended outcome, and when those failures cannot be attributed to the intervention of some chance agency".[56] Although this definition was published in 1990, a very similar one was published in 1991, although without attribution, in Human Error,[55] a synthesis of a 1983 North America Treaty Organization (NATO) sponsored conference. This was the second conference, on the Nature and Source of Human Error, and was held in Bellagio, Italy, with the participants being the who's who of thinking about error, including Rasmussen and Reason.

Reason was also tackling error in relation to how we process information, describing the "basic error-shaping properties" of our thinking. He determined there was a "surprisingly limited number of forms of errors". This is despite the fact that we observe our errors appearing in a variety of ways, for example, in the different decisions we make and actions we undertake in our lives. They may all look different to us but there are only three types: slips, lapses, and mistakes.[57] Reason related these types to Rasmussen's three levels of cognitive performance,[16] showing that errors could arise from "all three levels of performance". Slips and lapses lay at the SB-level, rule-based mistakes at the RB level and knowledge-based mistakes at the KB level. He also classed each of the three types of errors according to where they originated in the information processing schema: storage, planning, or responding (execution[57]).

Slips occur when there is a failure in the execution stage of processing. When we make a slip it is usually obvious to us and to others, for example, with the error seen if we trip over a doorframe or heard when we make a slip of the tongue.

Lapses, in comparison, are failures in our memory, in the storage stage of information processing. The result of the failure is that an action does not occur. Because of this, we might or might not notice when we make a lapse. This noticing might be in the moment, for example, forgetting the name of someone you know, as becomes obvious when you are not able to introduce the individual properly. Another example is that of forgetting one's lunch on the kitchen counter when leaving for work and remembering only when stimulated by hunger. Additionally, some lapses are never noticed.

While slips and lapses mean our actions did not go as intended, *mistakes* occur when our actions do go as intended, but our plan for the action did not achieve the outcome we desired. The problem with mistakes lies in our more complex and higher-level cognitive processes of planning, although at different levels. Additionally, in comparison to slips and lapses, mistakes are often even more difficult to detect.

We make RB mistakes when a pre-established plan is applied inappropriately, referred to by Reason as a "failure in expertise".[57] This can happen in one of three ways: application of a bad rule, mis-application of a normally good rule, or failure to apply a good rule.[16] An example of an RB mistake would be driving at the posted highway speed limit of 110 km/h during bad driving conditions. Applying this 'good rule' during good driving conditions is correct, but applying this rule during poor driving conditions would be an RB mistake.

KB mistakes, in contrast, occur in novel situations when we have a "lack of expertise".[57] These are truly error-provoking situations.[16] Because we are in a new situation, we do not have a pre-established plan we can apply. We end up having to make up a plan. And if we develop the wrong plan, then we are faced with a knowledge-based mistake, as shown in our next driving example. On our way to work, we get caught in a traffic jam. Instead of waiting in the traffic, we make a decision to take a different route. However, we are unfamiliar with this part of the city and we end up stuck on a road from which we cannot exit. As a result, we are forced to back-track and to find another route to get to work and arrive late.

Why Do We Make Errors?

But why do we make errors? The short answer is that there are no reasons because reasons imply choice and "errors are not choices".[55] Reasons give us descriptions of "why something happened", for which we provide a subjective explanation of our "goal or intention". Particularly with mistakes, we do not usually have a good reason as to why we made them, as detailed below, although we often rationalize our actions. However, as John Senders and Neville Moray, both Professors of Industrial Engineering at the University of Toronto, emphasized, if we can account for why we chose to do something, and the "account [of it] is sensible in light of the evidence available", then what we chose to do was not an error.[55]

The longer answer is that we make errors in the same way that we successfully make decisions and carry out actions. This is all based on how we try to retrieve information stored in our memory. To do this, we employ two mechanisms, similarity-matching and frequency gambling, as our primary search mechanisms.[57] Both are automatic, unconscious, and continuously operative.

The first mechanism is the "similarity-matching heuristic", described in Chapter 1, best explained as our habit of *furiously pattern matching*.[58] Similarity-matching occurs when the initial search cues are detailed or highly specific. We then match these conditions to the characteristics of our stored memories (or knowledge structures) on a "like-to-like" basis, depending on how closely our current situation matches the knowledge we have.[57] The result is an error known as *cognitive bias*, as what we find when we search often *confirms* what we already believe or value.

The second mechanism is our ability to resolve conflicts between information that is "partially matched" by choosing a solution used "frequently in the past within that particular context". This is known as the "frequency-gambling heuristic".[57] When the search cues match several partially matched memories, our minds "gamble" that the most frequently used knowledge item in that particular context will be the one that is required.[57] But that answer is not always right.

Some kinds of errors are most likely to occur when we are doing something routine and in a familiar environment.[58] Invariably, because the tasks are so automatic, we are able to do them and think about something else.[49,59] This is the case with Reason's slips and lapses, which are most common when we are in either of two situations. One situation reflects a change, either when we have a change in the task to be completed or a change in our circumstances. Both types of changes reduce the normal automaticity of the task. The degree of change will reflect our tendency to make errors. If only one or two things change, either in steps in the task or with its circumstances, then we are forced to think about what we are doing and we are more likely to make errors.[59]

The other situation is when we are not paying attention, because we are either preoccupied or distracted or because our ability to pay attention is decreased. Our attentional resources have a limited capacity, known as "attentional capture",[60] to continue to monitor the initial task we were undertaking. Any or all of these factors could possibly have contributed when the technicians were mixing the CRRT solution. Although the solutions were prepared in a sterile room, under a fume hood, staff in the Central Pharmacy would play music in a large workspace without dividers for task privacy. The latter, especially of popular songs, can easily capture our attention and distract us. Similarly, problems with large workspaces, with extraneous noise and multiple people talking, are well-recognized.[61] These points all explain why the occurrence of slips and lapses is quite predictable although, as stated above, we might not notice that we have made a lapse in some part(s) of our thinking or doing.

The changes described above can also provoke us to make mistakes at the rule-based level, for example, when we recognize that the situation has changed. We then sometimes resort to previously memorized and practiced or written protocols and procedures ("rules"[57]), for example if we need to anesthetize a patient for an emergency in an X-ray suite, in which the lights have been dimmed to allow the radiologist to view the video screens more easily. These rules may be either good or bad. The former are driven by our "assumptions" of the situation but there is sometimes a mismatch between what we assume and the reality of the situation. The latter bad rules represent our habits, often learned and adopted to "get the job done",[62] but with potential unwanted results for our patients.

At other times, we move from experiencing problems with SB performance directly, to seeking knowledge-based solutions, (rather than only after trying RB solutions) when we do not know what to do. In his revised "Generic Error Modelling System" (GEMS), Reason stated that we conduct "automatic searching of the knowledge base" concurrently as we attend to our actions,[57] a more dynamic view of how our minds constantly try to seek solutions.

Once we are working in the KB domain, different factors can contribute to our making KB mistakes. One of these factors is our having an incomplete or inaccurate mental model of the task or situation, which often occurs when we are learning what to do. We also have (limited) attention spans, which can be affected by our emotions and fatigue. In fact, the list can be expanded to include almost anything that interferes with our ability to think our way through problems, either resorting to random trial-and-error or logically working from first principles through what we know.

While we can predict the occurrence and types of errors we are likely to make, measuring them is not so easy, nor accurate. In actuality, we are in error when we produce reports of 'numbers of errors'. As we described above, Rasmussen commented in 1983 that "frequently" errors were only "identified after the fact". Many errors are not even recognized at all, such as many of our lapses. Errors are ubiquitous in their occurrence and unknown in their frequency, although Reason suggests that errors are "neither as abundant nor as varied" as we might think, and are also "much rarer than correct actions".[16]

Yet, in some very specific situations, usually highly mechanized, we are able to determine specific errors were made, for example, turning a dial one way instead of another. It is also possible to train observers to count errors, but not all will be observed – because of the fallibility of the human, error-prone observers. Thus, it would seem faulty to count that which often cannot be observed.

How Not to Use the Word Error

The above descriptions, slips, lapses, and mistakes, apply to the three recognized types of human error. Yet, in the much of the (medical) literature on patient and healthcare safety, we see other errors described, defined, detailed, and apparently counted. These other types include 'medical error', 'honest error', 'honest mistake', 'medical mistake', and 'critical error'. Despite their popularity, creating these subtypes by adding a modifier to the word error, such as 'medical' 'critical' or 'honest', is neither helpful nor accurate, something the three of us have believed for the past two decades or so. Confusingly, the term 'medical error' is also sometimes interchanged with others, such as adverse event. These terms are variably used to describe the *cause* or mechanism of harm, the outcome for a patient, and sometimes an *excuse*. To be clear: a mistake is a type of error; an error is one factor that may contribute to harm; and the outcome for a patient is harm.

As Senders stated in 1994, a "medical error" is no more than "an error that happens in a medical setting and is made by someone who is engaged in a medical activity". He went on to say that "Much as human behavior in a medical setting is still behavior and not medicine, human error in a medical setting is still error and not medicine...If an error that was expressed in a medical setting instead happened to occur in a nuclear power plant, the only differences would be in the words used".[63] The context differs, as do the outcomes, but the errors are the same.

Another reason why the term 'medical error' is not helpful is because it does not explicitly consider the concept of violations. For at least the past 100 years, violations have been described in the medical literature. We conducted a rough survey of the numbers of errors versus violations over the last century as found on a simple search of "health care + errors" or "health care + violations" by decade. We found that, apart from the litigation-rich 1980s, the ratio of errors to violations was about five to one. We consider this important because, as we discuss in detail later, violations contribute to destabilizing a critical situation, which then might further destabilize in the presence of a few errors, thus evolving to an accident. Focusing on 'medical errors' has almost effectively smothered any discussion of violations in healthcare apart from that related to discipline and punishment.

To return to our discussion of the language of errors, the use of unhelpful additional (adjectival) modifiers, such as medical and critical, gives these terms implied judgment. This implication means the term no longer describes only an action. Instead, the term implies an individual (a doctor) has done something bad (made an error), which directly resulted in someone (such as a patient) being harmed. Our perception of the error is then influenced by thoughts of the negative outcome. This was shown three decades ago by anesthesiology safety researchers at the Virginia Mason Medical Centre, Seattle, Drs. Bob Caplan, Karen Posner and Fred Cheney, who studied anesthesiologists' opinions of cases when complications of care were deemed either temporary or permanent. Similarly, our opinion of the *critical* error has been biased. Our now biased view of what should be a factual description is also not supportive of a Just Culture. (This and other biases, and how they influence the way we view situations, were described in detail in Chapter 1.) We should not apply any moral judgments to errors – they are neither bad nor good. But we do so by associating the bad-ness or goodness of the outcome to the error we think was *causal*. As Reason described when writing about errors in everyday life versus on the flight deck of a commercial aircraft, the difference between the errors did not lie in the "nature of the error, but in the extent to which the circumstances of its occurrence will penalize it".[50]

Another term frequently seen in the literature is 'system error'. Although not negatively affecting a Just Culture, we also see this term as problematic. Simply put, systems cannot make errors. Only we as humans can make them. A bet-ter term is that of "system-induced errors", first introduced into the literature in 1975 by Earl Weiner, a psychologist and aviation human factors guru. He described the problems in the early 1970s underlying a spate of "Controlled Flight Into Terrain" (or CFIT) accidents, that is, accidents involving flying a perfectly serviceable plane into the earth without realizing what was happening. According to Wiener, the profession of human factors had already "recognized the concept of 'design induced errors'". Wiener extended the concept to a "large-scale system". His extensive list of contributing factors included "vehicles, [air] traffic control, and terminals", and extended through "community planning and government regulation", "terminology, "charts", the Air Line Pilots Association, the Federal Aviation Administration, the National Transportation Safety Board, to the "human factors profession" (of which he was a member). However, he clearly stated the purpose of his paper was "not to assign blame" but rather to look at the "unwieldy system" provoking errors that had "emerged as a result of piecemeal design".[64,65]

Noncompliance

Having described and discussed errors, we now address Reason's violations and sabotage.[56] These differ from errors in that they involve a deviation from standard operating procedures, policies, or procedures, which is usually, but not always deliberate. A deviation is rule-breaking or noncompliance, and our preference is to use either of these terms in healthcare, rather than violations. (In 2004, a group of us, who were working on policies in the Region to support a Just

Culture, made this decision based on feedback from other healthcare providers, leaders, and patients with whom we were working.)

To illustrate the important distinction between errors and the different types of noncompliance, we start with Reason's description of human actions. Whether "correct or otherwise", actions "entail three basic elements: plans, actions, and consequences".[66] Everything starts (or should start) with a plan that has an aim, intention, or outcome, and an outline of actions required to achieve the outcome.

We use the term, *intention*, purposefully, recognizing there are now different opinions with respect to its use in the Ergonomics and Human Factors (EHF) community.[67,68] In healthcare we operate within a regulatory framework that includes contracts and specific rules of conduct. We therefore require some way of delineating actions and behaviors that are acceptable or unacceptable within those boundaries. At the same time, our safety focus is not primarily on the *person* but on the entire system and our safety investigations are separated from those carried out to review the performance of specific individuals.

To return to actions and the planned outcome, both have related intentions. With respect to our actions, when we intend to do something but unwittingly do not do so or do something different, then we have made an error. For example, we would describe a respiratory therapist (RT), who intended to record a ventilated patient's respiratory values but did not do so because of being distracted by the alarm from another patient who became disconnected from the ventilator, as making an error.

We can also look at the intention for the results or outcome. Was there intention to do good or was there intent to do harm? In situations where the intention was to do good, actions of individuals represent a type of error (as above) or noncompliance. For example, the RT above had good intentions for the initial patient's outcome.

When rules are intentionally broken, they are classified as noncompliance. If the actions are carried out with the best of intentions for the outcome, this point then differentiates noncompliance from sabotage. If the intent was to not do good, that is to do harm, these actions are considered sabotage or, as we prefer to say, *willful intent to harm*.

Three Types of Violations

Reason defined three types of violations – necessary, routine, and optimizing.[15] Necessary violations were made when the rule could not be followed, for example a *necessary* tool was missing. Routine violations involved *routinely* bending the rules or corner-cutting, the purpose of which was to gain efficiencies by "taking the path of least effort between two-task related points". Optimizing violations deal with rules being broken for the individual's personal goals.

We illustrate the difference between Reason's types of violations with an example from healthcare. A Respiratory Therapist (RT) was asked to take an arterial blood gas (ABG) sample from a patient in the ICU. The written procedure directed the RT to take the sample, apply an identifying label, and carry the labeled sample directly to the laboratory next to the ICU and then analyze it. In actuality, the RT did not attach a label to the sample. If the RT did this because there were no labels available, then the violation would be considered necessary. If not labeling samples became a habit for the RT and colleagues, this would be considered a routine violation. If the RT measured an unlabeled sample because of wanting to do it quickly before going on a break, then this would be an optimizing violation, because it was done for the benefit of the individual and not the patient.

Over two decades ago, JMD saw the link between these three types of violations and Donabedian's three-part classification of the healthcare system: Structure, Process, and Outcome,[69] which has its parallels in the engineering model of Input, Process, and Output. Necessary violations were *driven* by problems in the structure of the system, and we therefore have renamed them as "Structure-driven noncompliance". Examples of drivers from the account above of the RT include the lack of ABG sample labels, the ABG machine being broken, or the procedure not updated for the latest ABG machine. Routine violations belong in the process part of the system, together with an individual's decisions and actions, including *routine* or habitual rule-breaking and associated corner-cutting, and are therefore named "Process-driven noncompliance". Finally, Optimizing violations relate to Outcome, where individuals deviate from policies and procedures for their own benefit – their own outcome – are "Outcome-driven noncompliance".

Why People Break Rules

As well as needing to understand types of violations so we can address their underlying problems and mitigate their negative effect on our patients and on our safety culture, we also need to consider why people *break rules*.

Reason's early research on violations identified three beliefs or "illusions" leading to noncompliance. The first was the "illusion of control" with a resulting overestimation of control of the outcome and with those breaking rules also having feelings of powerlessness in certain situations. These situations drove their rule-breaking, with the rule-breakers then conforming to what others were doing, such as speeding. The second was the "illusion of invulnerability" or an underestimation that their actions could result in an untoward outcome. The third, the "illusion of superiority", was an overestimation of their skill level, often combined with a belief that their noncompliance was not as bad as others' was.[60]

Rasmussen took a different point of view, stressing that workers did not follow procedures in a strict and logical manner. Rather, they followed the most useful and productive path at the time. He described these violations as "quite rational, given the actual workload and timing constraints".[70]

Different influences on noncompliance were described by Professor Rene Amalberti of the Cognitive Science Department at IMASSA in Bretigny sur Orge, France; Professor Charles Vincent of Imperial College and St Mary's Hospital, London, Dr. Yves Auroy of the Department of Anesthesiology & Critical Care Medicine, Percy Military Hospital, Paris; and Dr. Guillaume de Saint Maurice, Head of that Department. The authors considered motivation and attitude took into account what individuals believed the consequences of breaking rules could be, their social influences, and their beliefs about control, as well as personal beliefs and moral code. Flexibility and adaptation also influenced violations. In a positive way, the ability to adapt reflected an individual's intelligence and flexibility. However, adapting procedures to deal with work demands could lead to routine violations and a degradation in safety culture. Factors related to the organization also played into noncompliance, specifically the organizational culture as reflected by how people identified and responded to safety problems.[71]

The Effect of Noncompliance

Another concept relating to violations is their effect, specifically their role in either destabilizing a system's safety or its converse, helping a system recover. Rasmussen first wrote about this concept, describing the "existence of a natural migration of activities toward the boundary of acceptable performance". Workers carried out their tasks in a "work space" that had constraints related to administration, work function, and safety. Because the conditions of work underwent "normal changes", these changes influenced work "strategies and activity", with Rasmussen likening this to the Brownian motion of gas molecules. Workers adapted to the resulting changes in conditions and, balanced by their own "effort gradient" (toward "least effort") and management's "cost gradient" (toward "efficiency"), they could systematically move toward the edge of "functionally acceptable performance". Each boundary had an "error margin", which provided some tolerance and allowed recovery. However, these normal operations at the margins of performance could be exceeded by both errors and violations,[70] and result in what Amalberti described as "brutal migrations toward accidents".[72] This fits with Reason's thinking. Although he said violations were not "necessarily dangerous", he considered they were more likely than errors to destabilize a system,[15] altering the context of subsequent actions in a more negative environment and increasing the probability of errors being made.[15] The combination of the violations and the errors could, in turn, provide an additive factor to the accident-inducing equation.

In 2001, Amalberti adopted Rasmussen's model of "migration toward the boundary" to illustrate his thinking about the "trap of over regulation". A few years later, Amalberti and his colleagues (as above) used his "reference model of migration and transgression of practices", to illustrate the "initial safe space of action", with violations following, sometimes in response to production pressure. If violations became more routine and frequent over time, the whole system could *migrate to the boundaries of safety*.[71] We prefer the term, migration, to "practical drift", the term coined by Lt. Colonel Scott A. Snook, when he was at the United States Military Academy. Snook defined drift as the "low, steady uncoupling of practice from written procedure". Although Rasmussen also used the term "drift" in the same paper as "migration", he settled on the latter, using it for both "migration to the boundary" and to the "accident".[70] Most of the actions inherent in migration are conscious undertakings, rather than the implied *being carried along by the waves* image given by drift. Indeed, Rasmussen thought that *marking the boundaries* and giving workers this knowledge was more helpful than requiring larger safety margins,[70] reinforcing the idea of workers' consciousness of their actions.

Amalberti and colleagues considered that migration to the boundaries of safety then led to "normalization of deviance". This term was defined and detailed by Dr. Diane Vaughan, at that time a sociologist at Boston College, in her definitive and thoughtful account of the Challenger space shuttle launch tragedy. In the years leading up to the launch, Vaughan described the managers and engineers as having developed a "definition of the situation that allowed them to carry on as if nothing was wrong" despite facing evidence that "something was wrong". Noncompliance had become so commonplace that individuals did not even recognize their actions as being deviant. This was the embodiment of the *normalization* of the deviance.[73]

However, workers often use noncompliance to save situations and not only to either get the work done or to wreak havoc. Amalberti and colleagues described these violations that saved situations as a "necessary adaptation of professionals" who had to cope with the "conflicting demands of complex work situations". Indeed, in healthcare, noncompliance is unspokenly encouraged, when trying to look after patients in time and resource-limited situations. Although around the world there is an enormous range of these limitations, even in highly developed countries, limitations can be found to a relative extent. Patients must be cared for, no matter what the circumstances. Sometimes the circumstances arise because of the patients' conditions, whether due to their intrinsic genetics, anatomy, and physiology, or to extrinsic disruptions such as disease or trauma. Healthcare providers may need to break all the rules under some of these conditions, for example, operating to successfully extricate individuals trapped under concrete beams – without the standard equipment or drugs, including any monitors of patients' vital signs. As Reason summarized, such heroic recoveries require correctly assessing the situations' factors, synthesizing their significance, and anticipating multiple future possibilities.[60] Thus, noncompliance should not always be viewed as having a negative effect on safety. Despite that positive point, we focus on how to deal with noncompliance, specifically on doing so before patients are harmed.

Dealing with Rule-Breaking Before Patients are Harmed

Sometimes, the production pressure described by Amalberti and colleagues[71] can result from having to deal with constant or increasing workloads – without the necessary equipment, which is either lacking or broken or a shortage of skilled workers. Because these types of problems contribute to structure-driven noncompliance, structural deficiencies should be dealt with, by replacing or repairing missing or faulty equipment, or restoring the skilled workforce. This must be done before noncompliance in general becomes a daily occurrence, spilling-over to other personnel.

Importantly, we must avoid developing a workforce that accepts process-driven (routine) rule-breaking as the norm, with safety then taking second-place to *getting the job done*. These socially based and sometimes administration-endorsed types of noncompliance often have some (structural) contribution from overly specific procedures written by *experts* with no experience in carrying out the tasks. But there is a disconnection between how the work was set out and how it is actually performed. The social aspects of this type of noncompliance relate to the individuals who start to adopt informal ways of doing things, sometimes quite different from the written policy and procedures. These individuals are usually skilled and experienced, who might have a hierarchical position in a team or part of the workplace, and who have determined where corner-cutting can save time or effort. Such situations can occur in the absence of tight social control of the experts and if no action is taken to deal with this behavior, it can negatively influence other workers. In addition, should there be obvious signals of "impending danger", the results could be more severe than they might have been because of individuals denying or minimizing dangers, and delaying taking action.[74] Vaughan provided a good example of this in her recounting of the

Challenger disaster, where numerous managers and engineers carried on, as if nothing was wrong, despite evidence to the contrary that something was indeed very wrong.[73]

Understanding which parts of policies are problematic and changing them, as well as dealing with the noncompliant experts, must be undertaken. Doing so expeditiously might also decrease the possibility that some of these experts could start to adopt outcome-driven (optimizing) noncompliance for their own betterment, such as for "the thrill of it".[15] In this situation, some individuals become willing to violate even basic procedures, carrying out actions for their own betterment. This type of noncompliance represents crossing Reason's line between acceptable and unacceptable and can obviously contribute to patients being harmed. However, it is important to deal with such actions before patients are harmed. In safety significant industries, most instances of outcome-driven rule-breaking need to be considered in a similar vein as willful intent to harm – people or property, although there will obviously be differences for the worker's outcome. Some actions could result in the worker being referred to human resources versus other actions that could prompt calls to the police.

We therefore see this progression from structure-driven through process-driven to outcome-driven noncompliance (and then on to willful intention to harm) as a spectrum of actions and behaviors that must be dealt with in a Just Culture. Structure-driven noncompliance lies to the far left-hand side of the spectrum, with some of actions so far to the left they are actually errors. (For example, earlier we described an RT who did not record a patient's values because of distraction.) In contrast, outcome-driven rule-breaking has definitely *crossed the line*, and, together with willful intent to harm, occupies the right-hand side of the spectrum. That leaves almost all process-driven noncompliance, which sits to the left of the line, although some of the seemingly socially influenced process-driven examples could potentially be misclassified and might actually represent outcome-driven rule-breaking.

Having now worked through the spectrum of noncompliant actions and a general way of dealing with them, we move to a discussion of willful intent to harm, the most dangerous type of action.

Willful Intent to Harm

Sabotage (willful intent to harm) is similar to noncompliance in that a rule is broken; however, it is different with respect to the intention for the outcome. In sabotage, there is a willful intent for a negative outcome, that is, to cause harm. This can mean damage to property or harm to individuals. In healthcare, willful intent to harm a patient is incredibly rare. But when it does occur, the news garners substantial media and public attention. This may lead to the perception by the public that it is more common than it actually is. (See also Chapter 1.)

In summary, we have shown in this chapter that we make errors, despite our best intentions for both the action and the outcome. Errors occur when something goes wrong in our information processing, decision-making, and responding process. This could be from a problem or failure in memory, in planning and decision-making, or in executing our plan. Psychological or emotional factors, as well as conditions within the situation and the contextual environment, contribute to errors. Simply put, errors are part of our human condition! Noncompliance is more oriented toward social factors, which lead individuals to greater or lesser degrees of rule-breaking, including willful intent to harm. We have emphasized the importance of determining what individuals' intentions were for their actions and their outcomes. However, should an individual's actions be found to be more focused on their personal needs than on their patients' needs, these actions should be carefully reviewed.

In the next chapter, we advance our discussion of the human condition, by detailing what our responses should be to patients and their families after a patient has been nearly or actually harmed. We describe what patients and families want, need, and deserve: respect, empathy, apology, disclosure, and support, as well as evidence that any deficiencies in the healthcare system that contributed to harm will be rectified where possible.

References

1. Braid D. Dialysis drug mix-up demands fatality probe. *Calgary Herald: Tragic Error at Foothills.* 2004 Mar 19;A5 (col. 1).
2. Slobodian L. Medical mix-up occurred before. *Calgary Herald.* 2004 Mar 20;A1 (col. 1) & A5 (col. 5).
3. Braid D. Fourth medical mix-up revealed. *Calgary Herald.* 2004 Mar 23;A1 (col. 5) & A11 (col. 1).
4. Canton M. CHR denies link of recent deaths to mistake in 2000. *Calgary Herald: Top News.* 2004 Mar 21;A3 (col. 1).
5. Cormier R. Antibiotic dosage error strikes fear in mothers. *Calgary Herald.* 2004 Mar 20;A5 (col. 2).
6. Calgary Health Region. Mixing the solution. *Calgary Herald.* 2004 Mar 19;A4 (col. 2).
7. Braid D. Medication error "very hard to make". *Calgary Herald.* 2004 Mar 25;A1 (col. 3) & A14 (col. 1).
8. Olsen T. Hospital tragedies boost CHR critics. *Calgary Herald: Inside Politics.* 2004;A6 (col. 5).

9. Toneguzzi M. Two patients dead in tragic error at Foothills hospital. *Calgary Herald*. 2004 Mar 19;A1(col. 6) & A4(col. 3).
10. Braid D. CHR's disclosure a hopeful sign. *Calgary Herald: Foothills Tragedy*. 2004 Mar 20;5 (col. 1).
11. Kirkey S. Medical mistakes leave deadly toll. *Calgary Herald*. 2004 Mar 19; A5(col. 5).
12. Canton M. Druggists feared worst at CHR. *Calgary Herald: City & Region*. 2004 Mar 23;B1 (col. 1) & B3 (col. 4).
13. Braid D. Reform for the patients. *Calgary Herald: City & Region*. 2004 Mar 26;B1 (col. 4) & B6 (col. 2).
14. Toneguzzi M. National expert will investigate mix-ups. Health region vows to learn from fatal mistakes. *Calgary Herald*. 2004 Mar 24;A1 (col. 6) & A3 (col. 1).
15. Reason J. *Managing the Risks of Organizational Accidents*. Aldershot: Ashgate Publisher; 1997.
16. Rasmussen J. Human errors. A taxonomy for describing human malfunction in industrial installations. *J Occup Accid*. 1982 Sep;4(2–4):311–33.
17. Atkinson RCC, Shiffrin RMM. Human Memory: A proposed system and its control processes. In: Bower G, editor. *Psychology of Learning and Motivation – Advances in Research and Theory*. New York: Academic Press; 1968. pp. 89–195.
18. Sperling G. The information available in brief visual presentations. *Psychol Monogr Gen Appl*. 1960;74(11):1–29.
19. Baddeley AD, Hitch GJ. Working Memory. In: Bower G, editor. *Recent Advances in Learning and Motivation*. New York: Academic Press; 1974. pp. 47–90.
20. Peterson L, Peterson MJ. Short-term retention of individual verbal items. *J Exp Psychol*. 1959;58(3):193–8.
21. Miller GA. The magical number seven, plus or minus two: Some limits on our capacity for processing information. *Psychol Rev*. 1956 Mar;63(2):81–97.
22. Thalmann M, Souza AS, Oberauer K. How does chunking help working memory? *J Exp Psychol Learn Mem Cogn*. 2019 Jan;45(1):37–55.
23. Bartlett FC. *Remembering: A Study in Experimental and Social Psychology*. Cambridge, England: Cambridge University Press; 1932.
24. Schank R, Abelson R. *Scripts, Plans, Goals, and Understanding: An Inquiry into Human Knowledge Structures*. Hillsdale: Lawrence Erlbaum; 1977.
25. Loftus EF, Miller DG, Burns HJ. Semantic integration of verbal information into a visual memory. *J Exp Psychol Hum Learn Mem*. 1978;4(1):19–31.
26. Graf P, Schachter D. Implicit and explicit memory for new associations in normal and amnesic subjects. *J Exp Psychol*. 1985 Jul;11(3):501–18.
27. Berners DJ. A treatyse of fysshynge wyth an angle. In: *The Book of St Albans*. St. Albans; 1486.
28. Klinzing JG, Niethard N, Born J. Mechanisms of systems memory consolidation during sleep. *Nat Neurosci*. 2019 Oct 26;22(10):1598–610.
29. Rich R. "Acoustic confusions" in short-term memory and auditory imaging. *Aust J Psychol*. 1970 Aug 1;22(2):185–92.
30. Cohen MA, Horowitz TS, Wolfe JM. Auditory recognition memory is inferior to visual recognition memory. *Proc Natl Acad Sci*. 2009 Apr 7;106(14):6008–10.

31. Unsworth N. Working memory capacity and recall from long-term memory: Examining the influences of encoding strategies, study time allocation, search efficiency, and monitoring abilities. *J Exp Psychol Learn Mem Cogn*. 2016;42(1):50–60.

32. Long N, Kuhl B, Chun M. Memory and attention. In: Wixed J, editor. *Steven's Handbook of Experimental Psychology and Cognitive Neuroscience*. 4th ed. Hoboken: John Wiley & Sons, Inc.; 2018;285–321.

33. Kaplan RL, Van Damme I, Levine LJ, Loftus EF. Emotion and false memory. *Emot Rev*. 2016 Jan 23;8(1):8–13.

34. Loftus EF, Hoffman HG. Misinformation and memory: The creation of new memories. *J Exp Psychol Gen*. 1989 Mar;118(1):100–4.

35. Loftus E. Planting misinformation in the human mind: A 30-year investigation of the malleability of memory. *Learn Mem*. 2005 Jul 18;12(4):361–6.

36. Malmberg KJ, Raaijmakers JG, Shiffrin RM. 50 years of research sparked by Atkinson and Shiffrin (1968). *Mem Cognit*. 2019 May 28;47(4):561–74.

37. Atkinson RCC, Shiffrin RMM. Human memory: A proposed system and its control processes. In: Bower G, editor. *Human Memory, Basic Processes*. New York: Academic Press; 1977. pp. 7–113.

38. Pollack I. Message uncertainty and message reception. *J Acoust Soc Am*. 1959 Nov;31(11):1950–1508.

39. Reason J. Safety in the operating theatre — Part 2: Human error and organisational failure. *Curr Anaesth Crit Care*. 1995 Apr;6(2):121–6.

40. James W. *The Principles of Psychology*. Vol. 1. Cambridge: Harvard University; 1890.

41. Wason P, Evans JSB, Johnson-Laird P, Wason P. Editorial. Obituary Peter Wason (1924–2003). *Think Reason*. 2003;9(3):177–84.

42. Wason P, Evans J. Dual processes in reasoning? *Cognition*. 1974 Jan;3(2):141–54.

43. Kahneman D. A perspective on judgment and choice: Mapping bounded rationality. *Am Psychol*. 2003;58(9):697–720.

44. Stanovich KE, West RF. Individual differences in reasoning: Implications for the rationality debate? *Behav Brain Sci*. 2000 Oct 9;23(5):645–65.

45. Kahneman D. *Thinking Fast and Slow*. New York: Farrar, Strauss and Giroux; 2011.

46. Wickens C, Hollands J. *Engineering Psychology and Human Performance*. 3rd ed. Upper Saddle River: Prentice-Hall Inc.; 2000.

47. Waterson P, Le Coze J-C, Andersen HB. Recurring themes in the legacy of Jens Rasmussen. *Appl Ergon*. 2017 Mar;59:471–82.

48. Rasmussen J, Jensen A. Mental procedures in real-life tasks: A case study of electronic trouble shooting. *Ergonomics*. 1974 May;17(3):293–307.

49. Reason J. Little slips and, big disasters. *Interdiscip Sci Rev*. 1984 Jan 18;9(2):179–89.

50. Reason J. How did I come to do that? *New Soc*. 1975 Apr;10–3.

51. Reason J. Absent minds. *New Soc*. 1976;4:242–5.

52. Norman D. Slips of the Mind and An Outline for a Theory of Action. Report #7905. Personnel and Research Training Programs, Office of Naval Research. Arlington, Virginia: Center for Human Information Processing, University of California, San Diego; 1979.

53. Larouzee J, Le Coze J-C. Good and bad reasons: The Swiss cheese model and its critics. *Saf Sci*. 2020 Jun;126:1–11.

54. Rasmussen J. Skills, rules, and knowledge; signals, signs, and symbols, and other distinctions in human performance models. *IEEE Trans Syst Man Cybern.* 1983 May;SMC-13(3):257–66.

55. Senders J, Morey N. *Human Error. Cause, Prediction, and Recovery.* New Jersey: Lawrence Erlbaum Associates Inc.; 1991.

56. Reason J. *Human Error.* Cambridge: Cambridge University Press; 1990.

57. Reason J. Modelling the basic error tendencies of human operators. *Reliab Eng Syst Saf.* 1988 Jan;22(1–4):137–153.

58. Reason J. Human error: Models and management. *BMJ.* 2000 Mar 18;320(7237): 768–70.

59. Reason J. *Organizational Accidents Revisited.* Aldershot: Ashgate Publishing; 2016.

60. Reason J. *The Human Contribution: Unsafe Acts, Accidents, and Heroic Recoveries.* Aldershot: Ashgate Publishing Limited; 2008.

61. Haapakangas A, Hongisto V, Varjo J, Lahtinen M. Benefits of quiet workspaces in open-plan offices – Evidence from two office relocations. *J Environ Psychol.* 2018 Apr;56:63–75.

62. Reason J, Hobbs A. *Managing Maintenance Error. A Practical Guide.* Aldershot: Ashgate; 2003.

63. Senders J. Medical devices, medical errors, and medical accidents. In: Bogner M, editor. *Human Error in Medicine.* 1st ed. Hillsdale: Lawrence Erlbaum; 1994.

64. Wiener EL. "Controlled Flight into Terrain (CFIT)" accidents: System-induced errors. *Proc Hum Factors Soc Annu Meet.* 1975 Oct 21;19(1): 95–101.

65. Wiener E. Controlled flight into terrain accidents: System-induced errors. *Hum Factors.* 1977 Apr 1;19(2):171–81.

66. Reason J. *A Life in Error.* Aldershot: Ashgate Publishing Limited; 2013.

67. Shorrock ST. 'Human error': The handicap of human factors, safety and justice [Internet]. Hindsight; 2013 [cited 2022 Feb 9]. 32–37 p. Available from: https://skybrary.aero/sites/default/files/bookshelf/2568.pdf

68. Read GJ, Shorrock S, Walker GH, Salmon PM. State of science: Evolving perspectives on 'human error'. *Ergonomics.* 2021 Sep 2;64(9):1091–114.

69. Donabedian A. Evaluating the quality of medical care. Part 2. *Milbank Mem Fund Q.* 1966 Dec;44(3(suppl)):166–206.

70. Rasmussen J. Risk management in a dynamic society: A modelling problem. *Saf Sci.* 1997 Nov;27(2–3):183–214.

71. Amalberti R, Vincent C, Auroy Y, de Saint Maurice G. Violations and migrations in health care: A framework for understanding and management. *Qual Health Care.* 2006 Dec;15(suppl 1):i66–77.

72. Amalberti R. The paradoxes of almost totally safe transportation systems. *Saf Sci.* 2001 Mar;37(2–3).

73. Vaughan D. *The Challenger Launch Decision: Risky Technology, Culture, and Deviance at NASA.* Chicago: Chicago University Press; 1996.

74. Pidgeon N, O'Leary M. Man-made disasters: Why technology and organizations (sometimes) fail. *Saf Sci.* 2000 Feb;34(1–3):15–30.

Chapter 3

"Don't Make Me Sue You."

The decision to go public on March 18th had been made some days earlier after disclosure had been provided to both families. Time was also needed to organize all the arrangements, including letting the families know the Region would be informing the public – but not with any information about the patients' identities.

One of the Executive Medical Directors had been appointed to provide disclosure to both families. Importantly, he was also to be their link with the Region for further information as it became available. Because he was responsible for the Region's Community Portfolio, the EMD-COM was least likely of all the Executive Medical Directors to oversee staff who could have been involved in either patient's care. In addition, he was very calm and sincere in his manner, the right kind of person to talk with the families and to provide disclosure of the events and details. The EMD-COM wanted to offer his condolences and support.

Several days before the Press Conference, the EMD-COM had driven to a town outside Calgary, to meet with the widow and family of the man who had died. The EMD gave them the details of what had happened, the existence of another patient, and invited questions, which he answered. He told the family they had every right to sue the Region and gave them the business card of the Region's Legal Counsel, offering support. In fact, Jack was later quoted in an interview that he was prepared to discuss compensation with the families of the victims, but when the time was right. He acknowledged the tragedy of the

DOI: 10.4324/9781003185307-4

deaths for the families and expressed his heartfelt sadness and sympathy for all they had experienced.[1]

A few days before, the meeting with two of the sisters from Kathleen's family had been quite different. Thirteen months previously Kathleen had undergone a routine hip replacement in a Calgary hospital, which had gone terribly wrong. The history of those events overshadowed everything. And the Executive knew nothing of them.

The day after Kathleen's hip operation was a Saturday and to the family members at her bedside, it was clear that something was not right. But the orthopedic surgeon on call was not the one who had operated, and he was in the OR, busy with trauma cases.

The family's escalating pleas for help transformed into demands, which did not sit well with the nursing staff. After an overly long period of time without a suitable response, the family made a plan as to how they would get Kathleen what they knew was much-needed medical attention. In their desperation they'd decided to wheel their mother, in her hospital bed, out of her room, into an elevator, and down to the main floor to get her admitted to the hospital's emergency department. The plan was aborted when the surgeon finally arrived. The family members met him in a hallway, placarded with a pre-existing sign reading "Abuse of staff would not be tolerated". Tense words were exchanged between the surgeon and the family. One of the daughters then asked the surgeon to assess Kathleen. He did so and quickly announced that her condition was grave.

The family was correct. Her hemoglobin (blood count) was less than half normal, and her electrocardiogram (ECG) was also abnormal. It was likely Kathleen had suffered a major postoperative hemorrhage. There was now a flurry of activity. Kathleen was transferred to the OR, for a second operation. Postoperatively she went directly to the ICU, where she spent eleven days, and was diagnosed with having had a heart attack. She eventually recovered and left the hospital, fortunately without memory of the events or her ICU stay.

Up to and after Kathleen's discharge from the hospital there was no mention or explanation of the postoperative events from the hospital or three months later from the orthopedic surgeon when Kathleen saw him in follow-up after the operation. It was as if nothing had ever happened.

At this point, Kathleen had recovered more fully although she still had no memory of the events. But the family did. They were very upset about the ongoing lack of any apology or disclosure and therefore considered suing. There seemed to be no other way of finding out what had happened and why. The legal members of Kathleen's family talked with her about filing a statement of claim. As lawyers and judges, the Prowse family had no need of support to initiate a legal suit against the Region. As they joked together, they could write a statement of claim over breakfast. Shocked and horrified, Kathleen would not hear of it. She reasoned that, at her age, she was going to need more care, not less, from the Region. And she certainly did not want a black mark on her file. But she – and the rest of the family – had lost trust in the Region.

None of this – the previous operation, the disastrous postoperative period, and the loss of trust – was mentioned in the disclosure discussion with the CMO and the EMD-COM.

However, in the days, weeks, and months to follow, the Region's Executive was forced to look at both the immediate events leading up to her death and those events of the previous hospitalization. The Region had a lot of work to do to gain any degree of credibility and trust with the family. The plea, of "Don't make me sue you", was uttered by one of the daughters in a later meeting with Jack. She needed him to understand that those previous events had harmed not only her mother but their whole family. And then the lack of any disclosure or discussion had further harmed them. There had not even been a simple apology, of the kind that one person would offer another, when hearing that something terrible had befallen the other person. And then their mother had died.

Apology, Disclosure, and Support

Healthcare organizations exist to offer diagnosis, treatment, and comfort to patients. However, despite all best intentions, things can go wrong with any aspect of care. When that happens, and patients suffer complications, are injured, or die, we need to look after them, help them, and care for them, as well as their family members. After the two patients died from incorrectly mixed dialysate solution, Regional leaders found themselves in crisis management mode. For many of them, this was early on in their introduction to many aspects of healthcare safety. The Region had no playbook to guide it in helping the family members of the patients who died – there were no Region-wide policies or procedures on disclosure.

The absence of disclosure was not unique to the Region. In the early 2000s, many healthcare providers and leaders, as well as malpractice insurers in Canada and the United States, still believed apology and disclosure would lead to successful litigation. When the Region was struggling to decide how best to respond to the deaths of the two patients from the potassium chloride mix-up, apology and disclosure were not commonplace in Canadian healthcare organizations.

The concepts of apology and disclosure were not, however, completely foreign to some doctors and some administrators in the Region. Physicians such as the (then) Chief Information Officer, the CMO, the Head of the Critical Incident Review Committee, WF, JMD and others knew about, taught, and included apologies and disclosures in their medical practices. In fact, two decades previously, JMD and her Department Head at the time had written that any problem "should be fully discussed with the patient or relatives", although this recommendation was "contrary to the usual legal advice". They added, "withholding information", which would "certainly emerge sooner or later", would be "counterproductive" and "not doing what is right".[2]

Over the next several years, this process of doing what is right was accepted by more and more staff, who initially were reluctant to participate, fearing litigation should patients be told the truth. The concepts were then integrated into the Critical Review Policy when the Calgary Regional Health Authority (CRHA) was established.[3] The Policy was most successfully implemented at the FMC. (This was where those Regional leaders, who in 2004 understood and demanded apology and disclosure, all practiced.) But a reorganization of the CRHA in the early 2000s to the Calgary Health Region meant some policies were lost.

In the United States in 1995, the Department of Veterans Affairs (VA) was probably the first large healthcare system to enact a disclosure policy, possibly prompted by the success of the VA system in Lexington, Kentucky, which had been following such a policy since 1987.[4] The patient safety standards for the Joint Commission on Accreditation of Healthcare Organizations (JCAHO) were implemented in 2001. These standards required healthcare organizations to have a disclosure of harm policy. JCAHO's equivalent in Canada, the (then) Canadian Council on Health Services Accreditation (CCHSA), now Accreditation Canada, did not implement its requirement for organizational disclosure policies until 2006 and the Canadian Patient Safety Institute published its first edition of its Disclosure Guidelines in 2008, preceded by the Health Quality Council of Alberta's Disclosure of Harm Policy in 2006.[5]

What Patients and Families Experience after a Patient Suffers Harm

When our patients are harmed, they most often suffer some type of physical injury, frequently accompanied by psychological effects, including fear, anxiety, distrust, and anger. Suffering harm equates with one or more kinds of loss: of life, of bodily functions, of independence, and of trust. As a result, many patients and families who experience significant loss proceed through a grieving process. Some individuals, if referred to a psychiatrist, can even end up with a formal medical diagnosis of Major Depression and Post-Traumatic Stress Disorder.[6]

However, if we can intervene quickly to meet the needs of patients and families after such an event, this may help with their grieving process. Most patients and families usually return to relatively normal, daily psychological functioning, although this may take a variable period of time. However, when the needs of patients and families are not met in a timely way, they can then suffer a second type of psychological harm, compounding, prolonging, and worsening the grieving process. This secondary harm ("second harm") can be an important factor contributing to the development of "complicated grief".[6] In our experience, many patients and families are often capable of forgiving the first type of harm but are much less often able to forgive the second.

Just above we described harm as equating with one or more kinds of loss, ranging from life to trust. However, differing definitions of harm used by healthcare providers, organizations, or regulators can lead to variable disclosure conversations with patients about exactly what they suffered. Some healthcare providers and organizations may believe that some part of suffering or loss was a 'necessary component' of the treatment. Others may believe that harm refers to anything the patient suffered. For example, the College of Physicians & Surgeons of Ontario (CPSO) refers to harm as an "outcome that negatively affects a patient's health or quality of life". However, the CPSO adds a clause potentially restricting that definition. "Harm may or may not relate to material risks discussed during the informed consent process".[7] Individual providers could interpret these statements in different ways. Consider the example of a surgeon who preoperatively discussed with a patient the possibility of damage to a ureter during bowel surgery or perforation of part of the bowel during laparoscopic surgery, and then the damage or perforation occurred. Some individuals might defend the position that the patient had not been harmed. Clearly, from the patient's perspective, this would appear to be a case of the healthcare system and the provider protecting themselves. Other healthcare providers and leaders might accept the perspective of the patient and conclude that the patient was indeed harmed. They would then proceed with a disclosure conversation and after a system analysis, offer an appropriate apology. This latter perspective is one taken by the College of Physicians & Surgeons of Alberta (CPSA). The CPSA's definition of harm is an outcome that "negatively affects the patient's health and/or quality of life",[8] and does not add any modifying clauses. Regulators and healthcare organizations should strive to have clear, unambiguous definitions of important patient safety terms that respect the perspective and opinions of patients. In the absence of a patient-oriented perspective, we can only advise caution for healthcare providers and patients who work or seek care in jurisdictions where policies of the hospital or organization do not match those of the regulator.

What Patients Need and Expect

Just what do patients and families need *and* expect after a patient has been nearly or actually harmed? (Here we use 'harm' to refer to when breakdowns in care occur that contribute to a patient being injured, physically or psychologically.) Patients and families then have three major requirements: first, they need to feel the emotional responses of *respect and empathy*; second, they expect to be given a sincere *apology* and *disclosure with transparency*; and third, they require *support*, both financial and non-financial. We describe each of these in turn.

Respect

As described in the Prologue and the narrative in this chapter, thirteen months before Kathleen required urgent heart surgery, and immediately after her hip operation, her daughters tried to convince the hospital staff that something was seriously wrong with their mother. However, they were not believed. Even the fact that two family members were qualified healthcare providers did not stimulate a different response. In short, their opinions were not respected.

In the nearly two decades since then, we have learned a lot about the stories patients and their families tell, which are similar yet very different to the stories we tell about them. Our stories are those we put together from what we have learned about the patient, the family, and things like laboratory results. We then recount these stories in notations in a patient's chart, perhaps in a letter asking for a second opinion or at rounds as we summarize the patient's condition at the bedside. However, our stories are *our* opinions.

Patients and their families also tell stories of what they have lived and experienced, which offer *their* opinions. As Dr. Patricia Trbovich, a Human Factors Engineer at the University of Toronto, and Professor Charles Vincent, of the Department of Experimental Psychology, University of Oxford, said, patients and their families are "our primary informants". Additionally, families are an important source of potentially life-saving information. They often detect clues, such as what the patient is saying or how things are being said, that reflect physiological deterioration.[9] Often these observations are missed by the hospital staff because the family knows the patient better than anyone else and sees the early start of the patient's downward trajectory. It is only in having both parts – and not sides – of the full account can we start to fully know the patient, including what is important, what matters. By not believing the patient or family, we are effectively saying we do not respect them, and that their opinions do not matter.

The experience the Prowse family had is not unique. We know from studies of hospitalized patients who have suffered harm, that often, they or their family members were not believed when they said to hospital staff the equivalent of "Mother doesn't look right…".[9,10] Patients and families reported dismissive attitudes from hospitals and a lack of responses from the clinical team,[11] similar to those experienced by Kathleen Prowse's family during her first hospitalization. We now also know that by listening to such observations and messages, and incorporating them into our early warning response systems, we can often save patients – before they actually need saving. This was observed by Mandy Odell, Karin Gerber, and Melanie Gager, three senior nurses at the Royal Berkshire NHS Foundation Trust in Reading, England. In 2006, they set up the first program in England in which patients and families could contact intensive care teams directly, should they be concerned about their or their family member's condition.[9] This type of program has now been developed and implemented successfully in several other countries, including Australia and the United States, as described in a systematic review of results by Gill and colleagues in Australia.[10]

To ensure these patient and family-activated programs, as well as the patients' and families' stories are heard and believed, we must truly accept the patient and family as equal partners in the care team and that they are equal partners in providing that care. To do so, we must respect not only their opinions but also respect them as unique individuals. They have entrusted themselves or their family members into our care, and we must return that trust by welcoming, valuing, and respecting them.

Empathy

Strictly defined, empathy means our abilities as humans to understand what others are feeling or experiencing, by placing ourselves in their contexts. Sometime between 675 and 725 BCE, Homer, the eighth-century Greek epic poet, wrote "Yet, taught by time, my heart has learned to glow for other's good, and melt at other's woe".[12] The word empathy itself, however, did not enter language for another twenty-five centuries. Rudolf Lotze, a German physician, philosopher, and logician, writing about the history of beauty and artistic taste, coined a German term as a translation from the Greek meaning passion or state of emotion.[13] Then, in 1909, EB Titchener, an English psychologist, translated the term into English, commenting, "I see gravity, modesty, courtesy, stateliness [in someone], but also feel them. I suppose that's a simple case of empathy…"[14] Over the next several decades, empathy lost its aesthetic connections and was taken up by psychotherapists.[15]

Our use of empathy has continued to evolve, particularly in how it compares with sympathy. Simply put, empathy is not the same thing as sympathy, which means feeling sorrow for another's experience or situation. Empathy, in contrast, takes a proactive approach to comprehensively understanding what another individual feels and what they experienced.[16] This involves "putting in the work to educate oneself and to listen with a humble heart to understand another's experience from their perspective, not as we imagine we would feel". Additionally, expressing empathy is not about us and what we think we might do in a situation in which we have never been and might never be. Rather, empathy is the "kindred connection from a place of deep knowing that opens your spirit to the pain of another as they perceive it".[16,17]

If we are able to demonstrate empathetic communication, then this will help us to form and then express our understanding, as well as our responses to the individual's feedback, as Wilkerson describes. To be empathetic, we must listen closely to the description that the patient and/or the family gives us. Only they know what they experienced and what their emotional reactions to being harmed were. We need then to reflect back a summary of what we heard. We do this to demonstrate that we have not only listened with our ears but we have heard with our brains – what was said and perhaps what was not said. We must also demonstrate that we appreciate all the feelings expressed, even if they are unpleasant, such as those of disappointment and anger.

Unfortunately, when attempting to express empathy, some of us, as healthcare providers and leaders, may claim we know what the patient or family has gone through. We might believe this to be true because of our previous experiences with other patients or we might say it in an attempt to communicate understanding. Additionally, statements such as "I know what you mean" or "I know what it must feel like" appear patronizing and break down, rather than build, bridges between individuals. Ultimately, it is up to the patient or family to determine if their experiences and feelings were understood – based on how well a person or group of people listened and reflected back what had been said. With education and coaching, we can all learn to listen and communicate in a more empathetic way, thus demonstrating we understand the patient's and family's perspective.

When genuine empathy is communicated effectively, a patient/family feels heard and, again, respected. Empathetic listeners have described feeling the walls or barricades the patient or family member erected begin to disappear, replaced with a sense of respectful openness, and the situation no longer being one of us versus them.

Apology

As well as not being heard or understood, patients and families become even more upset and angry when they do not receive an apology. The most basic version of an apology is when we offer an apology extending our sympathy. A *sympathetic apology*, which healthcare providers and leaders provide to patients who have been harmed, is made in the same way we would apologize to a neighbor who had slipped on ice on the road – "I'm *so* sorry you are going through the pain and awkwardness of having a broken ankle". We are stating our *regret* – our sadness – for their injured condition and we are also reinforcing our human connection.

When we are formally apologizing, in addition to expressing sympathy, we also express *remorse* – our distress at the patient's and family's suffering. We must also be clear about *what* we are apologizing for, in the same way we need to be clear about what we are disclosing. An effective formal apology has two parts. In the first part, we express regret and remorse for what happened, and what the patient and family had to and could be continuing to experience. In the second part, we take and state appropriate acceptance of our responsibility for the events that took place and the factors that contributed to the events. These two parts may (need to) be delivered at different times. The first part can be given during the first conversation with the patient and family, and repeated in subsequent conversations and meetings. We should only offer the second part once we have a complete understanding of the events contributing to harm.

The art of expressing regret (our sadness) and remorse (our distress) is not just in what we say but also in how and when we say it. If we have been successful in making an empathetic connection with a patient or family, either as an individual or as part of a (disclosure) team, then our expressions of regret and remorse are much more likely to be interpreted as genuine and meaningful. Having an empathetic connection with someone means that we have been able to understand the patient and family's experience and related emotions, and to communicate these back to them. In contrast, if we were to make similar expressions of regret and remorse before establishing an empathetic connection, then the patient or family could interpret these as our simply going through the motions and not truly meaning or caring about we what we said.

As for accepting appropriate responsibility for the events that took place and for the important antecedent factors, we must include these for our apologies to be complete. This is one reason why, especially in complex events, we should often have a disclosure team, members of which can meet several times with the patient and family, rather than having one discussion with the patient and family.

As individual healthcare providers, any of us can accept responsibility for the decisions we made and the actions we did or did not take. However, we cannot and should not take responsibility for factors in the healthcare system over which we have little or no control. For example, an Emergency Room nurse can accept responsibility for not reacting in a timely way to a patient's abnormal lab result but should not take responsibility for the laboratory turnaround time being longer than expected. That is part of the roles and responsibilities of healthcare leaders.

Thus, for those of us holding leadership positions, it is more appropriate to apologize for deficiencies such as staffing levels, the care environment, equipment, and organizational policies. Conversely, as leaders, we should not be in a position of apologizing for the actions of our healthcare provider colleagues who are not present to speak for themselves. Apologies for wrongful actions or lack of actions are more meaningful when they come from these who were involved, rather than from an administrator.

It can sometimes be challenging to determine where the right degree of responsibility lies. This can exist on a spectrum between falling on one's sword and accepting more responsibility than is reasonable, *versus* denying all responsibility for one's actions or actions made by leaders at the highest levels of the organization.

Some healthcare providers and organizational leaders might try to use a pseudo or partial apology in place of a complete one. "We are (or, I am) sorry this happened, but this is a recognized complication of the procedure". Worse, sometimes apportioning blame to a specific individual or to the organization is dressed up to look like an apology. "We are sorry the surgeon (*who is not in attendance*) made this error. It was a terrible error". or "I am sorry the pharmacy could not get the proper medication to you in a timely way so I chose a different medication that you reacted to". The most deplorable type of pseudo-apology made is when some blame is saved for the patient. "I am sorry you had a heart attack during your operation but if you had not been such a heavy smoker it probably wouldn't have happened". We would all be wise to stay far away from such statements because, ultimately, they further damage our relationships with our patients and their families.

Decisions about what to apologize for and the degree to which responsibility is accepted are not always easy ones to make. In healthcare, unlike industry, there is not always a clear line between the right versus the wrong way to do things. Additionally, in healthcare we sometimes must harm our patients to heal them. For example, to inject treatments or to measure certain bodily functions, we insert sharp (and sometimes quite large) needles. We use sharp knives to cut into the body and remove or replace parts. We prescribe medications with terrible side-effects. We administer radiation and toxic chemicals in the treatment of different types of cancer. We try to do all these things, for the purpose of healing, recognizing the "intimacy, complexity and sensitivity of the services" we provide, and the "trust, compassion and empathy that underpin" healthcare.[18]

Before we perform these procedures, however, we provide our patients with information about what we plan to do, what they should anticipate in the way of harm, and what could go wrong, a process we describe as obtaining informed consent. This process (and not our patients' signatures on the Consent Form) implies we have foreseen the harm our patients might experience. This is a challenging area. How can we tell the difference between the harm we anticipated as a normal part of the treatment and that which could have resulted from deficiencies in the way the treatment was carried out? We know there is a spectrum of performance in providing care, even in care that is considered acceptable. Similarly, there is a spectrum of the harm we normally anticipate and one of the harm we do not anticipate. The difficulty often lies in deciding between these ranges of performance, anticipated harm and unanticipated harm.

Healthcare providers sometimes do not complete actions either correctly or completely because of making errors. This is not the only possibility, as the healthcare provider might have broken one or more rules. In those events in which a healthcare provider made errors and might have also broken rules that contributed to the event, we think it is reasonable and expected that the healthcare provider accepts responsibility, and offers remorse and regret for their actions or inactions. However, healthcare providers are only one part of the healthcare system and we must keep in mind there are always other system factors contributing to errors being made, as well as to some rule-breaking. Having a system-focused review of the event can help with understanding these system factors. These other system factors can also directly contribute to a patient being harmed, and therefore should be addressed by a healthcare leader during the disclosure conversation.

Disclosure

Many patients who have suffered harm, as well as their families, will be able to recall hearing only deafening silence from healthcare providers and organizational leaders after the events that led to the harm. This is what Kathleen Prowse and her family also experienced, following Kathleen's hip operation when she suffered severe bleeding and a heart attack. Even after Kathleen's life-threatening condition had been diagnosed and treated, neither the orthopedic surgeon nor any of the Region's leaders responded correctly – or at all. There was not even a sympathetic apology. Remarkably, Kathleen's family was prepared to give the Region a second chance.

As important as an appropriate apology is for the patient and family, on its own it is insufficient. Disclosure and its related supportive actions are also required. Disclosure is the formal communication we as healthcare providers and sometimes healthcare organizational leaders have with patients and families following harm. While both apology and disclosure provide descriptions of what happened to patients, our descriptions with disclosure will be longer, providing more detail than with apologies, acknowledging that something untoward occurred, and explaining what happened and why. When sharing this information, an apology can be interwoven. Thus, although apology and disclosure have similarities, they are not synonymous but are linked by their intended purpose of helping patients and families deal with the consequences of harm. Both should be provided with empathy.

Without complete knowledge of what happened to their loved one, patients and families will consider our responses to the harm they experienced to be completely inadequate and will often become frustrated and angry. That anger mounts when their questions are not answered, contributing to patients and families believing they have been denied information and that we, as healthcare providers and/or leaders in the organization, are hiding the details they want. This anger may then drive families to the media to draw attention to the problem, to lodge an official complaint, or to institute legal proceedings for damages (or do all three). Studies have detailed patients and families suing specific personnel and the institution as a whole, primarily to gain the information they were denied, with any financial payments then of secondary importance.

For example, in 1994, Charles Vincent and colleagues surveyed over 200 patients and relatives to learn why they were either taking or considering taking legal action after patients were harmed. The research team identified four themes: desiring accountability; feeling ignored or neglected and wanting an explanation; improving standards of care so that something similar would not happen again; and wanting compensation and an admission of negligence. When asked if there was anything that could have been done to avoid the need for legal action, over 40% of those surveyed replied "Yes" and listed "receiving an apology and explanation" as the most important.[19]

Patients and their families expect – and deserve – a complete recounting of the event in which the patient suffered harm. In this recounting, we should provide a truthful explanation of what happened, what had been done to help the patient by the time of the meeting, and information about providing any future care the patient might require. Additionally and importantly, almost all patients and families want to know what will be done to ensure the same thing will not happen to anyone else.[20]

Patients' experience with disclosure after an event is often vastly inferior to what they need.[21] One study describing patients' experiences was conducted in Australia by Rick Iedema, of the University of Technology, Sydney, several colleagues from around Australia, and Thomas Gallagher, from the University of Washington. Interviews were conducted between 2008 and 2010 of 39 patients who had suffered harm at a high level of severity (death, permanent, or short-term disability) and 80 family members from all over Australia. These interviews resulted in 100 stories, which yielded five major concerns about disclosure. These were "inadequate preparation", "inappropriate disclosure", "lack of follow-up support", "lack of appropriate closure", and "insufficient integration of open disclosure with improvement of patient safety".[22]

These concerns started with "inadequate preparation" for disclosure. Some of the healthcare organizations did not have a complaints (or concerns) mechanism that could activate a disclosure process and if there was one, the patients' adverse events were not readily acknowledged. The disclosure meeting times and locations were often unsuitable, and those able to attend rarely had a say about which staff members would or would not be there. Additionally, patients and families were not encouraged or even told they could invite a support person to the meeting, and at which the disclosure process was either not introduced or adequately explained.[22]

The second finding was summarized as the disclosure being "inappropriate". Staff present did not explain their role within the organization. Often an apology was not readily offered and the attitude of the staff was described as impartial. No clear explanations of what went wrong were provided and patients and families were not given an opportunity to express their views or ask questions about the event. No information was suggested related to services the patients and families might have wanted to access, nor were they provided compensation for costs incurred as a result of the event. There was a similar lack of information about whether or not other healthcare organizations were involved.[22]

After the meeting, there was a "lack of follow-up support". This included no arrangements for any more than a single meeting, no ready access to relevant clinical information, no invitations to be part of the investigation into the event, and no contact information for someone in the organization who could provide further information and support.[22]

Lack of support was followed by "lack of appropriate closure", with patients and families lacking vital information. There were no records of what was disclosed, explanations of what happened or planned improvements. Nor was there information about which, if any, alternative dispute resolution mechanisms were available when there was disagreement with the disclosure process or findings.[22]

Lastly, the patients and families felt there was "insufficient integration" of disclosure into any processes for improvement in safety. The adverse events were not recorded or investigated properly. Medical records were not up to date or complete, which slowed investigations and also led to disagreements about what happened and what was done. Patients and families were not included in any discussions about improvement. Significantly however, the patients and families were concerned about the staff, that those involved did not receive support from their colleagues and organization, thus limiting their acceptance and the effectiveness of disclosure.[22]

Unfortunately, despite publications such as that by Iedema and colleagues, many patients and families still continue to experience the same problems with disclosure. These are not limited to any one country but are to be found worldwide, although there are pockets of extremely good practice. This is similarly true with apology. Despite many jurisdictions having adopted apology legislation, expecting it would increase the likelihood of patients and families being offered an apology, this has not been a universal finding.[23]

The findings from Australia about disclosure, however, do help highlight the specific points an effective disclosure process should address. One of these points was the lack of invitations to be part of the investigation into the event. Patients and families should have a role in the review, and this role starts with them being the first individuals to be interviewed. They should also be asked about which recommendations for improvement they would want to see put forward and implemented. Patients and families should also be told that certain changes will take time.

The three of us have all had experience in providing disclosure, at times more effectively than at others. But we have learned there are several important points.

Simple Disclosure Versus Formal Disclosure

In the majority of events, a disclosure meeting involves a patient, the family, and/ or the support people they want present, as well as the individual providing care. With *simple disclosure*, the care provider should apologize, and acknowledge and explain what happened. For example, a nurse who was late in giving medications to two patients should apologize, acknowledge the medication was late, and explain why ("Called to help another patient who had fallen"). The nurse should also provide any information about whether there could be any possible side-effects ("Need to wait 30 minutes before eating"). Usually in these situations, this is the end of the disclosure process, unless of course the patient or family has more questions, or requires additional information.

However, in some cases, for example, if the patient has suffered more severe harm and/or if several care providers are involved, the disclosure process will involve planning and additional participants. The suggestions we offer below will help healthcare providers and administrators to work through the aftermath of untoward events more successfully with their patients and families, and their colleagues.

The Four "Ws" of Disclosure

When Disclosure must be timely. An initial conversation is important and should take place as soon as possible after it is recognized a patient has suffered harm. In the absence of much, if any factual knowledge, this initial conversation will likely only provide an acknowledgment that something happened – but with the promise of an investigation and the sharing of factual information when available. We must establish timelines for the disclosure process that are discussed with the patients and families. Missing agreed dates and times leads patients and families to question our credibility and commitment, and will further erode trust. Additionally, although we might be tempted during an initial meeting to speculate what could have happened, speculation that is ultimately proven to be unfounded further erodes any trust the patient and family still have, and therefore should be avoided.

Where Disclosure should take place in a private setting that has been suggested or agreed to by the patient/family. Most patients/families will not want to meet in the vicinity of where the patient was harmed, which could include the entire building rather than just part of it. Both the patient and family have likely been traumatized by the event. Taking steps to avoid or limit re-traumatizing them by requiring they meet in an unwanted location demonstrates a needed sensitivity and understanding of their suffering.

Who The presence of any or all of several factors indicates the need for a group of people to form a disclosure team. Some of these factors include: how severely harmed the patient might be; the number of healthcare providers involved in the event; the involvement of more than one service (such as Emergency,

Anesthesiology, and Surgery) or institution; the degree of relationship between any breakdowns in care and the harm suffered by the patient; the presence of multiple, important breakdowns in care by two or more providers; and the state of the relationship between the patient and family and the most responsible provider, especially if there is evidence of irreparable damage.

Building a formal disclosure team starts with three members. These are the most responsible healthcare provider involved in the event, a senior administrator of the healthcare organization providing the care who can address organizational responsibility, and an individual who will be the patient's main point of contact, such as someone from Patient Relations. This latter person will act as the single source of contact and support for the patient and family, who can be contacted with any additional questions or concerns that might come up after the meeting, and who can set up future meetings.

At least one of the three core team members should have experience and training in disclosure. If they do not, then a fourth person who does have this training should join the team. In particular, the lead spokesperson should be knowledgeable about and experienced in demonstrating empathy. Showing willingness to listen, to empathize, and to express regret signals respect for the patient and family's experience and helps to set a tone of reconciliation. Then, other specific individuals can be added to the team, according to the situations described above.

Finally, the patient and family should be consulted as to who they would and would not like to be present. For example, they may request a healthcare professional or another individual who could provide support, such as a social worker or spiritual representative. This request should be honored *if at all possible*. Conversely, if there is an individual whom the patient and/or family does not wish to be involved, for example, the individual who provided care at the time of the event, this wish should *always* be honored.

What   Before meeting with the patient and family, team members should anticipate what information they are likely to want to know. Additionally, a pre-disclosure discussion with the patient and family can help clarify what their questions, concerns, and goals are, and what they want to discuss. The disclosure team should also talk together before the disclosure meeting to be clear about what factual information is known, thus determining what can be disclosed and the best way to do this. All team members should also be clear as to how far an apology can go, based on the latest understanding of the event. Team members should be aware of and prepared to address culturally sensitive issues that could arise. All this preparation will help those in the disclosure team to meet the patient and family's expectations.

It is useful for the disclosure team to share a written timeline or chronology of events with the patient and family, which will explain when things happened. Relevant facts can then be added. The patient and family will also find it helpful to be given a report of the important system factors that contributed to the patient suffering harm.

If we are to provide a factual explanation, then we must have a systematic system-based investigation to gain a proper understanding about "What?" happened, "How?", and "Why?".[24] We recommend reviews be conducted by individuals who will not be part of a disclosure team. This separation is important because, should a patient or family member ask a question the answer to which is opinion rather than fact-based, a team member with knowledge of the investigation would be placed in a difficult and awkward situation. Depending on any legislative and protective governance under which investigations are conducted, an individual involved in the protected review might have to tell a patient or family that they cannot reveal information they know. Such a statement could be interpreted by the patient and family as the individual *willfully* withholding information and could lead to distrust in the disclosure process. Additionally, it is important never to speculate if the team does not know the answer to a question. Patients have said, "Tell us what has happened, not what might have happened".[25] It is therefore far better for team members to say they do not know but commit to providing factual information, if and when it becomes available.

There is another major concept about *what* is disclosed (and apologized for) we think requires discussion and that is when the focus of disclosure and apology is on 'medical error'. Part of the problem arises when respected medical publications repeat the premise that 'medical error' alone directly causes patient harm, including death. These statements influence people's beliefs and attitudes toward fault. The corollary is that our disclosures and apologies then focus primarily or exclusively on error, on asking who 'screwed up'? We perpetuate the naïve and rather misguided thinking that close calls and harm are the direct result of only that single error. But in reality, life – and events in which patients are harmed – are not this simple. Worse still, when we use this language and this approach, we perpetuate the inherent bias we as humans have toward cause and blame, thus directly undermining the principles of a Just Culture. In reality, harm is most often the culmination of a series of unrecognized factors and unfortunate events that unforeseeably come together to wreak havoc.

Additionally, using the term 'medical error' when disclosing shifts the focus from the patient to the provider. When we disclose (and apologize) for making a 'medical error', we are focusing on what was done *to the patient by the healthcare provider(s)*, and not what the patient *experienced and suffered* – which was harm. We need to ensure the focus is on the patient and the family, and to illustrate the importance of this, we recount a story from a few years into the Region's transformation.

In the early stages of development of the 2008 Canadian Patient Safety Institute (CPSI) Canadian Disclosure Guidelines, the phrase 'disclosure of medical error' was used. This information reached members of the Patient and Family Advisory Committee in the Region, who were very concerned. In 2006, the Health Quality Council of Alberta (HQCA) had published its own document, "Disclosure of Harm to Patients and Families",[5] work on which started in February 2004, triggered by the two deaths in the Region. The HQCA's approach to disclosure was focused on harm a patient and family had suffered, and not the 'medical error' made by a healthcare provider. Because of this, a small group of Calgary patient advisors went to Ottawa and lobbied against the inclusion of 'medical error'. As a result, the final CPSI document contained the statement, "These guidelines purposefully avoid the use of the term error". The shift in focus, from the provider to the patient, had been accomplished.

Thus, when our mental model of harm moves away from 'who failed, so who do we blame and therefore who pays?', we as healthcare leaders and providers will be able to have more realistic and complete conversations with our patients and their families. It also follows that individuals involved in the event will more readily accept appropriate responsibility for their part in the system that contributed to the patient being harmed.

Not Just a Single Meeting

The importance of disclosure is also underscored by the fact that holding only one or two disclosure meetings, such as an initial and then a formal one, does not mean that our conversations and discussions with the patient and family have ended. Disclosure is a series of discussions that, in some cases, may go on for a few years. In general, after the formal disclosure, we should present plans for follow-up and, after discussion, ensure that the patient and family agree. They will also find it important to learn of ongoing plans to acquire additional information, the status of recommendations for improvement, and/or actual improvements started or implemented. In our experience, patients and families very much want to learn about and help ensure what is being done to greatly reduce the probability of something similar happening again to the patient or to other patients.[20] Once again, the team should offer to explain this rather than assume that the patient and family want to hear about it. 'Do not assume anything' should be a fundamental principle for all of us.

Support

Do not assume anything also applies to patients' and families' need for support. In addition to facing barriers to obtain information, patients and families often experience challenges in getting healthcare providers and organizational leaders to understand their need for support. This can be both financial and non-financial. An important part of a complete disclosure response is for providers and leaders to acknowledge this need proactively, and not wait for a patient or family to ask.

Financial Support

Financial support can be in the form of either reimbursement or compensation. The former is defined as, the "act of paying someone for expenses with or without an admission of fault".[26] These expenses could cover travel costs to allow one or more family members to be with a patient. Expenses could also cover other out-of-pocket costs, for example, childcare, parking, meals, or accommodation, as well as lost wages. By providing reimbursement proactively, we can help to re-establish the relationship and trust between the patient and family and the healthcare organization and some of its specific personnel. In our organizations, we should be able to offer such reimbursement immediately following an event in which a patient is harmed, without prejudice, and before the findings of any detailed investigations are available.

In the United States, the concept of reimbursement is slightly more complicated because of legislation related to 'never events'.[27] These were first described in 2001 by Dr. Ken Kizer, in an interview in which he described patients' tragic outcomes that should *never* happen[28] but did and continue to do so. The list included patients being injured or dying after a fall while in hospital. Many states, firstly Minnesota, followed with legislation to require mandatory reporting of these events. Because of the costs, both financially and in terms of human lives and suffering, this type of legislation was followed by an announcement in 2008, made jointly by the US Department of Health and Human Services and the Centers for Medicare and Medicaid Services. Hospitals would not be refunded if patients developed any one of eight Hospital-Acquired Conditions (HACs). These HACs were "conditions which would not occur, so long as the hospital and its staff (were) engaging in good medical practice".[27] Although we appreciate the thinking behind the concept of 'never events', we have difficulties using a term that includes the modifier 'never' for something that occurs all too often. In a poll one of us ran about a decade ago, the response of patients who were asked about the term was one of dismay and even anger.

As for patients living in the USA, changes to reimbursement had implications for patients. Hospitals were required to treat them but billing them became complicated. Many hospitals opted for disclosure of the harm and withholding billing for costs, as in Minnesota, where legislation required hospitals not to bill patients who suffered a 'never event'. Private insurers followed the lead of Medicare and Medicaid, either not reimbursing if a patient suffered a 'never event' or reimbursing only some basic costs.

To return to the discussion of support being offered, the disclosure team may not be ready to discuss compensation. But the team should not avoid the subject, which might require a follow-up discussion. However, if we do offer fair compensation for the harm a patient suffered, once the results of a systematic analysis are available, we could help avoid litigation and reduce the stress felt by the patient and family, as well as the healthcare providers. We will also build back trust.

We know that because opportunities for healing do not usually present themselves in courtrooms. Having patients and families, healthcare providers and healthcare leaders become adversaries within the legal system and/or the media runs counter to what we believe is needed. We fully accept that in certain situations, successful ligation by patients and their families will provide necessary funds to help patients who were harmed receive whatever ongoing treatment and care they believe is required. In the Region in 2004, senior executives proactively discussed legal settlements with the families so that they did not have to go through the painful process of suing the Region. However, we also know that many patients and families initiate litigation for the sole purpose of trying to discover what happened, how, and why. This should not be required. If patients are harmed, then they have a right to know what happened. They should not need to ask and should be given the information as quickly and completely as is possible. By providing full disclosure to the families, the Region was able to fulfill what we think is a requirement and also to start to rebuild its relationships with them.

Early adopters of this approach, which was combined with open disclosure, included the Foothills Medical Centre in Calgary, the VA Medical Center in Lexington Kentucky,[4] and the University of Michigan.[29] Published commentary[20] on and analyses of their liability claims showed benefits of this approach over the more traditional deny and defend approach. These successes encouraged other organizations in the United States to follow suit.[30] But even the new approaches are variable and their success is based on legal metrics, such as the number of successful claims, costs of claims, and total liability costs. These metrics do not capture what patients and families experience. Similarly, countries that have established no fault compensation for patients injured as a result of an adverse event generally report better outcomes for institutions and patients.[31]

The model in much of Canada is that some healthcare providers (mainly doctors) are not employees of the healthcare organizations in which they practice. Rather, they work under a fee-for-service program, in which doctors bill their patients' provincial or territorial government. Thus, when patients and families seek compensation, they must contend with at least two different defendants – one for the organization and another for the physicians, each with separate legal counsel. Such complexities create challenges and can add to delays in reaching a fair resolution in a timely manner. Much more remains to be done to fairly address compensation requests from patients and their families.

Non-Financial Support

Even without any monetary concerns, following an adverse event, patients and their families often struggle to cope. Organizations that proactively recognize what is needed and offer it before being asked will experience a more rapid and complete restoration of trust and confidence in its relationship with the patient and family. We should offer pragmatic types of support, such as coordination to provide accommodation and transportation for family members, if patients have to remain in a care setting and their families have no place to stay. Patients and families will find it helpful if they are ensured access to spiritual support and/ or psychological support, for example, from social workers, psychologists, or psychiatrists who either work for the organization or who are in private practice. Patients may require immediate and ongoing care and rehabilitation, depending on the injuries suffered, as well as alternative care providers. Arrangements for these, as well as delivery of primary and/or specialist healthcare, as required in the future, should be set in place.

Finally, a patient and family might have a different perspective from healthcare providers involved in the event and/or the healthcare leaders about how and why the patient came to suffer harm. Different healthcare providers might not completely agree with one another and might not agree with healthcare leaders. It is important to anticipate and then acknowledge this possibility because it can affect how the facts about the event are interpreted. Different perspectives can contribute to important differences between what a patient and family might be expecting to hear, and what is actually said by healthcare providers and leaders. This is one reason why listening to a patient and family describe their experience and their understanding is important. Providing empathy for them is still possible and desirable, in fact, more important when there is incomplete agreement about how events unfolded. Empathy does not require agreement but it does require understanding. The goal of a disclosure conversation is not to convince everyone to agree on one interpretation of events. Still, it can be important to know how far apart different individuals might be in their interpretations. This should not be seen as a problem, but rather an opportunity for further shared discussions, leading to better understanding and healing for all.

In summary, in this chapter we have described how disclosure conversations are an important part of responding to adverse events in healthcare. How these conversations are conducted is also vital, as this affects how patients and families, healthcare providers, and leaders feel emotionally after the event. These emotions have knock-on effects on healing for all involved, as well as for the organization's culture. In addition, we have stressed that an apology without empathy will not help with the grieving process, nor will compensation without disclosure or an apology. We all need to know how to structure an apology, connect this with an open and transparent disclosure, and offer the right types of support.

When health systems' leaders and their providers believe patients are harmed as the result of a complex interplay of system factors, their attitudes and language may shift from trying to find a single root cause and assigning blame. This also changes the disclosure conversation. The shift will have positive effects for the healthcare providers, patients, and families involved, resulting in fairer treatment for all, and importantly providing a critical ingredient for a Just Culture. This is the right thing to do for our patients and families. We believe it is also the right thing to do for an organization's leaders and providers.

References

1. Braid D. Pharmacy staff to answer for deaths. *Calgary Herald: Exclusive.* 2004 Mar 21;A1 (col. 1).
2. Strunin L, Davies J. Doing what is right in anesthesia. *CMAJ.* 1986 Jun;134(11): 1232.
3. Davies JM. Risk assessment and risk management in anaesthesia. *Baillieres Clin Anaesthesiol.* 1996 Jul;10(2):357–72.
4. Kraman SS, Hamm G. Risk Management: Extreme honesty may be the best policy. *Ann Intern Med.* 1999 Dec 21;131(12):963–7.
5. Health Quality Council of Alberta. Disclosure of harm to patients and families. Provincial Framework [Internet]; 2006 July [cited 2022 Feb 9]. Available from: https://hqca.ca/wp-content/uploads/2018/05/DCL_Framework.pdf
6. Trew M, Nettleton S, Flemons W. Harm to healing – Partnering with patients who have been harmed. *Can Patient Saf Inst.* 2012 Jan 1;21. [cited 2022 Feb 9]. Available from: https://www.patientsafetyinstitute.ca/en/toolsResources/Research/commissionedResearch/HarmtoHealing/Documents/Harm%20to%20Healing.pdf

7. Disclosure of Harm [Internet]. College of Physicians and Surgeons of Ontario; 2019 [cited 2022 Feb 9]. Available from: https://www.cpso.on.ca/Physicians/Policies-Guidance/Policies/Disclosure-of-Harm

8. Disclosure of Harm [Internet]. Standards of Practice. College of Physicians & Surgeons of Alberta. 2020. [cited 2022 Feb 9]. Available from https://cpsa.ca/wp-content/uploads/2020/05/Disclosure-of-Harm.pdf

9. Odell M, Gerber K, Gager M. Call 4 Concern: Patient and relative activated critical care outreach. *Br J Nurs*. 2010 Dec 9;19(22):1390–5.

10. Gill FJ, Leslie GD, Marshall AP. The impact of implementation of family-initiated escalation of care for the deteriorating patient in hospital: A systematic review. *Worldviews Evidence-Based Nurs*. 2016 Aug;13(4):303–13.

11. Brady PW, Zix J, Brilli R, Wheeler DS, Griffith K, Giaccone MJ, et al. Developing and evaluating the success of a family activated medical emergency team: A quality improvement report. *BMJ Qual Saf*. 2015 Mar;24(3):203–11.

12. Homer. *The Odyssey. Book 18*. Heinemann W, editor. New York: G.P. Putnam's Sons; 1919.

13. Lotze. *Geschichte der Aesthetik in Deutschland*. Cotta J, editor. Munich; 1869.

14. Titchener EB. *Lectures on the Experimental Psychology of the Thought-Processes*. New York: The MacMillan Company; 1909.

15. Depew D. Empathy, psychology, and aesthetics: Reflections on a repair concept. *Poroi. An Interdiscip J Rhetor Analy Invent*. 2005 Mar 1;4(1):99–107.

16. Price A. Commentary: My pandemic grief and the Japanese art of kintsugi. *BMJ*. 2021 Aug 10;374:n1906.

17. Wilkerson I. *CASTE: The Origins of Our Discontents*. New York: Random House; 2020.

18. Macrae C, Stewart K. Can we import improvements from industry to healthcare? *BMJ*. 2019 Mar 21;364:11039.

19. Vincent C, Phillips A, Young M. Why do people sue doctors? A study of patients and relatives taking legal action. *Lancet*. 1994 Jun;343(8913):1609–13.

20. Davies J. On-site risk management. *Can J Anaesth*. 1991;30(8):1029–30.

21. Mazor KM, Greene SM, Roblin D, Lemay CA, Firneno CL, Calvi J, et al. More than words: Patients' views on apology and disclosure when things go wrong in cancer care. *Patient Educ Couns*. 2013 Mar;90(3):341–6.

22. Iedema R, Allen S, Britton K, Piper D, Baker A, Grbich C, et al. Patients' and family members' views on how clinicians enact and how they should enact incident disclosure: The "100 patient stories" qualitative study. *BMJ*. 2011 Jul 25;343:d4423.

23. McMichael BJ, Van Horn RL, Viscusi WK. "Sorry" is never enough: How state apology laws fail to reduce medical malpractice liability risk. *Stanford Law*. 2019 Jan;(1):341–409.

24. Duchscherer C, Davies J. Systematic systems analysis: A practical approach to patient safety reviews. Calgary, Alberta; 2012. [cited on 2022 Feb 9]. Available from: https://d10k7k7mywg42z.cloudfront.net/assets/5328a610f002ff2140000338/HQCA_SSA_Patient_Safety_Reviews_FINAL_June_2012.pdf

25. Davies JM. Disclosure. *Acta Anaesthesiol Scand*. 2005 Jul;49(6):725–7.

26. Conway J, Federico F, Stewart K, Campbell M. *Respectful Management of Serious Clinical Adverse Events (2nd Edition)*. IHI Innov Ser White Pap [Internet]; 2011 [cited 2022 Feb 9];52. Available from: http://www.ihi.org/resources/Pages/IHIWhitePapers/RespectfulManagementSeriousClinicalAEsWhitePaper.aspx

27. Rowland H. When never happens: Implications of Medicare's Never-Event Policy. *Marquette Elder's Advis.* 2009;10(2):341–82.

28. Kizer KW. Kenneth W. Kizer, MD, MPH: Health care quality evangelist. Interview by Brian Vastag. *JAMA.* 2001 Feb 21;285(7):869–71.

29. Kachalia A. Liability claims and costs before and after implementation of a medical error disclosure program. *Ann Intern Med.* 2010 Aug 17;153(4):213–21.

30. Pillen M, Ridgely M, Greenberg M, Hayes E, Driver N, Hodgson A. Longitudinal Evaluation of the Patient Safety and Medical Liability Reform Demonstration Program: Demonstration Grants Final Evaluation Report. Rockville, Maryland; 2016. [cited 2022 Feb 9]. 83 p. AHRQ Publication No. 16–0038-2-EF. Available from: https://www.ahrq.gov/sites/default/files/wysiwyg/professionals/quality-patient-safety/patient-safety-resources/resources/candor/psml-demo-grants-final-report.pdf

31. Kachalia AB, Mello MM, Brennan TA, Studdert DM. Beyond negligence: Avoidability and medical injury compensation. *Soc Sci Med.* 2008 Jan;66(2): 387–402.

Chapter 4

"All Intensive Care Units in Calgary Were Notified to Look Out for Similar Difficulties."[1]

At the Press Conference on March 18th, the media was informed the Region had alerted other health facilities and hospital pharmacies. These institutions, in the province and across the country, needed to know the details to minimize the possibility of the same tragedy occurring elsewhere.[1] Issued on March 12th by the Region's Director of Pharmacy Services, the email began with a simple statement that he was writing to inform the recipients about a pharmacy compounding error that had occurred in the Region. The email was written with the hope that it might avoid a "similar occurrence" in other facilities. The Director went on to detail the problems.

The email had its desired effect. A newspaper report on March 28th described responses from across the country. Some of these responses detailed differences in package sizes, storage, preparation, and both double and random checking of the final solutions. Sadly, other deaths related to potassium chloride were also reported, although none under similar circumstances to those in the Region. A Senior Vice-President from the Chinook Health Region in Lethbridge noted the usefulness of the email. They had used the trigger of the email to review their

DOI: 10.4324/9781003185307-5

methods and "implement more stringent controls". The senior VP added they could "always use these opportunities to learn".[2]

The newspapers also praised the Region for doing the right thing by going public about the deaths and their circumstances. As one columnist wrote, they "made a horrible mistake" but gave credit to the FMC and Region for having "... owned it, where lesser people might have tried to get away with it".[3]

This was quite a different reaction from in the past, when the Region had steadfastly avoided the press. Two previous deaths were described in one of the newspapers. The first, in 1997, was a ten-year-old girl who'd gone to hospital with her mother because of abdominal pain. After waiting for two hours, they left before the girl was seen and assessed, because of overcrowding and slow care. She returned, underwent emergency surgery for a ruptured appendix, but died about twelve hours later, of sepsis. A Fatality Inquiry was called and the Region implemented 20 of the 22 recommendations.[4]

The second patient was a young man, also with abdominal pain. He'd gone to two busy Emergency Departments in 2001 but left both of them without being seen. When finally in the Operating Room of a third hospital, he apparently suffered an asthma attack and died.[5] Again, a Fatality Inquiry was held. The Judge concluded that the young man's death was not from the wait. But what did take the Judge's attention was that the Region frustrated the Inquiry with its "late, misleading and incomplete information".[4]

Over the span of four years, the Region had started to learn the importance of ensuring others elsewhere did not die because of the same problems. The only way the Region could do that now was to hold a Press Conference and release at least some of the information to the appropriate bodies. And in holding a Press Conference, the Region was also effectively informing the public – through the media.

In addition to deciding that other institutions and the public should be informed, Jack considered it vital everyone who worked in the Region should also be informed – and by the Region itself. It was bad enough for people to learn bad news. But if that had to be done, then it was important the news came directly from the Region, as quickly as possible, and not via the press. That had been accomplished back on March 18th, with a Region-wide email sent within minutes of the start of the first Press Conference. This *internal informing* of the Region, of deaths and their circumstances, was also new to the Region.

Additionally new to the Region was the idea of holding a second Press Conference to continue to describe and explain the events surrounding the deaths. On the morning of March 20th, another meeting of the CEO, Executives, and Communication representatives was called at Southport. JMD, who'd been away for two weeks, was asked that morning by the CMO to join the team managing the safety disaster. She agreed with continuing to inform the public, including providing explanations of what had happened, what changes had been made, and what changes were planned.

The CMO, the EMD-SW, and the Director of Pharmacy spoke with the press that Saturday afternoon, an event that was then described in the press as "rare".[6] The briefing team was also there in part to allay fears about the safety of Intermittent Hemodialysis (IHD), the most common form of treatment for chronic kidney failure. They emphasized there was no connection between what had happened with the two patients who died and the Region's hemodialysis program. In addition, the trio answered questions about the Central Pharmacy's preparation and production concept of using two pharmacists and 33 pharmacy technicians, assistants, and aides to do the bulk of the work, which was to produce "3,300 prescriptions and 1,600 doses of intravenous medication" each day. They accomplished this using a "technician checking technician" and with the Director of the Pharmacy saying, "We didn't foresee that those checks would fail." However, the Region was reported as having initiated plans to remove all sources of potassium chloride from the nursing units.[7]

What was not new to the Region was having a paper-based internal reporting system. Healthcare providers could use the forms to report problems when providing care to patients, with "each incident report represent[ing] an intentional effort by someone to share some unsatisfactory aspect of patient safety that they hope[d] to improve through action".[8] The idea behind reporting is to try to have problems in the system fixed, before anyone is harmed, whether patient or healthcare provider, but there are different ways to run a reporting system. The Region's system, which had been in place for a few years, was not confidential. Nor had its effectiveness been tested.[9] But the attitudes of Regional employees towards reporting were about to be made public – and the results were not complimentary to the Region.

In July 2003, the Region had initiated a Patient Safety Collaborative initiative, cochaired by WF, in his role as the Medical Director of Quality Improvement and Health Information. This new concept had three goals, the first of which was to create a culture of safety throughout the region. The survey was the starting point. The goal was to help those in QIHI, and the Region itself, understand what the safety culture was like in different parts of the Region and amongst different types of healthcare providers. Nearly 7,000 surveys were sent to senior executives, nursing leaders, health region staff, and doctors, asking a series of questions about things such as if healthcare providers thought problems in healthcare were identified – or not.

The results from the just under 2,000 returned surveys became available in March 2004, at about the time of the Region's initial Press Conference announcing the deaths of the two patients. The Region's Executive became concerned that survey results could be leaked to the media. By now the Region had moved into a proactive mode related to the press. WF and others on the Executive did not want the Region to go back to its old reactive ways. Again, a decision was made to go public with the results – the Region's third Press Conference in eight days.

This time, one of the Quality Improvement physicians was chosen for the Press Conference on March 25th. She was well-spoken, believable, and tough – and would not be intimidated by television reporters or newspaper columnists. She was joined by the Quality Improvement Consultant responsible for the Patient Safety collaborative, someone very familiar with the project.

The media's reception of the news was less alarmist than at the first Press Conference and more focused on the results presented by the two women. One columnist noted the Region was endeavoring to be more transparent about all aspects of the safety of patients' care and that most Regional employees and doctors supported the impetus to report problems. The comment was made, however, that the results were "not flattering" to the Region.[10]

Nearly 70% of respondents thought problems were not reported and almost 80% thought that these problems represented a "significant risk" to their patients.[11] Another question had asked where most problems occurred. The majority of survey respondents thought the "bulk" came from drugs that confusingly sounded alike, and from misreading labels. No comment was made about the irony of the second goal of the Region's Patient Safety Collaborative having been to "design, implement and disseminate a safer medication system".

That a large percentage of these medication-related problems were not reported was supported by other results. Just under half the respondents reported "embarrassment" being a barrier to reporting. Some good news was that fewer than 10% were worried about suffering "negative consequences" if they reported making a mistake.[11]

An Editorial questioned if the Region's culture was discouraging reporting. This was thought unlikely as the reporting system was voluntary and less than 10% of respondents feared "negative consequences". Interestingly, the editorialists suggested the Region impose consequences for the "act of concealment". They also agreed with the senior physician who had fronted the Press Conference at which the survey results were released. She'd encouraged patients to "be team members in their own care and demand explanations". Citing this as "sensible", the editorialists suggested patients in hospital had a "right" to receiving an "accurate diagnosis, competent treatment and suitable medication". They added, however, not all patients were able to "challenge the professionals to whom they (were) entrusted". As a final comment, the editorialists suggested that "workload, competence and system design" were all important things to be tackled. However, a "flawed" culture would outweigh the benefits of those worthwhile improvements.[12]

A Professor of Medicine in the Faculty of Medicine and former Intensive Care Unit specialist spoke positively about the survey and its results. He thought these gave the Region the ability to "work to create an environment in which workers are comfortable coming forward with admissions". He was clear, however, not to equate reporting with whistle-blowing. The most important thing was to make suggestions about things to improve the system, thus decreasing the potential for lethal problems.[11]

But the president of the largest union of provincial employees described the culture as "scapegoat". He thought it would be difficult for workers to overcome this culture when wanting to report. He did agree the primary focus should be on "patient care" and improvements, which would help, and the Chair of the Canadian Patient Safety Institute was quoted as making the important link between "trust" and "100% compliance" in reporting.[13] The Region had work to do.

In fact, the Region had assembled a group of healthcare providers from the front lines, as well as Executives. Their task was to learn what other workers thought the problems were – in every hospital and facility in the city.[11]

One way that the Region's system had been designed to maximize reporting was by making it voluntary. The Quality Improvement Consultant coordinating the Patient Safety Collaborative, who spoke at the Press Conference, commented that if the system were to be made mandatory, then reporting of problems would be lessened.[11]

This concept of reporting freely had been clearly emphasized a few days previously, when a columnist interviewed Jack Davis. He hoped that the Region's employees and doctors knew the Region's Executives wanted problems that posed a threat to patients brought to light. Ideally this would be in the Region where its new culture meant that reporting was not to be feared. Jack mentioned that the events and media coverage of the previous days had been difficult on those who provide care in the Region. He wanted to motivate healthcare providers, and not put them off reporting by frightening them. But he stressed they also wanted to see the problems identified, despite the media coverage. The columnist shared this opinion, writing that healthcare providers came into healthcare to look after patients and not to harm them and then hide their actions.[10]

The Board Chair was also strongly in favor of being open, releasing a statement to the press. He assured readers he wanted to ensure they received information about the healthcare system and predicted the Region would be on the forefront of patient safety. Recognizing that going public had been painful, he emphasized it was the "right thing". But better than words to the grieving families would be the Region's actions and learning from the events. Finally, "commitment" was essential – to "do better" and "to support each other and set patient safety as our core objective".[14]

It's Mainly About Sharing Information

To many of us, *culture* is a nebulous term that has more of a feeling to it than an operational description. One view of culture is that it represents what people believe, what they think, and how and why they act in certain ways. In organizations, the leaders and governors play an important role in establishing and promoting a culture – determining what is important, who and what will get their attention, and conversely, who and what they will ignore.

We believe the starting point for a discussion of culture in healthcare is the appreciation of the interdependence of organizational culture, safety culture, and Just Culture. How information is acquired, controlled or managed, and shared reveals much about leaders' beliefs, attitudes, and values. An indispensable source of safety information can and should come from reports originating with individuals who are directly or indirectly involved in the provision *and* the receipt of care. However, this information is only useful if an organization knows how to use it to be able to make decisions about and implement required fixes. Thus, when a healthcare organization's culture is in keeping with its values, then the organization will keep informed its most important stakeholders – the patients and the public who have entrusted their health to them, and the people who work for or with them.

Types of Organizations

Professor Ron Westrum classified organizations according to how they processed information and how information flowed through these organizations. Westrum, a sociologist at Eastern Michigan University, considered organizations as "pathological" if they viewed information as a "personal resource, to be used in political power struggles". Within those organizations, individuals would withhold, dole out or use information "as a weapon to advance particular parties within the organisation".[15]

Next were "bureaucratic" organizations, which resorted to using standard operating procedures and communication channels under any and all circumstances. This type of organization would even employ procedures and channels for normal operating procedures during emergencies, despite the possibility the channels might fail in a crisis and needed information be delayed or lost.[15]

Organizations classified as "generative" focused on the question "Who needs the information now?" and endeavored to ensure "needed information [was delivered] to the right person in the right form and in the right time frame". Generative organizations were led by individuals who emphasized that the organization's goal was to accomplish its mission and to do so required critical safety and quality information. Ideally such information would be delivered before it was needed, that is, proactively,[15] before any system breakdown and before anyone, patients and/or staff, were harmed.

Healthcare organizations which are considered generative would likely also have a strong safety culture because they understand the necessity of putting safety critical information in front of decision-makers. Safety-oriented organizations also know the importance of sharing safety information with stakeholders to keep them as safe as possible and to maintain their trust by being transparent. We refer to this as *informing* – sharing information both internally and externally outside the close circle of insiders, who are traditionally thought of as those who 'need to know'. When organizations freely and openly share safety information with stakeholders they set an expectation for the converse to happen. This converse, when stakeholders share safety information with an organization, is referred to as *reporting*, and its importance to a safety culture will be addressed later in the chapter.

Informing

When organizations openly share safety information with stakeholders, they communicate important unspoken messages about their values. Bold actions that match strong values are an important demonstration of culture. Organizations that regularly inform are those that prioritize safety above all else. Such organizations also understand that transparency, as shown by informing, fosters trust, a critical ingredient of safety.

Minimizing Harm

Truly, the most important reason to inform is to minimize harm. There is a tragic example in aviation illustrating why reporting and informing is so important. This example is not recounted as an exhortation to learn from other industries[16] but to illustrate in part how tragedy can also drive enormous safety improvements. In 1974, two different aircrews misinterpreted the same aeronautical chart, which resulted in their descent towards a mountain. The first crew was fortunate, having good weather conditions and able to see the mountain, allowing them to correct their course. The second crew was not. Flying in worse weather conditions and in the clouds, they were not able to see the mountain and crashed. The resulting inquiry brought to light the previous close call and became the final impetus to establish NASA's Aviation Safety Reporting System (ASRS), as described further on in this chapter. Once safety critical information is captured in an information system, it then needs to be shared so that other people might be saved.

This aviation example has many healthcare equivalents. In Calgary in 2004, we as healthcare providers and leaders alike were all shocked and horrified to learn that Kathleen Prowse was not the first patent to die after receiving the CRRT containing potassium. Admittedly, at the time of her death we did not know of the first, but it soon became obvious that more patients could die, both in Calgary and elsewhere in the country. This helped to provoke the feverish pace at which many individuals worked to ensure that those deaths did not occur. The other Regional hospitals' pharmacies and other ICUs were informed right away. Staff in the pharmacies and ICUs were not only notified but also instructed to look for the additional dialysate bags that had been manufactured in the same batch. Any such bags found were then returned to the Central Pharmacy and locked in the narcotics vault, until the investigation was over, when the bags were destroyed.

Maintaining Stakeholder's Trust

Sharing safety information helps to ensure that physicians and staff within the organization learn officially about serious events, in particular when there has been or could be media attention, as was done in Calgary at the same time that the first press conference was starting. When internal stakeholders receive this important information from the organization itself, rather than from outside sources, it fosters or maintains trust. Openly providing everyone in the organization with the same available facts about an event is a start to countering any mis-information from various sources, including social media, on which staff might otherwise rely. Salient messages about both the event and those that support Just Culture can also be distributed to staff and physicians in strategically planned and timed internal communications, with updates provided as more information becomes available.

Sharing safety information and the resulting organizational learning is one of the components of a safety culture. Thus, important safety information is disseminated and the organization becomes more generative.[15] Stories and themes from the reporting system should be de-identified, appropriately packaged, perhaps with additional advisory or educational materials, and sent out widely throughout the organization.

For example, one story from 2004 the Region did not but could have shared internally was the immediate response in the Central Pharmacy on the day Kathleen Prowse died. The problem with the CRRT was reported to the Manager of the Central Pharmacy, who took control of the situation, identifying many contributing factors. He informed other Regional pharmacy sites and directed managers there to return potentially problematic dialysate bags to the Central Pharmacy, thus partly mitigating the immediate threat from the hazard.

Closing the loop on the combined reporting and informing occurred when all bags of the dialysate containing potassium were accounted for.

Apart from informing internal stakeholders, various external stakeholders should be notified. These include the media – and through them – the public who are and represent current and future patients. Informing also includes communicating with other healthcare organizations and appropriate associations/regulatory agencies beyond those that have mandatory reporting requirements.

Thinking Outside the Circle

However, many healthcare organizations are hesitant to share safety information with the media and with the public. This reluctance is understandable, given that the media (and the justice system) have yet to adopt the perspective of "systems thinking".[17] Despite this reluctance, many organizations have found sharing information shows transparency and builds trust. It also creates an opportunity for us as leaders to demonstrate to our staff that it is acceptable to talk, even publicly, about untoward events.

Informing can include sharing information regularly about the quality and safety of the healthcare we provide, as well as providing information when patients have been seriously harmed. Organizations wanting to do this may encounter challenges and barriers in doing so, including opposition from their lawyers and resistance from people within the organization. Some of these individuals will be driven by the perception of an increasing possibility of litigation or by the potential for negative media attention. Proactively sharing information with the media following an event in which a patient is harmed, however, can help an organization 'get in front' of the event and to share information in a planned and strategic way. This is considered highly preferable to 'chasing the story' later, once the media has learned about the event from other sources, including the patient and family. Thus, informing can be an important strategy for managing an organization's reputation.

Organizations that regularly share safety information may be able to normalize the conversation, resulting in decreasing negative media attention over time. A good example of this is from the State of Victoria in Australia, where a very forward-thinking expert in quality and safety would routinely discuss publicly released healthcare reports with newspaper editors and other individuals from the media. This helped to normalize the conversation with the media and thus in the eyes of the public, increasing the perception of organizational transparency.

The Region made a purposeful decision to share information with the media and the public, after the families had received their initial disclosure. At the time, going public was quite uncommon and considered risky but Jack made the decision to do so because of the desire to take accountability and to show transparency. He and his executive also wanted to reassure the public that the Region was not hiding anything.

Sharing information with healthcare agencies and other healthcare organizations is important for two reasons. First, we must ensure other healthcare systems know about critical safety issues to minimize the probability of a similar event happening elsewhere. Second, we want to help support change more broadly. When one organization steps forward and does this, it helps to demonstrate and foster transparency and a safety-oriented culture. Ideally, such actions provide the impetus for other organizations to follow suit in the future.

In the Region's example, information about the CRRT and the associated deaths was shared with other external stakeholders. The Health Ministry (then called Alberta Health & Wellness) was informed immediately after the event was identified and before the Region released any information to the media. As well, the two relevant professional colleges were also informed – the (then-named) Alberta College of Pharmacists and the College of Physicians and Surgeons of Alberta. The Region's Director of Pharmacy informed the pharmacies in all major hospitals across Canada that had a similar practice of compounding their own dialysate solutions, in case they could have a similar event. Information was also shared with regulatory agencies, including Health Canada, partly in an attempt to drive regulatory level changes in how pharmaceutical manufacturers labeled their products. Other external safety organizations, such as the Health Quality Council of Alberta and the Institute for Safe Medication Practices Canada, were also informed. Organizations such as these can play a role in further distributing safety information.

When the Region took the bold steps it did to inform others about the potassium chloride-related deaths, it signaled a change in its values and in its understanding of a safety culture. Before that, the Region would clearly not have been mistaken for a generative organization. Indeed, it had all the hallmarks of a system vulnerable to failure.

Vulnerable Organizations

Before the potassium-related tragedy, the Region had been through previous experiences with patients whose poor outcomes had become the subject of judicial Fatality Inquiries. In addition, the Region, like other acute care healthcare organizations, had had experiences with patients whose IVs had mistakenly been flushed with potassium chloride rather than with sodium chloride. Fortunately, in those events the patients had not died. But none of these negative experiences had forced the Region to stop and seriously question the way it conducted the business of healthcare. Poor outcomes for our patients, even when unexpected, are often a combination of factors where less than optimal care blends with underlying disease. This is one reason why healthcare organizations and their providers might fail to grasp the full extent of what is considered avoidable harm to patients. Organizations can easily operate under the delusion that they are safe and that their patients are generally safe. This misguided belief and attitude were well described as an organizational syndrome two decades ago.

In 2001, Reason and his colleagues, Dr. Jane Carthey, a human factors specialist and Lecturer, and Professor Marc de Leval, a senior pediatric cardiac surgeon, both at the Great Ormond Street Hospital for Children and the Royal London Hospital, coined the term "vulnerable system syndrome" (VSS). This organizational syndrome described a set of core organizational pathologies that reflected its culture and vulnerability to adverse events,[18] in the same way one would describe a patient's syndrome and underlying factors for a disease or illness.

The trio's conclusions were drawn from the investigations of disasters in several complex, high-reliability industries. The three interacting and self-perpetuating pathologies they described were assigning blame to those providing care, refusing to believe there were problems in the system that provoked weaknesses, and the tunnel-visioned acceptance and following of indicators focused solely on production and costs. Reason and colleagues argued that all organizations, to some degree, suffer from the VSS. Analogous to a patient who, when told of a problem must accept some type of change in therapy or lifestyle, an organization must first recognize the existence of the problem, accept it, and then commit to learning how to operate differently.

Learning how to 'do differently' is referred to as "second-loop learning", a concept developed in the early 1970s by Professor Chris Argyris, an Organizational Behavioral psychologist at Harvard Business School and philosopher Donald Schön, Ford Professor of Urban Studies and Education at MIT. They considered that learning requires us to detect and correct our errors. When we do something that does not work, we look for another way to do things – another strategy involving an action. Usually before we carry out this second action, we do not question ourselves as to our intrinsic values, our goals, the plans we made, or the rules by which we work. Argyris and Schön described this as "single-loop learning" and proposed another way of 'doing', which was to stop before acting again and to self-question all the factors that guide us, including any assumptions we hold. This is "double-loop learning" and requires the organization to change its foundational beliefs, its rules, regulations, and goals[19,20] – and therefore its culture. These changes will then facilitate the organization to 'do better'. These experiences thus provide the organization with knowledge of the various changes and actions, of how and what to do and what not to do. This organizational learning can occur at all levels of the organization and is related to Reason's fourth requirement for a safety culture, that of a "learning culture".

Thus, although there could be old cultural reasons for certain actions, organizations can learn new ways of behaving. As Argyris and Schon comment, some of this requires an organization to actively undertake learning, for example, to incorporate lessons from tragedies into new policies and procedures. But organizations can also unlearn[21] old habits. This requires as much, if not more, active participation from everyone, for example, learning not to blame, by unlearning – and then learning to take a "less 'blamist' approach". In safety-oriented organizations, this new approach could lead to "more information about malfunctions"[22] and is also one of the lessons required if we wish to escape from the Blame Cycle.

Safety Culture

In contrast to organizations deeply affected by the VSS, both Westrum and Reason considered that generative organizations are helped to achieve their goals by the free flow of information flow. One of these goals is reaching maximum organizational safety health, through being informed and therefore having a safety culture. This concept of a safety culture (and not 'culture of safety') emerged in 1980 but was not defined until 1988. Although contained in a report from the nuclear power industry, that definition is worth quoting here as it clearly declares the over-arching importance of safety. That report said safety culture is "… that assembly of characteristics and attitudes in organizations and individuals which establishes that, as an overriding priority, nuclear plant safety issues receive the attention warranted by their significance".[23]

A slightly later definition was produced in 1993, the result of a joint meeting between the Advisory Committee on the Safety of Nuclear Installations (ACSNI) Study Group on Human Factors and the UK's former Health and Safety Commission. The safety culture of an organization was considered the "product of individual and group values, attitudes, competencies, and patterns of behavior that determine the commitment to, and the style and proficiency of, an organization's health and safety programmes. Organizations with a positive safety culture are characterized by communications founded on mutual trust, by shared perceptions of the importance of safety, and by confidence in the efficacy of preventive measures".[24]

While this definition appears more healthcare-applicable, it is also more focused on the individual working in the organization, rather than on the collective of the organization. Both the health and safety of all working in an organization are important, but good health can be rudely interrupted by an organization that is not safe.

The 1991 report from the Nuclear Safety Advisory Group also added that Safety Culture reflected the ever-important structural issues, one of a Safety Culture's two components. Structural issues represented the framework based on the organization's policies and planned managerial responses. The other component was from what individuals did in response to working according to the framework. Individuals were required to carry out correctly "all duties important to safety" and to do so with "alertness, due thought and full knowledge, sound judgement and a proper sense of accountability". This is the embodiment of the often-used definition of culture as "the way we do things around here"[25] and what Dr. Nick Pidgeon, of Birkbeck College, University of London, described as "everybody in an organization ... regard[ing] the policing of hazards as a personal as well as a collective goal".[26]

Practically speaking, if an organization is striving to be informed, that is to collect safety information and use it to improve, a "safety information system" is required to collect and analyze the data, something that many healthcare organizations are still trying to implement. Traditionally, healthcare organizations have relied on data that are reactive in nature – telling about hazards and harm after the fact, which represent "lagging indicators".[27,28] (These often provide information about single, isolated untoward events.) Sometimes "coincident indicators"[27] are used to shed light about the organization's current safety state, such as emergency department waiting times. Until recently, rarely has healthcare embarked on using "leading indicators",[27] from consolidation of information from reactive sources, as well as systematic proactive analyses, looking for hazards and hazardous situations. Leading indicators can and should be used predictively, to look for the source of the next accident. Obviously, much greater analysis and therefore greater associated resources are required to be predictive than reactive. However, aviation has validated the business case for such expenditure.[29] Dissemination of the derived information is then critical. These requirements are at the heart of an "informed culture", which Reason equated to a "safety culture". Information is thus the *currency of any organization*.

For organizations with a well-developed safety culture, individuals are expected to work in a way that supports and improves the organization's safety. This requires workers to report safety issues from which the organization can generate its safety information, which then requires developing a "reporting culture". In turn, this requires an organization to have a climate or culture in which all members of the organization were prepared to report problems and close calls as they carried out tasks. (Reason did not mention reporting accidents.[30])

Reporting

Reporting is defined as healthcare provider(s) telling the organization about a safety concern for patients or an event in which a patient was nearly or actually harmed. Reporting can also include when healthcare organizations report to an outside organization, often for mandatory reasons. (More on this later in this chapter.)

Safety reporting is considered a fundamental aspect of safety management. Many healthcare organizations have invested, some quite heavily, in systems to facilitate safety reporting within their organization. In the early 2000s, there was a particular focus on reporting systems, with many organizations abandoning paper-based systems, and replacing them with electronic ones, which were anticipated to help organizations better manage their safety information.

Electronic Reporting Systems in Healthcare

In 2000, the United States' Institute of Medicine (IOM) identified reporting systems as an important part of organizations' safety programs.[31] As a result, many American states enacted legislation requiring reporting systems be instituted. A few years later, the Patient Safety and Quality Improvement Act of 2005[32] was passed by the US Senate, in an amendment to The Public Safety Act. This established a framework for reporters using voluntary safety reporting systems and also provided federal privilege and confidentiality protection for patient safety information.[33]

In 2003, the UK National Health Service (NHS) launched its National Reporting and Learning System (NRLS). The UK established its National Patient Safety Agency (NPSA) in the same year. The role of the NPSA was to manage the reports submitted to the NRLS and to support distribution of safety information gleaned from these reports. By 2009, the NPSA had received more than a million safety reports into its NRLS,[34] but in 2012, after a reorganization of quality and safety agencies by government, the functions of the NPSA were transferred to the NHS Commissioning Board Special Health Authority.

In May 1987, an Australian group of anesthesiologists established the Australian Patient Safety Foundation (APSF), with one of its ten patient safety-oriented aims focused on coordinating reports and studies of critical incidents.[35] Anesthesiologists in Townsville, Queensland adopted the Critical Incident Review technique, first developed in aviation[36] and then pioneered in anesthesiology (and healthcare) in Boston by Dr. Jeff Cooper, a biomedical engineer in the Department of Anesthesia at the Massachusetts General Hospital.[37] Soon, other Australian centers were publishing results.[38,39] The APSF's anonymous and voluntary reporting system was the Australian Incident Monitoring Study (AIMS), spearheaded by Dr. Bill Runciman, Professor and Head of the Department of Anaesthesia and Critical Care at the University of Adelaide and the Royal Adelaide Hospital. With an initial participant reporting base of 90 hospitals and (private) anesthetic practices in three Australian states, by 1993 AIMS membership had expanded to every state and New Zealand. In the late 1980s and early 1990s, this type of nation-wide reporting and case discussion was unique, not only in anesthetic practice but in healthcare. The APSF grew,[40] with reporting run through the Patient Safety Institute.[41] Unfortunately, problems beset these organizations and neither they nor AIMS are now operational, with Australian states having established or acquired their own electronic safety reporting systems.

During this same period in Canada, there was no national patient safety reporting system, nor were there any province-wide reporting systems. In 2008, British Columbia was the first provincial healthcare system and Calgary was the first regional system in Canada to embark on establishing state-of-the-art electronic reporting systems designed to support safety culture. In Calgary, the paper-based incident reporting system was replaced by an electronic safety and learning reporting system. This change stemmed from recommendations made during the reviews of the two potassium-related deaths. Also necessary for the research into and development of the reporting system was a significant financial investment. As well as being electronic and more efficient, the new system was very different from the former incident reporting system. The new reporting and learning system was confidential, mainly narrative-based, to make reporting simpler, more focused on hazards that represented a threat to patients and providers, and designed to support learning.[42] When the regional health authorities in Alberta were abolished and replaced with a single, provincial health system in 2009, Calgary's electronic reporting system was adopted and implemented provincially. Some changes to the design were made, including allowing reporters to determine if their manager could receive their reports with their names on it, a step recognized as not being ideal but necessary at the time to support change management.[43]

As of 2021, in countries such as Australia, Canada, and the United States, there are many safety reporting systems at local levels (hospital-based or primary care-based), within health authorities and integrated health systems, at provincial/state levels, as well as national systems. Although these represent a significant step forward from the previous paper-based incident systems of the past, challenges still exist with the broad sharing of safety information to support learning and improvement.

Purpose of Reporting Systems

Reporting systems vary in their purpose and functional design. When we think about establishing one, we need to be clear about both requirements, especially the primary purpose of the reporting system, as this will affect some important decisions for its functional design and related processes. The primary purpose of reporting systems is to facilitate the sharing of important safety information. As healthcare providers, we need to be able to tell *our story* of what happened to a patient. Through sharing this safety information, organizational leaders and healthcare providers within their organization become aware of hazards that lie in wait for their patients. These hazards are those things that have contributed to or have the potential to contribute to patients being harmed. Effective safety reporting systems also support the analysis, dissemination of, and learning about safety information.

Reporting is actually more than just 'reporting'. Having workers report their problems is also a fundamental part of their safety habits and actions, thus reinforcing the organization's safety culture, as described at the beginning of this chapter. Therefore, the way safety reporting systems are designed and used is critical to enhancing safety and also to driving safety culture.

Design of Reporting Systems

Reporting systems can be functionally designed to be *accountability* or *learning* systems. Those designed for accountability are set up for exactly that – to hold healthcare organizations accountable to a higher, usually regulatory, body. These systems most often have criteria as to what should be reported and may even have specific timeframes for reporting requirements. This type of requirement could be coupled with sanctions for 'unsafe' practices, which in turn could drive some organizations to be reluctant to report events that could be concealed.[44] Although their primary purpose is for accountability, such systems can also support learning if information is analyzed and shared broadly. For example, the Joint Commission 'strongly encourages' organizations to self-report sentinel events, which includes events leading to severe temporary harm, permanent harm, or death. Summaries of sentinel event data are available. Additionally, information from reported events are aggregated, de-identified, and shared for the purposes of safety learning in the form of *Sentinel Event Alert Newsletters*.[45]

Learning systems are designed with the primary purpose of fostering safety learning and improvement, the third characteristic of Reason's Just Culture. Learning systems generally aim to receive a broader range of patient safety information when compared to accountability systems. Rather than events in which a patient was harmed, learning systems often facilitate reporting of hazards or hazardous situations, which could lead to a patient being harmed in the future and close calls, in which a patient was nearly harmed. To truly support learning, analysis and sharing of information is required. (See below.)

While accountability systems can also support learning, it is difficult for a system with a primary purpose for learning to also be an accountability system. This is because if organizations or individuals are held to account for something they report, future reporting is likely to be stifled and thus so will learning.

There is an aviation example that illustrates this point, from a country with legislation that required reporting. But, if a pilot did something 'wrong', then the protection that came with safety reporting could be removed and repercussions could result. This did occur, which resulted in significant under-reporting to the point of no reporting. Fortunately, this legislation was changed several years ago and reporting has resumed. (Reporting systems in aviation will be discussed further, later in this chapter.)

The second design feature is mandatory versus voluntary reporting. Accountability systems are often mandatory. Occasionally, an organization will set up its own internal mandatory system. Most often, organizations will be mandated to report to government or to another regulatory body. For example, in Canada there is now a mandatory requirement for hospitals to report serious adverse drug reactions and medical device incidents to Health Canada, based on legislation that came into effect in December 2019.[46] Known as Vanessa's Law, the *Protecting Canadians from Unsafe Drugs Act* is named after Vanessa Young. Vanessa was a fifteen-year old girl who died of a heart rhythm abnormality in 2000 after taking a commonly prescribed medication for acid reflux, which was later removed from the market. Her father, Terence Young, campaigned for better regulation and safety of prescription drugs,[47] and Vanessa's Law was finally enacted by Canadian parliament in 2014. The mandatory reporting requirements came into effect on December 16th, 2019.[48]

In contrast, learning systems are usually voluntary. These allow an organization's people to choose what and when they report. Reporting is encouraged, not required. There are no penalties for not reporting and no ramifications result from reporting.

The third functional design consideration for reporting systems is for them to be external or internal. The latter exist within an organization, often behind the organization's fire walls, and only accepting reports from individuals working within that organization. The size of the reporting system will depend on the size of the organization – whether a single hospital or clinic or healthcare system with multiple facilities. An organization should be able to facilitate further investigations, for example, if a series of similar problems are reported from different facilities. The organization then also has the ability and the authority to institute changes for rectifying and improving parts of the system.

In contrast, reporting systems that are external are administered by an organization external to the individuals and/or organizations subscribing to the system. A common example is that of nationally based systems. Some reporting systems are hybrids, where an internal reporting system submits reports, usually de-identified and for the purposes of learning, to a larger, external reporting system.

Effective Safety and Learning Reporting Systems

In its *Draft Guidelines for Adverse Event Reporting and Learning Systems*, the World Health Organization (WHO) described seven characteristics of successful reporting systems. The WHO did acknowledge the long experience of other domains, such as aviation, in identifying these seven characteristics, which we have grouped into three. First and foremost, reporting systems should be *non-punitive*, with reporters free from retaliation and punishment, either personally or to others because of reporting. The best way to ensure a system is non-punitive is for it to be *confidential*. Thus, reporters may be required to submit their names, the patient's name, and/or contact information (including the organization) to the *independent* group running the system. The group holds that information in confidence, that is they do not share it and use it only if the reporting analysts need to follow-up. They might need additional information, sometimes to clarify what was reported, which then will facilitate the organization being able to learn from the report. At that time, the identities of the patient, reporter, and others are not shared and, in external systems, even the name of the organization is also not made public. Additionally, the group managing the reporting system is independent of any authority to punish the reporter (or those included in the report), and also independent of any organizations with such authority. Of note, a confidential system is different from an anonymous system, which allows individuals to submit a report without including their names or other details, such as position and contact information. When reports are anonymous, analysts cannot contact those reporting for clarification, as can be done in a confidential system. Additionally, some 'person-focused' managers may disregard and dismiss anonymous safety reports, on the grounds that those reporting are troublemakers.[49] In contrast, a confidential system provides reassurance that no disciplinary action can result, while still facilitating follow-up and gathering of additional information from analysts.

Second, reports must undergo *expert analysis* by individuals who understand the clinical aspects and who can also analyze and code reports based on system-related factors. The combination of independence and expert analysis is important for credibility. Reports must be analyzed in a timely and expeditious manner. The overall reporting system, analysis, and resulting recommendations must be oriented toward and focused on the system, not on individuals or their performance, but on reducing and not perpetuating similar actions. Recommendations and learnings must also be disseminated in a timely manner.

Third, reporting must be seen to be *responsive*, in that safety improvements are undertaken. The overall reporting system must therefore be capable of analyzing reports and recommending changes, and the organizations must then implement system improvements.[44] The best improvements are those that are studied and tested before implementation, so as to 'build better', rather than to shore up intrinsically problematic design. Information from analysis of the reports should also be disseminated broadly.

To facilitate reporting, reporters must consider it easy. This can be accomplished by keeping the required information to a minimum. Having more open-ended questions than prescribed tick-boxes or multiple drop-downs allows reporters to tell their story fully, including their perceptions, judgments, decisions, and actions. This type of reporting facilitates gathering more information about an incident but does take more analytical resources.[49] Narrative-based reporting systems require analysts to effectively conduct text word searches to process data and yield useful information, which previously meant hours carrying out hand-searches in health records. Natural Language Processing (NLP) has made it much easier to learn from narrative-based reports, categorizing unstructured free text and linking information in health records with that in reports.[50]

We must add one caveat to our comments on reporting, particularly when reporting a problem involving a patient, and more importantly, when reporting into an anonymous system. Reporting, even into a confidential system, does not replace the need for reporters to ensure the event has been included in the patient's health record and that other healthcare providers are aware of what happened to the patient. We are familiar with cases in which that was not done. The absence of information in the health records had negative consequences for the patients, who went on to suffer second and third episodes of harm before problems were recognized and rectified. Charting the events and discussing them with colleagues are both necessary so that certain aspects of immediate care of the patient and safety management of the event, as well as disclosure and follow-up, can be undertaken.

Finally, a robust safety reporting system should be based on a model of the system. This model can be used to *map* where reports come from, and should drive the way reports are categorized for analytical purposes.[9,51] A reporting system that uses a model of the system will better support analysis and pulling out of safety information to support organizational learning.

Reporting Systems in Aviation

Not surprisingly, most of aviation's long-standing reporting systems espouse the characteristics described above, such as being non-punitive (not looking for blame or fault), confidential, and run by an independent group. They are system-oriented and well-resourced for expert analysis and distribution of safety information.

In the United States in 1975, NASA developed and established the Aviation Safety Reporting System (ASRS), for voluntary and confidential reporting "from any person who has observed or been involved in an occurrence which he or she believes poses a threat to flight safety".[52] Reports were not restricted to aircrews or affiliated personnel but were accepted from anyone involved in aviation, including the public, theoretically, even those on the ground. The ASRS dealt with the problem of reporters breaking certain rules by establishing a Waiver of Disciplinary Action with specific requirements. These included the rule-breaking having to be inadvertent, not deliberate, and not involving a criminal offence. Pilots, for example, were also required to file a report of what they did within ten days of the event. Fulfilling these requirements would then *protect* the pilots against suspension of their flying certificate. Further protection was also embedded in the system by having it run by NASA at the NASA Ames Research Center in California and not by the regulator of aviation, the Federal Aviation Authority in Washington DC. The ASRS became very successful and is now the Aviation Safety Program (ASRP). Summary reports of de-identified events deemed educational or otherwise noteworthy are sent out freely to anyone wishing to subscribe to the newsletter (Callback). The database is similarly accessible by those who would like to research a particular topic.

In the early 1990s, British Airways (BA) developed its own reporting system, known as BASIS or the British Airways Safety Information System. BA required mandatory reporting of "safety related events" by all personnel.[53] Mike O'Leary, then a Captain at BA, was involved in the design, development, and implementation of BASIS, which had a series of reporting modules for flight crew, including *"Air Safety Reports"* (ASR). Asking for more information than mandated by the UK Civil Aviation Authority in its incident and accident reports, BA's BASIS was more than a 'count the numbers' database. BASIS was purposefully designed to help those involved in safety answer three important questions: "How safe are we?", "Can we prove it?", and "Where should we put our resources to become even safer?"[54] O'Leary described how reports were handled with respect to breaking rules, which was accomplished through having a documented agreement between British Airways and the British Airline Pilots Association (BALPA). In addition, BA published a statement to the effect that individuals would only be disciplined if they were found to have done something that no reasonably prudent employee would have done with a comparable degree of training and experience.[53]

Some countries also have voluntary systems, complementing legislated and therefore mandatory systems for reporting accidents and incidents. Certain of these country-based systems are part of a larger body, the International Confidential Aviation Safety Systems (ICASS) Group, membership of which is by invitation. ICASS "promotes confidential reporting systems as an effective method of enhancing flight safety in commercial air transport and general aviation operations". The objectives of the ICASS Group are to assist with setting up and operating a confidential reporting system, facilitating exchange of safety information between similar systems, and helping determine solutions to "common problems in the operation of such systems".[55] Unfortunately, there is no equivalent in healthcare.

One interesting healthcare example of a healthcare reporting system modelled on aviation (the ASRS, as above) is the Patient Safety Reporting System (PSRS), which is non-punitive, confidential, voluntary, and independently managed by NASA. The PSRS is considered complementary to healthcare providers' organizational or other reporting systems, particularly as it offers an opportunity for the reporting of safety concerns and close calls,[56] which many healthcare-based reporting systems still do not offer.

Underuse of Healthcare Reporting Systems

Given all of these benefits, why are reporting systems underused? There are many reasons for this. First, harm, hazardous situations, or hazards may not be identified as such, and thus not seen as something that should be reported. If recognized as a safety issue, individuals may be unsure of how to access the system or how to use it. Time constraints or forgetting to submit a report during a busy shift have also been identified as barriers. As well, electronic systems may have technical issues,[34] which can become a frustration to reporters, as well as hamper efforts to effectively analyze reports and share information broadly. Other factors negatively affecting reporting include a fear of blame, a lack of feedback, and a perceived lack of value.[34]

If organizations were to ensure their reporting systems embodied the characteristics of successful systems as described by the WHO, then this would help to address many of these barriers. Also, organizations could make efforts to enhance safety culture, especially the specific components of just and learning, and build trust to enhance reporting.

The concept of trust as it applies to reporting cannot be minimized for having a successful reporting system. In 1996, when Mike O'Leary was a Captain at British Airways and Dr. Sheryl Chappell, a psychologist and Human Factors specialist, was Chief Scientist for the ASRS, they noted the enormous importance of trust in confidential reporting. Reporters' candid introspection in the confidential reports they made of close calls and other incidents was considered vital. The reports were described as allowing corrections to be made in the aviation system, minimizing subsequent recurrences of events, and decreasing accidents. With incomplete trust, reports would be incomplete and with no trust, similarly there would be no reports. Trust was paramount.[49] O'Leary and Chappell went on further to say that trust must be actively protected, even after years of successfully operating a safety reporting system.[49] Thus, should any discipline appear to or actually result from reporting, then this will have a drastically negative effect on future reporting and also on the organization's safety culture.

One mechanism to engender trust is to have the reporting system operated independently from those in authority or regulatory agencies. Also known as "neutral program operation",[49] many aviation reporting systems are set up like this. In healthcare, independence of the reporting system can be achieved by having a system that is managed by a department, such as a patient safety office, independent from those with 'hiring and firing' authority.

When Reporting Systems Work Well

Progressive healthcare systems promote receiving reports from everyone in the organization, be the leaders or workers. This can be a reflection of safety culture. Healthcare organizations, however, consistently see differences in reporting behaviors amongst their provider groups. Physicians, in particular, have been recognized as being low contributors to safety reporting systems, with many systems receiving the majority of reports from nursing staff followed by allied health providers, including pharmacists. A study in Australia of anesthesiologists' perceptions of safety reporting identified concerns with the amount of time required to report, being blamed by colleagues and potential for disciplinary action. Interestingly, the majority of those participating in the survey were not in agreement with a number of anticipated factors, including the need to be perfect, putting their own interests before those of their patients, or being inhibited by peer competition.[57]

Differences between nurses' and physicians professional cultures were identified in another study, although the data were collected about two decades ago. These professional identities were felt to explain difference in reporting between these two groups. Nurses were found to more habitually report than physicians. This was attributed to the nurses' professional culture being more accepting of directives and protocol-driven work, compared to the physicians' culture of less transparency and less reliance on directives.[58]

More innovative reporting systems are configured to facilitate input of important safety concerns and information from patients and families directly into the same reporting system that staff, physicians, and volunteers use. Interestingly, the healthcare version of the aviation ASRS, the PSRS (described above) is at present not designed to accept reports from patients. In contrast, the American aviation ASRS has been able to accept reports from members of the public from the time of its inception in 1975. We are proponents of reporting systems that accept reports from anyone who has concerns about the safety of the healthcare system, including patients and their families. They should not be relegated to using a 'patient concerns intake system', which is not focused on safety and is used for patients to *complain* about various aspects of their care.

In addition to learning about fatal or other adverse outcomes, effective safety reporting systems should also strive to capture events in which patients suffered what could be considered 'minor harm'. Just as importantly, innovative systems promote the reporting of events in which patients were not harmed. These are close calls (and not the confusingly named 'near misses') and hazards that lurk in the infrastructure of the system. Another clarification is that events labeled as 'no harm' need to be carefully appreciated as the term actually means there was 'no evidence' that the patient suffered harm – at the time of reporting.

Information about the details of a close call or discovery of a hazard represents a "free lesson",[30] that is, an opportunity for an organization to understand where future patients could be harmed and to mitigate this proactively. Free lessons are termed 'free' partly because the event is free of the angst, sadness, and waste associated with events in which patients (and sometimes personnel) are harmed. In the Region, the new reporting system did just that – focusing on reporting of hazards, close calls, and events in which patients were not harmed, and not just on the events in which patients suffered harm.[42]

Effective Use of Reporting Systems

While the merits of safety reporting systems are quite clear, they need to be used appropriately to support patients' safety. Reports must be analyzed, safety information must be shared broadly in a confidential manner and improvements to the system must result from the reports. Unfortunately, many healthcare organizations have not realized the benefits from their reporting systems as much as they had hoped and planned. Many struggle to use information from the reporting system in a meaningful way, including prioritization of safety improvement efforts and evaluation of safety improvements.[59]

One of the challenges is how to best use the information (or data) from safety reporting systems. Information from these systems should be used to identify safety hazards or system deficiencies. Although it may be tempting to do so, organizations should not use the numbers of specific events or types of reports to measure the prevalence of safety events. These numbers are not a metric of how safe an organization is. This is because what is collected by a reporting system is a reflection only of what has been *reported*, not what actually *occurred*. Many incidents go unreported. To try to link numbers of events or numbers of patients harmed as found in the reporting system to the safety – or danger – of an organization would be similar to trying to measure how many people exceeded the speed limit on a highway from the number of speeding tickets issued. Because of this, metrics from a safety reporting system cannot be used to measure rates of events in which patients were harmed, to compare organizations, or to measure changes over time.[60] Comparisons within an organization, for example, hospital to hospital or unit to a similar unit, should also not be made for this same reason.

However, the total number of reports received, shown as trends over time, may be valuable as a surrogate metric of safety culture. Indeed, some organizations have been able to positively correlate higher safety culture survey results with higher reporting rates.[34] As well stated by Pham and colleagues, for safety reporting systems we should "make the measure of success system changes, rather than events reported".[60] Furthermore, instead of focusing on quantitative metrics, reporting systems should carry out more qualitative analysis, mining reporters' stories to identify safety issues. To correctly measure and monitor patient safety means not relying solely on a voluntary reporting system. Instead, measurements require the use of multiple sources of information, such as surveillance of electronic health systems, and adverse event triggers and chart reviews, as well as collecting safety information from patients, families, and healthcare providers. Together, these different measurements are part of a robust safety management system.

The Original Just Culture

Although it has long been accepted that reporting is required for the organization to learn about safety problems and to make improvements (learning culture), it is also true that those who report must feel safe to do so. Thus, Reason arrived at the requirement for a Just Culture. He defined this as "an atmosphere of trust in which people are encouraged, even rewarded, for providing essential safety-related information – but in which they are also clear about where the line must be drawn between acceptable and unacceptable behaviour".[30] For example, an organization in which nurses are fired for making three errors (and not breaking any rules) when dispensing medications would not garner trust. (This edict is commonly known as 'three strikes, you're out'.)

The reality is that the errors workers make represent a valuable source of safety information but are the least likely to be reported for a myriad of reasons. Reason did examine difficulties in having workers 'confess' their errors and those of their colleagues. Early approaches to this challenge were to adopt a no-blame approach to reporting. However, Reason emphasized the problems of either punishing all errors or having a no-blame approach to all actions contributing to an accident, including those actions of individuals who endeavored to cause harm. Aviation's "no-fault" system for reporting close calls was perhaps an early forerunner of the no-blame approach.[61,62] The main problem with a reporting system without blame relates to a very small proportion of reports in which workers might state that they had intentionally broken rules, often because they thought their way of doing things was better, faster, or cheaper. Alternatively, the individuals might have been acting on personal impulses and not, at least in healthcare, putting their patients first. Reason therefore considered that providing a *blanket amnesty* on certain actions, including purposefully hurting people or damaging equipment, was inappropriate.[30] This meant that organizations had to draw a line between acceptable and unacceptable actions. Individuals who crossed the line with their actions or behaviors were to be dealt with appropriately. This was also part of the original description of Just Culture by Reason, and if these concepts were well defined and proactively communicated to workers, they would contribute to the atmosphere of trust and not dissuade others from reporting. In fact, Just Culture was predicted to have a positive effect on morale, particularly when other workers saw that the system was no longer turning a blind eye to those who crossed the line.

In his original description of Just Culture, Reason did not enter into discussion about the specifics of drawing the line. In 2007 and 2009, Sydney Dekker, then Professor in the Lund University School of Aviation, Ljungbyhed, Sweden, considered who should draw the line when considering the difference between "acceptable performance and negligence" in medical care[63] and when considering culpability.[64] While we do not think negligence should be included in patient safety and we choose not to use the term 'culpability' in our work, we do believe these papers offer some starting points for discussion.

First, Dekker made the point that what observers might call errors were not – to those who made them. Rather, they were "deliberate strategies intended to manage problems or foreseen situations".[63] However, we are not concerned about errors, which can be said, when considering a spectrum of actions, to be far to left of the line. Our concern lies with those actions that are far to the right and those neighboring that area. These actions represent those involving breaking well-designed rules and putting the care-provider's benefit ahead of the patient's. Second, Dekker asked who should "draw the line"?[63] We believe there are four distinct parties in the healthcare system who have a responsibility to do so. First is the regulatory body – the licensing College (or equivalent) – which sets certain basic, and some moral, standards, such as not entering into a sexual relationship with a patient. Second is the organization, which through its employer-employee contracts, can determine certain behaviors, including aspects of hygiene, attendance at work or on call, and putting the patient first. Third, professional groups can set normative standards for specific actions and behaviors. As Dekker has noted, healthcare is unique, because it is "channelled through relationships between human beings – a discretionary space into which no system improvement can completely reach". He describes the space as being ambiguous, uncertain and with moral choices.[63] But peers who inhabit this space understand what is acceptable or not, and they have an important role and duty in helping determine this. Fourth, patients have the sometimes unrealized role and power to respond to care that appeared to have crossed their line. More importantly, patients have the right to refuse (if possible) care that appears to be unacceptable. We believe the latter provides a very good example of how patients can contribute to establishing and maintaining a Just Culture that is "forward-looking and change-oriented".[64]

It is important to emphasize three additional points about the line. First, it has to be defined for workers proactively, that is, individuals should know about the line long before they are caught up in events leading to patients being harmed. Second, the definition should be as clear as possible while understanding that some noncompliant actions will need to be assessed, taking into account the context of system factors at the time of the event(s). But organizations and regulators can commit to undertaking investigations that will include this system view of events when circumstances dictate. Third, in healthcare many professionals have two masters – the healthcare organization who employs them or provides an appointment to them, and their profession's regulator. Thus, if something goes wrong, a health professional may face different lines set by these two masters, a situation which can undermine the atmosphere of trust, the Just Culture, in healthcare.

In summary, safety culture is fundamental to how information is handled within the organization, with generative organizations striving to identify, share, and respond to vital safety information. This process of informing needs to include all stakeholders, for their safety and for maintenance of trust in the organization. Reporting is required for an organization to learn about safety problems and make improvements (learning culture). Thus a reporting culture must be fostered, and this will only exist when there is an atmosphere of trust in the organization and the regulators that is accepted by providers and users of the system. This is the hallmark of a Just Culture. In the next chapter, we recommend expanding the notion of Just Culture to include the fair and compassionate treatment of healthcare providers who find themselves caught up in events leading to patients being harmed.

References

1. Toneguzzi M. Two patients dead in tragic error at Foothills Hospital. *Calgary Herald*. 2004 Mar 19;A1 (col. 6) & A4 (col. 3).
2. Gray D. Hospital patient deaths produce ripples across the country. *Calgary Herald: City & Region*. 2004 Mar 28;A11 (col. 1) & A12 (col. 3).
3. Hannaford N. Canadian hospitals: Unsafe at any need? *Calgary Herald: Comment*. 2004 Mar 20;A21 (col. 5).
4. Calgary Herald Staff. Recent medical mistakes in Alberta. *Calgary Herald: Foothills Tragedy*. 2004 Mar 20;A4 (col. 1).

5. Braid D. Dialysis drug mix-up demands fatality probe. *Calgary Herald: Tragic Error at Foothills.* 2004 Mar 19;A5 (col. 1).

6. Canton M. Pharmacy system needs overhaul: Expert. *Calgary Herald: Top News.* 2004 Mar 21;A3 (col. 1).

7. Canton M. CHR denies link of recent deaths to mistake in 2000. *Calgary Herald: Top News.* 2004 Mar 21;A3 (col. 1).

8. Macrae C. Author response: From analysis to learning. *BMJ Qual Saf.* 2016 Feb;25(2):134.

9. Davies JM, Steinke C. Concepts of safety reporting. *Can J Anesth/Can d'anesthésie.* 2015 Dec 28;62(12):1233–8.

10. Braid D. Reform for the patients. *Calgary Herald: City & Region.* 2004 Mar 26;B1 (col. 4) & B6 (col. 2).

11. Canton M. Hospital staff believe many mistakes hidden. *Calgary Herald.* 2004 Mar 26;A1 (col. 1).

12. Calgary Herald Editorial Board. The hazardous bed. *Calgary Herald: Opinion.* 2004 Mar 27;A22 (col. 1).

13. Toneguzzi M. Stop health-care blame game. *Calgary Herald.* 2004 Mar 27;A1 (col. 1) & A16 (col. 2).

14. Tuer D. It is vital we learn from these mistakes. *Calgary Herald.* 2004 Mar 24;A3 (col. 4).

15. Westrum R. A typology of organisational cultures. *Qual Saf Health Care.* 2004 Dec 1;13(suppl_2):ii22–7.

16. Macrae C, Stewart K. Can we import improvements from industry to healthcare? *BMJ.* 2019 Mar 21;364:l1039.

17. Read GJ, Shorrock S, Walker GH, Salmon PM. State of science: Evolving perspectives on 'human error'. *Ergonomics.* 2021 Sep 2;64(9):1091–114.

18. Reason JT, Carthey J, de Leval MR. Diagnosing "vulnerable system syndrome": An essential prerequisite to effective risk management. *Qual Saf Health Care.* 2001 Dec 1;10:Supplement 2(ii21–5).

19. Argyris C, Schön D. *Theory in Practice. Increasing Professional Effectiveness.* San Francisco: Jossey-Bass; 1974.

20. Argyris C, Schön D. *Organizational Learning: A Theory of Action Perspective.* Reading: Addison Wesley; 1978.

21. Hedberg BLT, Bystrom PC, Starbuck WH. Camping on seesaws: Prescriptions for a self-designing organization. *Adm Sci Q.* 1976 Mar;21(1):41–65.

22. Horlick-Jones T. The Problem of Blame. In: Hood C, Jones DKC, editors. *Accident and Design: Contemporary Debates on Risk Management.* London: UCL Press; 1966. pp. 61–71.

23. International Nuclear Safety Advisory Group. Safety Culture. Safety Series. 75-INSAG-4; 1991.

24. Advisory Committee on the Safety of Nuclear Installations, Health and Safety Commission. *ACSNI Human Factors Study Group. Third Report. Organizing for Safety.* London: HM Stationery Office; 1993.

25. Deal T, Kennedy A. *Organization Cultures: The Rites and Rituals of Organization Life.* Boston: Addison Wesley; 1982.

26. Pidgeon N. Safety culture and risk management in organizations. *Cross-Cultural Psychol*. 1991 Mar;22(1):129–40.

27. Cheng P, Lempert L. Rates of change and cyclical magnitude. *Summaries of Papers Delivered at the 118th Annual Meeting of the American Statistical Association*, Chicago IL, December 27–30, 1958. *J Am Stat Assoc*. 1959 Jun;54(286):484–509.

28. Vincent C, Carthey J, Macrae C, Amalberti R. Safety analysis over time: Seven major changes to adverse event investigation. *Implement Sci*. 2017 Dec 28;12(1):151.

29. Macrae C. Making risks visible: Identifying and interpreting threats to airline flight safety. *J Occup Organ Psychol*. 2009 Jun;82(2):273–93.

30. Reason J. *Managing the Risks of Organizational Accidents*. Aldershot: Ashgate Publisher; 1997.

31. Kohn L, Corrigan JM, Donaldson MS (eds.). *To Err is Human: Building a Safer Health System*. Washington, D.C.: National Academies Press; 2000.

32. Health Information Privacy. Patient Safety and Quality Improvement Act of 2005 Statute and Rule. HHS.Gov US Department of Health and Social Services. [cited 2022 Feb 9]. Accessed from: https://pso.ahrq.gov/resources/act

33. Milch CE, Salem DN, Pauker SG, Lundquist TG, Kumar S, Chen J. Voluntary electronic reporting of medical errors and adverse events. An analysis of 92,547 reports from 26 acute care hospitals. *J Gen Intern Med*. 2006 Feb;21(2):165–70.

34. Hutchinson A, Young T, Cooper K, McIntosh A, Karnon J, Scobie S, et al. Trends in healthcare incident reporting and relationship to safety and quality data in acute hospitals: Results from the National Reporting and Learning System. *Qual Saf Health Care*. 2009 Feb 1;18(1):5–10.

35. Runciman WB. The Australian Patient Safety Foundation. *Anaesth Intensive Care*. 1988 Feb 24;16(1):114–6.

36. Flanagan JC. The critical incident technique. *Psychol Bull*. 1954;51(4):327–58.

37. Cooper JB, Newbower RS, Long CD, McPeek B. Preventable anesthesia mishaps: a study of human factors. *Anesthesiology*. 1978;49:399–406.

38. Currie M, Pybus DA, Torda TA. A prospective survey of anaesthetic critical events: A report on a pilot study of 88 cases. *Anaesth Intensive Care*. 1988;16:103–7.

39. Williamson JA, Morgan CA. Incident reporting in anaesthesia. *Anaesth Intensive Care*. 1988 Feb;16(1):98–100.

40. Webb R, Currie M, Morgan C, Williamson J, Mackay P, Russell W, et al. The Australian incident monitoring study: An analysis of 2000 incident reports. *Anaesth Intensive Care*. 1993 Oct 22;21(5):520–8.

41. Spigelman AD, Swan J. Review of the Australian Incident Monitoring System. *ANZ J Surg*. 2005 Aug;75(8):657–61.

42. Davies J, Duchscherer C, McRae G. A new reporting system: Was the patient harmed or nearly harmed? In: Anca J, editor. *Multimodal Safety Management and Human Factors. Crossing the Borders of Medical, Aviation, Road and Rail Industries*. Aldershot: Ashgate Publishing Limited; 2007. pp. 61–71.

43. Flemons W, McRae G. Reporting, learning, and the culture of safety. *Healthcare Q*. 2012;15:12–7.

44. WHO World Alliance for Patient Safety. WHO draft guidelines for adverse event reporting and learning systems [Internet]. Geneva, Switzerland; World Health Organization; 2005 [cited 2022 Feb 9]. Available from: https://apps.who.int/iris/bitstream/handle/10665/69797/WHO-EIP-SPO-QPS-05.3-eng.pdf

45. Sentinel Event Alert Newsletters [Internet]. The Joint Commission. [cited 2022 Feb 9]. Available from: https://www.jointcommission.org/resources/patient-safety-topics/sentinel-event/sentinel-event-alert-newsletters/

46. Health Canada. Mandatory reporting of serious adverse drug reactions and medical device incidents by hospitals - overview [Internet]; 2019 [cited 2022 Feb 9]. Available from: https://www.canada.ca/en/health-canada/services/drugs-health-products/medeffect-canada/adverse-reaction-reporting/mandatory-hospital-reporting/drugs-devices.html

47. Young TH. *Death by Prescription*. Oakville: Mosaic Press; 2013.

48. Health Canada. Module 1: Overview of Vanessa's Law and reporting requirements. Mandatory Reporting of Serious Adverse Drug Reactions and Medical Device Incidents by Hospitals [Internet]; 2008 [cited 2022 Feb 9]. Available from: https://www.canada.ca/en/health-canada/services/drugs-health-products/medeffect-canada/adverse-reaction-reporting/mandatory-hospital-reporting/education/module-1.html

49. O'Leary M, Chappell S. Confidential incident reporting systems create vital awareness of safety problems. *ICAO*. 1996;57(1): 11–13, 27.

50. Young IJB, Luz S, Lone N. A systematic review of natural language processing for classification tasks in the field of incident reporting and adverse event analysis. *Int J Med Inform*. 2019 Dec;132:132.

51. Wolfson M. Social proprioception: Measurement, data and information from a population health basis. In: Evans RG, Barer ML, Marmer TL, editors. *Why Are Some People Healthy and Others Not?* 1st ed. New York: Aldine DeGruyter; 1994. p. 32.

52. Billings C, Lauber J, Funkhouser H, Lyman E, Huff E. NASA aviation safety reporting system quarterly report number 76-1; April 15, 1976 through July 14, 1976 [Internet]. Washington, D.C.; National Aeronautics and Space Administration; 1976 Sep [cited 2022 Feb 9]. Available from: https://ntrs.nasa.gov/api/citations/19760026757/downloads/19760026757.pdf

53. O'Leary M. The British Airways human factors reporting programme. *Reliab Eng Syst Saf*. 2002 Feb;75(2):244–55.

54. GAIN Working Group B. Analytical methods and tools. Guide to methods & tools for aviation safety analysis [Internet]. Second; 2003 [cited 2022 Feb 9]. Available from: https://skybrary.aero/sites/default/files/bookshelf/1577.pdf

55. The International Confidential Aviation Safety Systems Group. The International Confidential Aviation Safety Systems (ICASS) Group. Aviation. The Australian Transport Safety Bureau [Internet]. Australian Transport Safety Bureau. [cited 2022 Jan 8]. Available from: https://www.atsb.gov.au/voluntary/repcon-icass/

56. The Patient Safety Reporting System. PSRS program overview. Welcome to the PSRS [Internet]. NASA; [cited 2022 Feb 9]. Available from: https://psrs.arc.nasa.gov/programoverview/index.html

57. Heard GC, Sanderson PM, Thomas RD. Barriers to adverse event and error reporting in anesthesia. *Anesth Analg.* 2012 Mar;114(3):604–14.

58. Kingston MJ, Evans SM, Smith BJ, Berry JG. Attitudes of doctors and nurses towards incident reporting: A qualitative analysis. *Med J Aust.* 2004 Jul 5;181(1):36–9.

59. Pronovost J, Morlock L, Sexton J, Miller M, Holzmueller C, Thompson D, et al. Improving the value of safety reporting systems. In: Henriksen et al., editors. *Advances in Patient Safety: New Directions and Alternative Approaches (Vol 1: Assessment).* Rockville: Agency for Healthcare Research and Quality; 2008. PMID: 21249856.

60. Pham JC, Girard T, Pronovost PJ. What to do with healthcare Incident Reporting Systems. *J Public health Res.* 2013 Dec 1;2(3):e27.

61. Hall D, Hecht A. Summary of the characteristics of the air safety system reporting database. Ninth Quarterly Report NASA. TM70608.; 1979.

62. Pidgeon N. Safety culture and risk management in organizations. *Cross-Cultural Psychol.* 1991 Mar;22(1):129–40.

63. Dekker SWA. Criminalization of medical error: Who draws the line? *ANZ J Surg.* 2007 Oct;77(10): 831–837.

64. Dekker SWA. Just culture: Who gets to draw the line? *Cogn Technol Work.* 2009 Sep 19;11(3): 177–185.

Chapter 5

"But What Are We Going to Do? Hang a Pharmacist?"[1]

Messages of support were expressed for the healthcare workers involved in the two deaths. At the Press Conference, the CMO was close to tears when he talked about how they would feel "great pain and loss" and which could "affect them for a lifetime".[2] Another reporter described the CMO's pain as "utterly genuine".[3] The EMD who'd provided the information at the Press Conference was also described as sharing his "pain and sympathy".[4] And an Internal Medicine specialist and patient safety expert, contacted by the media to comment on the deaths, said he felt with his heart for those involved.[5]

One columnist wrote movingly of what he imagined the Pharmacy workers were feeling. He described the individual or individuals somewhere in the city or its outskirts "suffering agonies and despair", which many of us could not even begin to imagine. He suggested their emotions would be profuse and formidable, while offering sympathy for them and for the families of the two victims. Chillingly though, the reporter's final sentence conjured up a less sympathetic idea: "…no one, except maybe professionals in other far darker areas of life, sets out to work in the morning to deliberately cause death".[1]

And indeed, the technicians were feeling greatly distressed. On Monday the 8th of March, the VP-SW and the EMD-SW had travelled to the Central Pharmacy to meet with the technicians, the Regional Pharmacy Operations

DOI: 10.4324/9781003185307-6

Manager, and the Director of Pharmacy. Everyone involved was very upset and the technicians were distraught. The two Executives had reassured them that they would not lose their jobs as long as the VP remained in her position. The technicians were then instructed by the Director and the Regional Operations Manager to go home. This instruction was in line with the standard operating procedures of Human Resources and the Union contract. The technicians would be on paid leave. However, they would also be isolated from their workplace friends and colleagues.

When reporters checked at the Central Pharmacy, they were told morale had dropped drastically when the problem with the two chemicals was discovered. Some workers had taken time off and many were feeling terrible. Others refused to say anything, citing instructions to avoid the media. The Pharmacy was painted as "grim, sombre, awful".[6]

The President of the Union to which the technicians belonged stated she hadn't heard from any of those working when the mix-up was discovered. She described herself as having been "distressed" and that she and her colleagues hadn't known the identities of those isolated at home. Wanting to offer help, she had asked her organization to phone all 120 Calgary pharmacy technicians.[7]

Nevertheless, columnists' expressions of well-placed sympathy were not endless and calls for accountability were also heard. To one columnist, the need for what he declared was 'accountability' was clear. "A head or heads have to roll. It's simply a matter of justice, of public safety and public confidence".[1] Countering this, a local well-known and well-respected Professor of Orthopedic Surgery asked a salient question: "What are we going to do? Hang a pharmacist?"[1] He continued with his explanation that, with those workers gone, others would come in taking the same roles, using the same bottles. The catastrophe would occur again. The surgeon added that, if the focus were on "finding someone to blame, someone to hang" then the problems in the system would not be corrected. And to this, the reporter's reply indicated that this indeed was the crux of the problem.[1]

Just over two weeks after being sent home on leave, on March 23rd, the pharmacy technicians were called back to meet with Regional administrators. Behind closed doors and accompanied by representatives from their union and the Region's Human Resources, as well as the VP-SW and the EMD-SW, the technicians were given an explanation of an internal evaluation that would be carried out over the next few days by an Administrative and Human Resources team.[8]

Once that was completed, the recommendations were to be forwarded to the CMO and the COO. The Region's Board Chair was quoted as saying the review was to "look at accountability and if there were any responsibilities that were violated". The overall message from the Region was that the technicians had "misread labels".[8] Additionally, the Board Chair said that up to that time the technicians had not been subject to any discipline.

But the technicians were to stay home longer than expected, while an External Review was carried out. The terms of their leave from work were also based on that investigation, which had been announced on the same day as had their Administrative Review. Months would therefore pass before they returned to work. Even then, they were to do "different jobs but in the same workplace".[9]

Supporting Healthcare Providers

Two patients dead after being dialyzed with an incorrectly formulated dialysate solution, calls from newspaper journalists for heads to roll, the leader of the province's official opposition party demanding the CEO be fired, and pharmacy technicians on an extended leave of absence pending one or more investigations. The Region had not proactively planned what its response would or should be to its healthcare providers in this type of situation.

Like many healthcare organizations, the Region did have an Employee and Family Assistance Program (EFAP) for its employees, but otherwise had no formal or even informal support system. Regional managers and administrators, however, would not have known if the EFAP psychologists had any experience working with traumatized healthcare providers who had been involved in an event leading to patients' deaths. Furthermore, the pharmacy technicians were to undergo an Administrative Review, which presumably would decide their fate. But there was also a forthcoming additional investigation, of system factors. How might this second review affect the first one? To add to the tension, the regulator, the (then-named) Alberta College of Pharmacists, was reviewing the role of the pharmacists who had supervised the technicians. At the time, pharmacy technicians were not regulated and were therefore not under the jurisdiction of the College.

Which precepts would guide these reviews and which approach or procedures would be used? Would the approach to be used for the search for system factors in the organization be similar to that of the regulators? And could the results of these reviews lead to discipline of the staff? No one knew.

How then might such a lack of knowledge about all these things affect healthcare providers' willingness to step forward in the future – to report hazards, poorly designed procedures and their errors? What could happen if the organization did not learn about the system deficiencies and weaknesses related to an event and therefore did not intervene before the next tragedy occurred? These questions reflect not only some of the personal problems suffered by the healthcare providers involved in the Region's two deaths but also some of the problems that underlie a Just Culture for all healthcare providers.

A Journey, Perhaps Toward Healing

After healthcare providers have been involved in an event in which a patient was harmed, they stand at the start of a journey, which may or may not lead to recovery. Susan Scott and her colleagues at the University of Missouri Healthcare started investigating "professional suffering" in the mid-2000s. For the subjects studied, being involved in an event in which a patient was harmed was a "life-altering experience that left a permanent imprint on the individual". This was true, independent of the healthcare provider's sex, professional role, or number of years spent in the specialty.[10] This life-altering effect is one of the similarities we see between the journey a healthcare provider takes and the one taken by a patient and their family.

As well as the losses suffered by the patients and families, healthcare providers also suffer a loss, which is psychological and emotional. The loss suffered by patients and families, however, is enormously different and cannot truly be compared any further, although the range of emotions is common to both. The experience of patients and families was discussed in Chapter 3, and we will comment below on some of the differences between what patients and families experience, and what healthcare providers experience.

Types of Healthcare Providers Involved

We know that it is difficult to estimate the possibility of a healthcare provider being involved in an event leading to harm. The possibility very likely depends somewhat on the provider's role, specialty, and years of experience. Although being involved always leaves an imprint on the individual, the way in which a provider responds emotionally to these events differs – also contributed to by role, specialty, and years of experience. Differences in the emotional response can be attributed to sex, gender, and other individual traits. One recent study of oncologists and surgeons determined that those who practiced surgery were no more likely than their non-surgical colleagues to suffer emotionally after an event. The opposite was initially postulated because of the higher rate of acute surgical complications compared with medical ones.[11] Also, women are considered more likely than men to suffer more untoward effects on their emotions and their careers. The difference is suggested as being greater if women have family responsibilities.[12]

These types of events and experiences can happen to anybody in their career – young as well as old – and experience is not necessarily protective. We all know of seasoned professionals who have had their confidence shattered, left the profession, or committed suicide after being involved in an adverse event, while some new to the profession have been involved in an event that left them so devastated that they chose to leave the profession. As healthcare providers, we have also personally been involved in events ourselves, and have experienced similar emotions and continue to have lasting memories.

Emotional Consequences

The commonality between the journeys of healthcare providers and those their patients unwillingly find themselves on lies mainly in the range of emotions that both experience. Many healthcare providers, involved in this type of event, report having suffered harm.[13–15] And they do suffer, mostly in silence.

With the experience of loss come many unwanted negative feelings and symptoms, which we know will change as our appraisal of an event changes. Common cognitive and emotional responses we might feel include troubling memories, anxiety or concern, inward directed anger, regret or remorse, distress, guilt, shattered confidence, fear of involvement in future events, and embarrassment. Many affected healthcare workers report difficulty sleeping and nightmares, and some even experience post-traumatic stress disorder (PTSD).[16] These emotional disturbances may also have physical consequences, such as weight loss, increased heart rate, and blood pressure. In essence, the experience – the journey – is a grieving process.

A Journey with Six Stages

Research carried out at the University of Missouri Health Care by Scott and McCoig enabled them to refine the concept of the journey many healthcare providers describe. They saw the journey as having six stages,[17] with the initial stage being "chaos and accident response". This *first stage* began the moment healthcare providers discovered they were involved in an event where a patient(s) was harmed, whether at the time of the event or later when told of the event and the patient's outcome. Providers' initial (cognitive and emotional) responses were considered to be proportional to their initial or "primary appraisal" of the event and their judgment of what the event meant to them.[18] Providers would then question themselves as to their roles in the event and how and why things could have gone wrong.[17] Their unanswered questions would increase their anxiety, and it was at this stage that they would start to feel a range of emotions and experience emotionally-related symptoms.

The *second stage* was one of "intrusive reflections", as the care providers faced the gut-wrenching reality of the patient's condition. Scott and McCoig used the evocative phrase, "haunted reenactments" as the providers relived what they did, how and why,[17] and interrogate themselves as to their decisions and actions. It was at this stage care providers might start to isolate themselves not only from their colleagues but also from their families and friends,[19] as they began to feel professionally inadequate. This latter emotion was no doubt underpinned by the "expectation of excellence" in which we as healthcare providers are inculcated, even before we enter clinical training.[14]

Stage three involved "restoring personal integrity". This was accomplished by talking with a trusted colleague, friend, or family member. At the same time, providers might have difficulties doing this because those to whom they spoke might not truly appreciate what they were saying. Accompanying these doubts were the questions providers often asked themselves – if anyone would (or should) trust them again. This questioning was made worse by gossip[17] and innuendo. The latter, such as increased 'casual' supervision or having the Department Head or manager send a colleague to 'lend a hand', can sometimes be worse than gossip. While these types of actions can be described as meaning well and trying to help, the messages may be interpreted and reaffirm what the providers have worried about – a lack of trust by others in their professional capabilities.

Investigations are common after untoward events and thus *stage four* was described as "enduring the inquisition". Investigations, whether by departments, quality of care/safety committees, or professional colleges, all have potential implications for the providers' future. Providers worry about loss of privileges or restrictions placed on licenses, as well as litigation, which brings its own set of examinations. All these concerns may be increased by not understanding or not receiving clear descriptions and instructions about the reviews.[17] This is probably what the pharmacy technicians in Calgary experienced, because the Region had not drawn an explicit line between acceptable and unacceptable behavior. Also, there were no pre-existing descriptions of the types of investigative reviews, and what personnel could expect might come of them.

In the *fifth stage*, providers started to concentrate on "obtaining emotional first aid". This was from personal connections, such as family, friends, and supportive colleagues, or from professionals, either provided by the organization or arranged privately. One drawback of talking with a personal support is that of privacy concerns, while a problem with the professional support could be the lack of understanding of exactly what the providers had experienced.[17]

The *last stage* of the journey was described as "moving on". (Please see later in the chapter for our views on the term.) This stage was unique to every individual and depended on several factors. This is why this stage had three possible outcomes: "dropping out", "surviving", or "thriving".[17] The choice of future paths will depend on a number of considerations, including how well individuals functioned psychologically before the event, and also how well they are guided through the grieving process.

As mentioned earlier, some healthcare providers may develop PTSD and/or depression. These conditions impair and may even stall attempts by providers as they try to regain a sense of well-being, as they emotionally survive. These conditions, and others, may contribute to them potentially changing what they do professionally. Being involved in an event in which a patient was seriously harmed has been shown to be an important contributor to the high rates of burnout that surgeons experience.[20] We believe that this finding is generalizable to other healthcare workers' experiences.[21,22]

How Healthcare Providers Cope

How do healthcare providers deal with how they feel after an untoward event? To manage the emotions and their related stress, some healthcare providers use specific coping strategies. Deciding what to do is the marker of the "secondary appraisal", with the individuals each asking separately, *what could they do to feel better.*[18] In this regard, stress was defined by Lazarus in 1966 as a relationship between individuals and the environments they assessed as relevant to their well-being, and in which their resources were strained or exceeded.[23] Coping was later described by Folkman and Lazarus as the "cognitive and behavioral efforts" we use to "manage (master, reduce, or tolerate) a troubled person-environment relationship".[18]

As to specific coping strategies, task, emotion, and avoidance-oriented strategies were applied to the results of a systematic review of coping strategies used by healthcare providers. *Task-oriented strategies* related to specific aspects of work, such as attempts to improve work performance, including closer adherence to policies, guidelines, and details. *Emotion-oriented strategies* were those of self-criticism as well as self-appraisal. Three important actions were considered representative of both task- and emotion-oriented strategies. These included informing others, apologizing and disclosing to the patient and family, and participating in discussions about offers of support.[24]

Less commonly, workers may use *avoidance-oriented strategies*. While Busch and colleagues reported that fewer than 10% of workers had resorted to using alcohol, drugs, or medication,[24] we believe this number seriously under-represents what actually occurs. Self-medication by healthcare providers has probably been a centuries-old problem, with the concept appearing in the English language in the late 1600s as a version of 'the doctor who treats himself has a fool for a patient'. Additionally, some healthcare workers reduce their clinical role following an untoward event, taking leave from work, or leaving the healthcare profession altogether.[25] Sadly, a few providers are unable to navigate the journey of healing after being involved in a serious event. Because of the associated guilt and shame, individuals may reach the end of their abilities to cope with their memories and their thoughts,[26] and even take their own lives.

Psychological Healing by Healthcare Providers

How well healthcare providers heal, following an event in which a patient is seriously harmed, depends on many factors. We need to avoid using language that overtly or covertly shames and blames our colleagues, provide them with useful psychological support, and conduct a fair assessment, all of which are known to help to restore providers' well-being. There are, however, other considerations.

The type and amount of support healthcare providers receive from their families, peers, colleagues, and their organization, as well as professional counseling, all play an important role in psychological healing. Affected individuals value understanding that others have had to endure similar experiences and survived. Informal conversations with those of us who have had this experience may be extremely beneficial, including immediately after the event. We can also demonstrate that people care about these providers. Having respected colleagues and supervisors be empathetic can be particularly valuable, as is their reaffirmation of trust in the providers' abilities to care for their patients.

Participation in disclosure and apologizing to the patient and family help to address feelings of guilt for the role providers had in events leading to patients being harmed. In complex cases, an individual healthcare provider may need assistance with disclosure and apology. As described in Chapter 3, the patient and family require an apology, disclosure, and support. Ideally, the first two requirements are provided by the healthcare providers involved in the event, and in the most serious cases, also by their healthcare leaders. Both the patient and family, and the healthcare provider(s), benefit when apology and disclosure are done effectively. Having the healthcare providers involved in the apology and disclosure can be an effective strategy to support and help them. Additionally, some will want to, and will benefit from, playing a role in the investigation of the event, including the development of recommendations for system improvements.

Self-compassion and self-forgiveness can be another vital component of healthcare provider healing.[27] Not surprisingly, personality traits are an important factor that shapes the way healthcare providers respond to being involved in a serious adverse event. Some may have a more natural tendency toward self-forgiveness. However, those with a strong leaning toward self-condemnation are prone to negative outcomes such as anger and depression.[28] These individuals would be predicted to need the most assistance reformulating the untoward event, their role, and their own loss. Self-exoneration can be mistaken for self-forgiveness. The former involves an individual not accepting responsibility, or minimizing the degree of harm, or not believing their actions were wrong.[28] Although this may superficially result in greater personal well-being, it would not be conducive to effective disclosure or apology. True self-forgiveness involves an individual accepting responsibility and working toward positive resolution. This can lead to greater well-being for the individual, while positively contributing to what patients and families need for their own healing.

Following a serious event, the needs of many healthcare providers and the needs of patients and families overlap in several respects and are interdependent. Offering effective support for both groups should be imperative for healthcare organizations, their insurers and their lawyers, professional associations, and regulators. In so doing, the organization is assisting in the healing of those involved, while advancing a Just Culture. Both groups need to regain trust, which takes time. Healthcare providers may need to regain trust in themselves, as well as trust that the system, which includes the organization and the regulator that oversees their professional practice, will assess what they did in a fair way.

Forgiveness

Somewhere along these paths of recovery, it may be possible for patients and families to feel able to forgive those involved in the event. This is more likely when their needs, as described in Chapter 3, are properly addressed. Forgiveness is not simple. It takes honesty, open-mindedness, as well as a genuine desire to forgive. Some believe that it is only with forgiveness that one can truly heal and feel peace.

Some patients and families are able to forgive, a few even without an apology. If a healthcare provider and organization respond well to the needs of a patient and family, there is an increased likelihood of them offering forgiveness at some point. This should neither be asked for nor expected, but if it is given, then this will also help with providers' healing.

Providers may then be able to self-forgive, separately from the patient and family. But if healthcare providers continue to be particularly hard on themselves, despite apologizing and remain living with intense self-blame, guilt, and shame, then self-forgiveness will be slow and will need to be encouraged. Learning self-forgiveness, as part of psychological healing, requires that healthcare providers reformulate their loss so it can be viewed in a different way. Ideally, they will be able to transform the loss into something positive. The highest level of functional recovery comes when people are able to forgive themselves for what happened and, if possible, to be forgiven by the patient and family.

Supporting Healthcare Providers

What can we do, as leaders and as colleagues of healthcare providers involved in an untoward event? Newman identified four primary needs for healthcare professionals following a patient harm event: talking to someone about the incident; validation of the decision-making process; re-affirmation of professional competence; and personal reassurance.[29] Healthcare providers have affirmed that a multidisciplinary peer support program is their preferred support option, and the majority indicate a preference for individual compared with group support. Most providers would like support to be available within a few days after the event, although some have described wanting support to be even more readily available.[30] However, the formal support programs of most organizations are external to the organization. Also, following a serious event, some healthcare providers do not believe they should expect to receive support because they made an error,[31] a form of self-recriminating response.

In the immediate aftermath of a serious event, some organizations provide Critical Incident Stress Management for healthcare workers. This technique was initially designed to help first responders cope with stressful traumatic situations. Systematic reviews of limited research studies have found little evidence of benefit, and some studies have shown evidence of psychological harm.[32,33] There is a lack of clear evidence either way on its effect when applied after events in which patients were harmed.

Some organizations have implemented a three-tiered interventional model of support. Tier 1 offers support at a local unit or department level, providing one-on-one reassurance to healthcare workers who are suffering following an event. Tier 2 consists of trained peer supporters if further assistance is required. Tier 3 support involves expedited referral to professional guidance as needed, for example an employee assistance program, a chaplain, a social worker, or a clinical psychologist.[30] Curricula have been developed in a small number of organizations for proactive education programs targeting different types of providers and different types of supervisors.[34]

There may also be a need to remove healthcare providers from providing care for a period of time. This may be necessary in the immediate aftermath of an adverse event to ensure the safety of other patients. Although this has been recommended, especially in some specialties such as anesthesiology, there is no evidence in the literature as to the effect on healthcare performance after a serious event. Thus, we recommend an approach of checking with individuals to see how they are feeling emotionally and asking them if they feel safe to continue to practice during their scheduled shift. Further, a screening process to ensure a lack of impairment, as well as to assess emotional and mental health after an event, should be beneficial to ensure the provider's ability to provide safe care to other patients. Screening may also help with triaging appropriate support, to reduce the probability of having a prolonged recovery and developing PTSD.[35]

Healthcare providers may be off work for much longer than just the shift during which the event occurred. Leave and its duration could be at the request of the personnel involved, who require time to support their mental health. Paid leave might also be part of an organizational process to have individuals away from work while an investigation of the event, and their performance, is conducted. In some situations, unions' collective agreements might come into play. However, a mandated leave, especially one resulting in a prolonged absence, could actually be detrimental to some individuals.[36] In the case of the pharmacy technicians, they were on paid leave for several weeks while the event underwent more than one review. The result of this delayed return to work was that at least one of the technicians found the prolonged period of professional isolation added to the stress, and the distress, that they experienced.

As described earlier, healthcare providers may benefit from providing an apology to the patient and family, as well as being involved in the disclosure process. We now recommend that, where possible, at least some of our healthcare providers meet with the patient and family members. This meeting should be planned as much as it can be for a process that is as variable as are the individuals involved, and their circumstances.

Fair Assessment

In addition to finding ways to psychologically support healthcare providers who are caught up in an adverse event, healthcare organizations and, where it is applicable, regulators can help address another source of anxiety and stress for healthcare providers – the review of an individual's actions. We have previously described the importance of organizations and regulators defining the line as precisely as possible and to proactively communicate what this means for healthcare providers. It is also critical that these same institutions commit to a fair assessment of an individual's actions should it become necessary. What exactly does this mean? A more detailed description is provided in Chapter 6 but briefly, fair assessment is based on three elements. First, only actions that are near the line will be formally reviewed and errors, not being close to the line will not be. Second, actions under review will be assessed within the context of system factors identified and understood through the completion of a system-oriented review. Third, reviewers will understand the biases that can affect judgments and reviewers will actively review these before making final decisions about assessments. Also, in the event that workers' actions are deemed to warrant some type of discipline, then a restorative justice approach will be taken. We believe all these elements together form an important part of a Just Culture for healthcare providers.

How Language and Beliefs Can Affect Healing

Why we seem preprogramed to blame and how that is antithetical to a Just Culture was discussed in Chapter 1. In Chapter 2 we described the misunderstandings that can arise from using the term 'medical error' and its related variants, and in Chapter 3 specifically with respect to disclosure of harm. We believe that language – the words we use – matters. The meaning that words carry or 'miscarry' when used improperly can have a huge effect. In looking after our patients and our providers, as leaders we think certain words and phrases currently used require a second examination. Here we review three terms used in relation to supporting healthcare providers – and leaders.

'Second Victim'

For the past two decades healthcare providers, who have suffered as a result of having been involved with, or contributed to a patient suffering harm, have been referred to as "second victims".[37] In this context, the patient, having suffered harm, is assumed to be the first victim. The origins of the word 'victim' are from the seventeenth century Latin word *victima* referring to a living creature killed and offered as a sacrifice.[38] Later uses in the eighteenth and nineteenth centuries refer to one who suffers some injury, hardship or loss, is badly treated or taken advantage of, etc. The etymology of victim starts to give some idea of the ongoing debate about using the term in the context of events in which patients are harmed.

The case for not using victim in healthcare has been eloquently argued by families and patients who have suffered harm. "There is a seductiveness to labelling yourself as a victim. Victims bear no responsibility for causing the injurious event and no accountability for addressing it. Victims elicit sympathy. They are passive. They lack agency. In fact, this passivity and lack of agency is why some patients and families whose lives have been devastated by medical harm avoid describing themselves or their loved one as victims".[39] Patients have the right to determine how they wish to be addressed, by their titles, such as Mrs. or Reverend followed by their last names, by their first names alone, or by a cultural appellation, such as Auntie. Similarly, they have a right to determine if they wish to be described as a victim or as a patient who was harmed.

There is even more debate about using the term, 'second victim'. Even if we, as healthcare providers and leaders were to accept that characterizing a patient and family as victims is appropriate, by applying the label of 'second victim' to the healthcare providers involved removes any requirement for those involved to take responsibility and accountability for the harm. Also, extending the victim description to those who were part of the events can, in the eyes of some, devalue the devastating suffering that their patients experienced. As mentioned earlier, it is impossible, nor is it right, to compare the suffering that patients and families experienced to that which the healthcare providers involved might have experienced.

We suggest that a different approach would be to describe patients and providers based on their distinct outcomes. Thus, we can talk or write about a patient who was harmed or who suffered harm. This can be physical, psychological, financial, or all three. Its severity can be described as ranging from minor to severe, to fatal. As for the healthcare provider, the harm they suffer is largely psychological, although it could be financial or reputational.

Responsibility and Accountability

For an individual to have responsibility means the person is deemed able to complete the task to a certain level of performance, that is, to carry out the actions and behaviors required. For an individual to take accountability, the individual is required to ensure that the task is actually completed as required and that the results of the task match those desired. Accountability cannot be assigned to an individual lacking responsibility, thus requiring consideration and determination of responsibility before that of accountability.

However, if an individual takes accountability for an untoward outcome because they did not complete an action correctly for which they were responsible, does it automatically follow that they should be punished? We hope we have convinced our readers that the answer to the question of accountability should be no discipline or punishment for most cases. To return to when Jack Davis was interviewed by a local columnist two days after the news conference where it was revealed that two patients had died as a result of an incorrectly prepared dialysate solution, he was quoted as saying he believed in a high degree of accountability for healthcare workers. Many in the media and the public took this to mean that those who erred would be punished. Following this line of thinking, is it not surprising then, that most of us, if we have done something incorrectly, are not eager to admit it?

The word 'account' dates back to the twelfth century use of the word 'counting' – reckoning of money received and paid, a detailed statement of funds owed or spent or property held. This originated from Old French *acont* and from Latin *computare* "to count up, reckon together". By the mid-sixteenth century, the term was also being used to suggest "answering for conduct". The suffix, –able, added a notion of "capable of, worthy of, requiring".[40] Thus a common, present-day definition of accountable in the context of one's decisions and actions is "liable to be called to account for responsibilities and conduct; required or expected to justify one's action, decisions, etc.; answerable".[40] Nowhere in the historical or present-day definition of the word is there a notion of blame, or of punishment. Therefore, we would strongly suggest that, in the context of adverse events, when someone is perceived to be accountable, this does not mean or imply that the individual will be punished or sanctioned. What it does mean is that the individual should explain what was happening at the time they acted or chose not to act, and the motivation(s) they had for the choices that they made.

'Moving On'

Another term that requires further mention is that of 'moving on' and its cousin, 'closure'. We would repeat the words of Scott and colleagues, that being involved in an event in which a patient is harmed is a "life-altering experience", which will leave a "permanent imprint on the individual".[10] The memories of the events and the aftermath might fade over the years and decades, but it would be the rare individual who appears completely unchanged. Recently, Dr. Amy Price, the Patient Editor for Research and Evaluation at *The BMJ*, and associated with the Centre for Evidence-Based Research at the University of Oxford, described the Japanese art of Kintsugi. She used this art form as a metaphor for dealing with grief, noting how kintsugi represents "healing, resilience, and restoration", with "treasured objects" of glass or pottery carefully and lovingly repaired with resin and gold, and the latter symbolizing "trust, permanence, and beauty".[41] In being repaired, the object becomes something different from what it once was, although now it is permanently altered, but still loved and treasured. We cannot remove the golden scar.

Ideally, tragic events lead to knowledge of the factors that contributed to the patient being harmed. Whether there are changes to the organization's infrastructure or not, all attempts should be made by the providers to learn from these events, at least about themselves.

In summary, we must remember that, in addition to supporting our patients and families, we must support our healthcare providers. They too have suffered a loss to which they must adapt, as well as a range of potentially disturbing and even life-threatening emotions, such as PTSD and depression. Unfortunately, the experience of many healthcare providers who need support in the aftermath of a serious event is that support, even if available, is both opaque and unstructured, potentially leaving them feeling there is simply no support. There are things, however, we can do as colleagues and leaders so they do feel supported. We can support them through specific programs and by our actions, as well as by the language we use. Words matter, whether we are talking with our patients and their families or with our colleagues and leaders – we need to ensure our *loose language* does not confuse or bias anyone. In the next chapter, we will provide ways to look at events in which patients have been harmed, which will be supportive to those individuals, foster a Just Culture, and also balance the need for appropriate accountability.

References

1. Gradon J. Facing up to double jeopardy. *Calgary Herald: City & Region*. 2004 Mar 22;B1 (col. 2)–B4 (col. 4).
2. Toneguzzi M. Two patients dead in tragic error at Foothills Hospital. *Calgary Herald*. 2004 Mar 19;A1(col. 6) & A4(col. 3).

3. Braid D. Dialysis drug mix-up demands fatality probe. *Calgary Herald: Tragic Error at Foothills.* 2004 Mar 19;A5 (col. 1).

4. Makowichuk D. Sorry. *The Calgary Sun.* 2004 Mar 19;4.

5. Kirkey S. Medical mistakes leave deadly toll. *Calgary Herald.* 2004 Mar 19;A5(col. 5).

6. Canton M. New pharmacy promised greater safety. *Calgary Herald.* 2004 Mar 20;A1 (col. 1) & A4 (col. 2).

7. Canton M. Druggists feared worst at CHR. *Calgary Herald: City & Region.* 2004 Mar 23;B1 (col. 1) & B3 (col. 4).

8. Canton M. CHR meets with pharmacy technicians. *Calgary Herald: Top News.* 2004 Mar 24;A3 (col. 1).

9. Toneguzzi M. Fatal flaws admitted, human errors, system blamed for drug mix-up. *Calgary Herald: City & Region.* 2004 Jun 30;B1 (col. 6) & B3 (col. 1).

10. Scott SD, Hirschinger L, Cox K, McCoig M, Brandt J, Hall L. The natural history of recovery for the healthcare provider "second victim" after adverse patient events. *Qual Saf Heal Care.* 2009 Oct 1;18(5):325–30.

11. Stukalin I, Lethebe B, Temple W. The physician's Achilles Heel—surviving an adverse event. *Curr Oncol.* 2019 Dec 1;26(6):e742–7.

12. Ozeke O, Ozeke V, Coskun O, Budakoglu II. Second victims in health care: Current perspectives. *Adv Med Educ Pract.* 2019 Aug; 10:593–603.

13. Seys D, Wu AW, Gerven EV, Vleugels A, Euwema M, Panella M, et al. Health care professionals as second victims after adverse events. *Eval Health Prof.* 2013 Jun 12;36(2):135–62.

14. Nydoo P, Pillay BJ, Naicker T, Moodley J. The second victim phenomenon in health care: A literature review. *Scand J Public Health.* 2020 Aug 13;48(6): 629–37.

15. Gazoni FM, Amato PE, Malik ZM, Durieux ME. The impact of perioperative catastrophes on anesthesiologists. *Anesth Analg.* 2012 Mar;114(3):596–603.

16. Busch IM, Moretti F, Purgato M, Barbui C, Wu AW, Rimondini M. Psychological and psychosomatic symptoms of second victims of adverse events: A systematic review and meta-analysis. *J Patient Saf.* 2020 Jun;16(2):e61–74.

17. Scott SD, McCoig MM. Care at the point of impact: Insights into the second-victim experience. *J Healthcare Risk Manag.* 2016 Apr;35(4):6–13.

18. Folkman S, Lazarus RS. If it changes it must be a process: Study of emotion and coping during three stages of a college examination. *J Pers Soc Psychol.* 1985;48(1):150–70.

19. Bacon A. Death on the table. *Anaesthesia.* 1989 Mar;44(3):245–8.

20. Shanafelt TD, Balch CM, Bechamps G, Russell T, Dyrbye L, Satele D, et al. Burnout and medical errors among American surgeons. *Ann Surg.* 2010 Jun;251(6):995–1000.

21. Lewis EJ, Baernholdt MB, Yan G, Guterbock TG. Relationship of adverse events and support to RN burnout. *J Nurs Care Qual.* 2015;30(2):144–52.

22. Tawfik DS, Profit J, Morgenthaler TI, Satele D V, Sinsky CA, Dyrbye LN, et al. Physician burnout, well-being, and work unit safety grades in relationship to reported medical errors. *Mayo Clin Proc.* 2018 Nov;93(11):1571–80.

23. Lazarus R. *Psychological Stress and the Coping Process*. New York: McGraw-Hill; 1966.
24. Busch IM, Moretti F, Purgato M, Barbui C, Wu AW, Rimondini M. Dealing with adverse events: A meta-analysis on second victims' coping strategies. *J Patient Saf.* 2020 Jun;16(2):e51–60.
25. Gupta K, Lisker S, Rivadeneira NA, Mangurian C, Linos E, Sarkar U. Decisions and repercussions of second victim experiences for mothers in medicine (SAVE DR MoM). *BMJ Qual Saf.* 2019 Jul;28(7):564–73.
26. Treiber LA, Jones JH. Making an infusion error. *J Infus Nurs.* 2018 May;41(3):156–63.
27. Cleare S, Gumley A, O'Connor RC. Self-compassion, self-forgiveness, suicidal ideation, and self-harm: A systematic review. *Clin Psychol Psychother.* 2019 Sep 13;26(5):511–30.
28. Cornish MA, Woodyatt L, Morris G, Conroy A, Townsdin J. Self-forgiveness, self-exoneration, and self-condemnation: Individual differences associated with three patterns of responding to interpersonal offenses. *Pers Individ Dif.* 2018 Jul;129:43–53.
29. Newman M. The emotional impact of mistakes on family physicians. *Arch Fam Med.* 1996;5:71–5.
30. Edrees H, Connors C, Paine L, Norvell M, Taylor H, Wu AW. Implementing the RISE second victim support programme at the Johns Hopkins Hospital: A case study. *BMJ Open.* 2016 Sep 30;6(9):e011708.
31. Schiess C, Schwappach D, Schwendimann R, Vanhaecht K, Burgstaller M, Senn B. A transactional "second-victim" model—experiences of affected healthcare professionals in acute-somatic inpatient settings. *J Patient Saf* [Internet]. 2018 Jan 30 [cited 2022 Feb 9]. Available from: https://journals.lww.com/journalpatientsafety/Abstract/2021/12000/A_Transactional__Second_Victim__Model_Experiences.49.aspx
32. Anderson GS, Di Nota PM, Groll D, Carleton RN. Peer support and crisis-focused psychological interventions designed to mitigate post-traumatic stress injuries among public safety and frontline healthcare personnel: A systematic review. *Int J Environ Res Public Health* [Internet]. 2020 Oct 20;17(20). doi:10.3390/ijerph17207645.
33. Bledsoe BE. Critical incident stress management (cism): Benefit or risk for emergency services? *Prehospital Emerg Care.* 2003 Jan 2;7(2):272–9.
34. Wade L, Fitzpatrick E, Williams N, Parker R, Hurley KF. Organizational interventions to support second victims in acute care settings. *J Patient Saf* [Internet]. 2020 May 13. doi:10.1097/PTS.0000000000000704.
35. Martin TW, Roy RC. Cause for pause after a perioperative catastrophe. *Anesth Analg.* 2012 Mar;114(3):485–7.
36. Manser T. Managing the aftermath of critical incidents: Meeting the needs of healthcare providers and patients. *Best Pract Res Clin Anaesthesiol.* 2011 Jun;25(2):169–79.
37. Wu A. Medical error: The second victim. *BMJ.* 2000 Mar 18;320:726–7.
38. OED Online. *Victim.* Oxford: Oxford University Press; 2020. Victim; [cited 2022 Feb 9]; [about 1 screen]. Available from: https://www.oed.com/

39. Clarkson MD, Haskell H, Hemmelgarn C, Skolnik PJ. Abandon the term "second victim". *BMJ*. 2019;364:l1233. doi:10.1136/bmj.l1233.

40. OED Online. *Accountable*. Oxford: Oxford University Press; 2020. Victim; [cited 2022 Feb 9]; [about 1 screen]. Available from: https://www.oed.com/

41. Price A. Commentary: My pandemic grief and the Japanese art of kintsugi. *BMJ*. 2021 Aug 10;374:n1906.

Chapter 6

"It Is Vital We Learn from These Mistakes."[1]

After Kathleen's death was determined to be related to unintentionally being dialyzed with potassium chloride, the Pharmacy carried out its own internal scrutiny to find the source of the mix-up. This was to be followed by an internal review of the Pharmacy by the Regional Critical Incident Committee. The purpose of that review was to ensure that hazards had been secured. The Region was therefore fairly confident that the problems in the Pharmacy had been found and rectified.

However, after the first Press Conference on March 18th, there were multiple calls for external investigations. First among these was one from the Official Opposition's Health Critic, who wanted a team from outside the province to investigate.[2] This review had to be a "probe" – completely independent of the Region and the province. Not only should the deaths be investigated, but so should the "workings" of the Region and the "patronage appointments" on its Board.[3]

The Minister of Health and Wellness had replied to this call for an external investigation, saying he felt "no need" for one. He stated the Region had undertaken all the necessary procedures, "tightening up safeguards", as well as providing full disclosure to both families. The Premier added "internal probes" would determine what had occurred.[3]

The Premier also said the Chief Medical Examiner (CME) was investigating the deaths, and it was likely the CME would "refer both cases to the Fatality Review Board".[4] The Minister of Health and Wellness commented, however, that the families "might not want the deaths of their loved ones given more publicity",[5] but he would accept the decision of the province's Attorney General.[3]

The next day, in response to press coverage, Kathleen's' family issued a brief statement. "Pending completion of the investigation by the Calgary Health Region, and the findings and recommendations of the Medical Examiner's office, the family would at this time decline to make any comment".[6]

The number of possible reviews external to the Region was starting to add up. The Minister of Health and Wellness mentioned the possibility of the College of Physicians and Surgeons of Alberta launching an investigation.[4] At the request of the Minister, the Health Quality Council of Alberta was also running its own review. The Minister was hopeful that investigations would be completed as quickly as possible. The government would then act on "any of the recommendations from the fatality review board regarding proper handling of this matter".[3]

Added to that list of investigations was an external review by the Alberta College of Pharmacists. The College had a legislated mandate under the Pharmaceutical Professions Act to investigate any errors in the dispensing of medications brought to the attention of the College. The aim was to look for any contributing factors and what needed to be done to avoid similar events anywhere in the province. This review was carried out on April 1st and 2nd. A Pharmacist and the Deputy Registrar of the Pharmacy toured the Central Pharmacy and met with the Director of Pharmacy and the Central Pharmacy staff to discuss the mix-up. They would then report back to the College Registrar.

There had also been discussions between the Registrar of the College of Pharmacists, the Region, the Minister of Health and Wellness, the Health Quality Council of Alberta, and the Canadian Patient Safety Institute. The Pharmacy College's approach was described by its Registrar as working "independently, but in co-operation with the other reviews". The outcome and recommendations from that review would then be shared with the public.[7]

A columnist raised a pertinent point. The "key question" was not "who made the mistake", but why the Region "allowed medications so likely to be confused to be stored in the same area, directly across an aisle from each other". He added a truth rarely acknowledged then in healthcare. When things were bad financially, "systemic problems" were "rarely fixed". Cuts in budgets focused administrators' minds on coping, and not on an accident that had yet to occur....[8]

Jack offered both agreement and a promise to make improvements to what were "increasingly demanding tasks". Procedures were complex and despite being completed perfectly "10,000 times" in the past, there was a "breakdown", which could be seen with "20–20 hindsight". Now the Region needed to review every process, every step. "We absolutely will get to the bottom of this.[9]"

After consideration, the Chief Medical Examiner decided not to refer the two cases to the province's Attorney General. There would not be a Fatality Inquiry.

However, an External Review was commissioned by the Region. The Region's Board Chair detailed that the lead individual on the review was the Director of Patient Safety at the Winnipeg Regional Health Authority. Working with him were two other external experts: a senior Pharmacist and a Human Factors expert. The aim of the review was to give the Region an external point-of-view of the Region's procedures, related to the safety of its patients. The review was to include how the Central Pharmacy operated, and how medications were prepared and then distributed.[10] The Terms of Reference stated that "Upon the conclusion of the review, the Region intend[ed] to make the results a matter of public record. The results [were to] be released to the Board and families of the deceased immediately prior to public release".[11] With the review due to start on April 1st the following week, the Board Chair, in a published statement, also promised the Region would make public the report, as well as act on the recommendations.[1]

An Editorial the next day welcomed the appointment of a national health-care safety expert to the external review. The authors, though, cautioned the investigation must be both complete and independent. They considered this would not be possible because the External Review expert, in reporting to the Region, would be required "to act in accordance with the mandate" given to him by the Region. That would make independence impossible.[12]

Systems, Systems Thinking and Investigating

Healthcare practitioners have a centuries-old history of investigating what happened to their patients – as they have tried to learn why treatments did or did not work, and why their patients improved, lingered, or died. Much of this investigation has focused solely on the patient and what happened, and much less on the myriad of possible factors that might have influenced the course of the illness or injury. To help describe these two basic approaches, we first explain systems, what they are, how they can be described in the form of a model, and why they are important in investigations and a Just Culture. We then review two linked approaches to investigations, both used when patients are harmed or nearly harmed. The first describes how to look at the system, in contrast to focusing on the person. The second outlines the necessary systematic approach to assessing individuals, within the context of system factors. We also link the concepts of systems and their investigations to a Just Culture.

Systems

We use the term 'system' quite commonly and across many different domains, including engineering, computer and software technology, social sciences, business, and biology, to name a few. To facilitate our discussion of healthcare systems, and how the concept of a system applies to a Just Culture, we start by defining systems.

To do so we go back to the mid-1950s, when the concept of General Systems was first developed. Two of those involved in this work were Arthur D. Hall, an American engineer, who coinvented the picture telephone in the early 1960s, and Dr. R.E. Fagen, a pioneer in high-speed computer systems. They defined a system as a "set of objects together with relationships between the objects and between their attributes".[13,14] In simple terms, what this often-referenced definition means is that a system has parts or components (the "objects"), which can be physical parts or abstract objects such as equations. These parts all have related properties (their "attributes").

We move forward to the 1960s and a definition provided by the Institute of Electrical and Electronics Engineers (IEEE) professional group in System Science and Cybernetics. They defined a system as "a large collection of interacting functional units that together achieve a defined purpose".[15] Thus, a system was made up of three main components, a set of things and/or rules ("functional units"), the way the things and/or rules were organized or interconnected, and a goal.

We now reach the twenty-first century and our final definition, from Dr. Donella Meadows, a Harvard-educated biophysicist. Pulling all the parts together, she defined a system as "a set of elements or parts that is coherently organized and interconnected in a pattern or structure that produces a characteristic set of behaviors, often classified as its function or purpose".[16]

Thus, in addition to its parts, their properties, and their interconnecting relationships, a system cannot be considered as such if it does not have its own inherent purpose. What this implies is that a system has functions or purposes distinct from its parts. Another interesting property of any system is that it can be subdivided hierarchically into subsystems, sub-subsystems, components, units, parts, and so forth. Any of these levels can be made up of objects, as a subsystem, component, unit, or part is an object in itself.

Different Types of Systems

There are a few ways we can describe and differentiate systems. Systems can be categorized as being natural or human-made, physical or conceptual, static or dynamic, closed or open, or discrete or continuous. The solar system is an example of a natural system, while the internet is an example of a human-made system. Physical systems are those containing physical objects and components, in contrast to a conceptual system, which is made up of concepts or ideas. Closed systems are isolated from their environment, as opposed to open systems that interact with their environment. A discrete system is one for which variables change instantaneously at separate points of time, while in a continuous system these variables are changing all the time. Some systems are neither completely discrete nor completely continuous and are therefore combined discrete-continuous systems.

We can also classify systems according to their complexity – simple, complicated, or complex. Simple systems are easily understood, as there is a single path to a single solution, with problems arising from an "expected production sequence".[17] Although complicated systems are more advanced than simple systems, they can still be deconstructed to identify their component parts and to be analyzed. They can also be controlled and may perform in a predictable way, for example, an engineered system. Complex systems are non-linear, do not have definable cause-effect pathways, and have multiple links and relationships between components. In complex systems there is "potential for unforeseen interactions to occur".[17] Systems with high levels of complexity have a high number of parts and a high number of system states, and because of these characteristics, they are difficult to describe and difficult to recreate.[18]

Complex adaptive systems are made up of many interactive parts that interact in different ways and have the ability to learn and to adapt,[18] with little central control.[19] The differing feature between complex systems and complex adaptive systems is the ability to adapt and to constantly change states or outputs resulting from changes in inputs. In complex adaptive systems, any single process within a system can be influenced by unseen factors or variables from both inside and outside the system.[20] The immune system is an example of a complex adaptive system. Our antibodies are highly mobile, responding to microbes and viruses that are constantly changing antigens, which antibodies (sometimes) recognize. To be effective, immune systems must constantly adapt to these changing inputs (antigens) by producing different antibodies, while also (hopefully) recognizing and not attacking our bodies.[19]

Coupling in Systems

Another way we can look at a system is by its coupling, which refers to the connection between components of a system and a system's responsiveness. This concept was borrowed from general systems theory (see above) by Dr. Robert Glassman, a psychologist and behavioral scientist,[21] and then from Glassman by Dr. Karl Weick, when he was a Professor of Psychology and Organizational Behavior at Cornell University.[22] A system that is tightly coupled means there is no slack or buffer and there are many time-dependent processes. What happens in one part of the system directly affects what happens in another part of the system. In contrast, loosely coupled systems are more flexible, have more slack, and have more than one way to achieve their goals.[17]

Coupling is particularly important when considering its application to safety. Loosely coupled systems have greater ability to make in-the-moment recoveries, while tightly coupled systems have fewer opportunities and must have buffers and redundancies designed into them for the sake of safety. The most dangerous systems are those that are both complex and tightly coupled.

How does this concept apply to healthcare? First, healthcare is a human-made system. It is complex, as well as dynamic and adaptive, meaning it is made up of many different interactive parts and is constantly evolving and changing. For example, the healthcare system includes patients and their families, individual healthcare providers, decision-makers, multiple health organizations with differing ways of doing things, and numerous regulatory agencies. All these components have multiple and dynamically changing interrelationships. In these dynamic and complex systems, patients, providers, and leaders "act locally, without knowledge of the system as a whole".[23] (This perspective has implications for investigations. During interviews of those involved, reviewers must bear in mind that multiple "different perspectives and worldviews exist",[23] even if they were all in the same room together at the same time.)

Furthermore, the healthcare system continues to change and evolve, often in unpredictable ways. In fact, healthcare's complexity is increasing, with increased specialization of personnel and organizations that use specialized equipment, technologies, and ever-improving methods.[20] Seeing healthcare as complex and dynamic, therefore, is central to effectively understanding and solving problems. From a quality and safety perspective, this means the "various dimensions of quality care are interconnected and thus interdependent".[20] Attempts to address one aspect of care, for example, by changing where and how pharmaceuticals are stored, could have a great effect on another part of the system, either positively or negatively. Recognizing healthcare is complex also has implications when choosing specific methodologies with which to analyze systems, such as root cause analysis and other linear or simple cause-and-effect approaches. These methods do not adequately address healthcare's complexity and hence are not strong analytical methods.

Systems Thinking

This concept is about understanding systems, the various types of systems and how they perform, and then applying this knowledge to address problems. Systems thinking is characterized by "identifying the multiple system goals and elaborating upon both its elements and the interconnections between these elements".[20] It involves understanding the structure of the system, the behaviors, and the inter-relationships between the system elements, as well as the goals and outcomes.

One well-respected author on systems thinking is Dr. Peter Senge, who was a Senior Lecturer at MIT when he described his belief that organizations had too great a focus on events, with less attention paid to patterns of behavior, and even less to system structure.[24] To effectively solve problems, he argued, organizations needed to focus on the *structure* of the system because it is at this level the underlying causes of behavior could be addressed. Senge's thinking aligned with Donabedian's Quality Triad of Structure, Process, and Outcome, with both identifying structure and patterns of behavior aligning with process and events equating to outcome. (Donabedian's Quality Triad will be described further in this chapter.)

The concept of complexity theory, or complex systems theory, is one that has gained popularity in many domains, including healthcare. Although complex systems are described above, 'complex systems theory' is not the study of 'complexity'. Rather, it is about understanding the behavior of systems – how they evolve, learn, and adapt. The theory also recognizes that problems are difficult to understand and solve because of complex system behavior.[18] Complex systems theory implies that simple cause-and-effect approaches to understanding problems do not work. Instead, the theory provides an analytical approach, which can be seen as a "model for thinking about the world". However, we have minimal empirical evidence to substantiate this theory as an approach that is more beneficial than others.[25]

Analyzing Systems

Systems analysis goes back many decades, emerging from Operations Research (OR) used in World War II. OR employed mathematical models as the basis for decision-making, often favoring integrated solutions, over those for isolated components of a problem.[26] In 1948, the Rand Corporation of America developed systems analysis under Dr. Edwin Paxton, a mathematician, whose "goal was to select 'next generation atomic bombs and aircraft'". Paxton considered that the costs of problems should be considered, to ensure consistent budgeting costing,[27] and included economists in the team of mathematicians and engineers. Systems analysis was described as providing a "framework for combining the knowledge of experts in many fields to reach solutions which transcend any individual expert's judgment".[28] Systems analysis was then adopted by other corporations, including General Electric, for air weapons systems analysis.[29]

A few years later, Deniston, Rosenstock, and Getting, of the University of Michigan School of Public Health, applied systems analysis to evaluation of programs in Public Health.[30] They were interested in assessments of the "appropriateness, adequacy, effectiveness, and efficiency" of various programs. The next year, Joseph Bower, a Professor of Business Administration at Harvard, considered the "revolutionary" application of systems analysis to social problems, describing it as employing models to clarify "input-output interactions that characterize the elements of a problem".[31]

Models of the System

To understand a system, and to analyze it, we need to start with a model. It therefore seems fitting to begin by quoting Professor George Box and Dr. Norman Draper, two British statisticians, who worked at the University of Wisconsin–Madison. They famously said "all models are wrong, but some are useful".[32] Because a model is a simplified representation of a system, inaccuracies will result from this simplification. Additionally, we all have hidden "assumptions and biases", some of which may negatively affect our modelling and its usefulness. Thus, successful systems thinking requires accepting that our models are wrong and having "humility about the limitations of our knowledge".[33]

One of the issues in analyses or investigations in healthcare is either the lack of a model to guide the analysis or use of an insufficient model, one that is quite wrong, and/or one that is not useful. The latter sometimes occurs when frameworks or methodologies from non-healthcare industries are applied to healthcare without appropriate modification to account for application to a radically different system.

The model we use for healthcare analysis, and to which we refer in this book, is the Winnipeg Model. This is a human factors model, which has been applied to many different healthcare investigations, reactively and proactively, and to investigations of one or multiple patients. JMD developed this model in the mid-1990s when working on a project requiring systematic classification of babies' deaths. The model was further developed for the Pediatric Cardiac Surgery Inquest, Winnipeg, Manitoba,[34] for which she was an Expert to the Crown in Human Error and Human Factors Analysis.

The Winnipeg Model was based on three previously existing models. The first of these was Professor Avedis Donabedian's 1966 model of Quality Assurance in health care, which he developed five years after he arrived at the University of Michigan at Ann Arbor. Donabedian was trying to describe and evaluate the then-current methods to assess the quality of healthcare, specifically the quality of care provided by doctors in their interactions with patients.[35]

Donabedian came up with his now-famous triad of Quality Assurance, formed by Structure, Process, and Outcome. To Donabedian, the Structure part of healthcare included the facilities in which care was provided and any associated equipment and their adequacies, the organization and qualification of the doctors, and the components of the administration and defined operations of the organizations providing care. Process represented the practice of medicine, from taking a history and performing a physical examination, to providing some form of treatment, and coordinating ongoing care. Outcome included patients' recovery, restoration of function they might achieve, and their ultimate survival. Also important to this triad of components was the concept linking the three: an "unbroken chain of antecedent means followed by intermediate ends which are themselves the means to still further ends".[35] Although Donabedian did not explicitly state it, this linking concept could be considered to tie Structure, Process, and Outcome together for the lifetime of a specific patient or even a group or population of patients, as they journeyed through the healthcare system. That healthcare was a system, and should be considered from that point of view, was also important in Donabedian's thinking.[35]

The second model incorporated into the Winnipeg Model was Reason's 1990 original "human contributions to accidents" model. This showed relationships in a complex system between these contributions and an organization's "basic elements of production".[36] Reason had described the "unsafe acts" that personnel committed, the "active failures" of any worker, especially frontline personnel interacting with various equipment or other components of the system. Traditionally, these individuals were thought to be the "principal instigators of system breakdown". Their actions seemed to interact with "local events", which many observers and investigators of the time considered sufficient to trigger an accident. But other factors were required. What made Reason's model exciting and provoking of an AHA! reaction, was his reaching back into the history of the organization. That was where the accident's precursors, the "fallible decisions" and "line management deficiencies" or "latent failures", made even decades previously, were to be found. In fact, to Reason, these latent failures were like "resident pathogens", lurking in the organization's structural crevices, and waiting to erupt into a cancer-like condition, should the numbers of pathogens increase and the organization be beset by stressors, breaking down its system defenses. Then, these "inadequate defenses" would be seen operationally as they failed to stop the progression that was the sum of all the contributory factors. With this model, Reason proposed that workers were not the primary instigators they were previously thought to be.

Starting in the early 1980s, JMD had been working on a method to improve investigations of deaths and other healthcare complications. From the late 1980s, one of the coauthors on that work was Dr. Rob Lee, a psychologist and Director of the (then) Bureau of Air Safety Investigation (BASI) in Canberra. He had obtained a copy of Reason's 1990 paper[36] and almost demanded she read it *immediately*. Like Lee, she saw the applicability of concepts in Reason's model to investigations. An international phone call later resulted in a working collaboration between Reason and JMD. Not long after, a patient died in the Operating Room in the FMC, before the start of the operative procedure. Fingers were pointed at the anesthesiologist. But having incorporated concepts from Reason into what was now a systems analysis investigation methodology, JMD and Reason, and another departmental anesthesiologist, Chris Eagle, were able to demonstrate many of the latent factors in the system. The patient and the anesthesiologist had unintentionally been set up for failure.[37]

The third model to be included in the Winnipeg Model was developed by Professor Bob Helmreich, a psychologist at the University of Texas at Austin, who was doing pioneering work in aviation safety, particularly in the area of Crew Resource Management. In 1990–1991, Helmreich had been the Expert to the Crown in Human Factors, crew resource management, and aviation accident investigations for the Commission of Inquiry into the Air Ontario Crash at Dryden, Ontario.[38] For the Inquiry he had developed a model showing how flight crews' behaviors were influenced and determined by four "simultaneously operating factors". These factors or "environments" were those of the "crew environment", "physical environment", "organizational environment", and "regulatory environment".[39]

What made Helmreich's model innovative and groundbreaking was formal inclusion of the "regulatory environment" as one of the contributing factors in an aviation accident in Dryden, Ontario.[39] This had not been done before and reflected the decision of Justice Moshansky, the Inquiry's Commissioner, and a pilot himself. From the beginning of the Inquiry, he had "anticipated possibly having to investigate" the role of the Canadian Department of Transport. He therefore insisted responsibility for the Inquiry be transferred from the Office of the Minister of Transport to the Privy Council to ensure and demonstrate investigative independence. He was also provided by the Government of Canada with a "broad mandate" to "permit an unbridled inquiry into the entire aviation system, in a search for systemic failures contributing to the crash". The regulator was therefore a contributory factor in the deaths of the twenty-two passengers and crew who died in the crash.

This outward extension of contributory factors in an accident – away from the personnel, where they worked and the equipment with which they interacted – was also novel in healthcare. JMD thought adding Helmreich's model to those of Donabedian's and Reason's would provide an additional dimension that was lacking. But there was one component missing in Helmreich's model, that of the passengers, and JMD saw parallels between passengers in aviation and patients in healthcare.

The Winnipeg Model therefore consisted of five basic factors. These were the people for whom the healthcare system provided care and their families; the personnel who provided the care; the environment(s) in which the care was provided, coupled with the equipment used; the organization(s) involved, including their administration (leaders); and the regulatory agencies involved, also including their administration (leaders) at civic, provincial and federal, and even international levels.

Each of these factors was considered to exist along the "arrow of time",[40] which also linked Donabedian's Structure, Process, and Outcome. Reason's "latent failures",[36] renamed by JMD as "latent factors",[40] were found in Structure, and the renamed "active factors" in Process, together with "local influencing factors" (previously "local triggering conditions"[36]). These latter factors were important in considering context when reviewing the actions and behaviors of both patients and personnel.

Investigating in Healthcare

Having reviewed systems and their models, we now move to using these concepts when investigating events in which our patients are harmed or nearly harmed. There are two basic approaches to conducting a review – using a person oriented review or a system oriented. Such reviews may also be conducted internally, externally, or in some situations, both.

A person oriented is used to understand an individual's decisions and actions, to categorize the types of actions, and to assess how they could have contributed to the outcome. Assessments of individuals may be done internally by the organization, or externally by a regulatory agency, for example, a professional regulatory organization. This type of review, however, is not always required. It may be necessary when there are concerns about performance or extreme behavior, in the form of personally-motivated rule-breaking or sabotage. The outcome of these investigations may be sanctions or discipline of individual(s). (We describe these in more detail later in this chapter.)

System oriented reviews are conducted to identify system contributions, which are then addressed to mitigate future harm to patients. It is always important to conduct this type of review when patients have been harmed, as such untoward outcomes present opportunities to understand how the entire system was functioning – or not. As clearly described by Professor Charles Vincent, then at Imperial College School of Science, Technology and Medicine in 2004, "The incident acts as a 'window' on the system",[41] helping show investigators what that small part of the system resembled at the time of the event. What a systems perspective gives investigators is the ability to conduct analyses without reducing the study of a system to the study of its parts in isolation.[26] This is vital, not just so that each of the parts can be seen in the context of the whole system, but also because, as Rasmussen explained, a "system is more than the sum of its elements".[42] Dissection of the system into its parts, without considering their integration, means important, linking information will not be discovered. Once investigations are completed, their results contribute to recommendations for system improvement. Investigations are therefore not simply just to understand how the event unfolded, they must be taken one step further to identify and recommend fixes to the system.

Internal Versus External Reviews

There may be reasons to consider having a review conducted by individuals from outside or by an external organization. This may be necessary, for example, if the organization does not have individuals with the training, experience, and skillset required to perform a high-quality review, a situation that remains unfortunately true in healthcare.[43,44] However, an organization may choose to commission an external review, despite having the ability to conduct its own. In these situations, the intention of the external review and its focus on the system should not differ to a review done internally by the organization. Reasons for an external review include seeking an external opinion, to gain a perspective that could be different than that seen from inside the organization. Another reason is to assure others, such as the public, that the review was objective and independent from the organization. As noted by Professor Carl Macrae, of the Centre for Health Innovation, Leadership and Learning, University of Nottingham, and Dr. Kevin Stewart, Medical Director, Healthcare Safety Investigation Branch, externally run safety investigations can help alleviate concerns of bias from those affected by the event, the public, the media, and other critics, as well as help ensure the results are not used for any punitively oriented purposes.[44]

In the Region's example, having reviews performed by different external groups served several purposes. These included ensuring objective analyses, garnering respected external opinions about safety, and building trust with families, the public, and the media.

Investigations may also be carried out by regulatory agencies, as part of their role and mandate related to accountability and/or safety. Accountability-driven investigations should always be done separately and independently from reviews looking at system safety. Examples of regulatory reviews include those conducted by a professional regulatory body, for example a provincial, state, or national/federal College of Physicians and Surgeons.

System Oriented Review: Systematic Systems Analysis

When conducting system oriented reviews in healthcare, we apply the Winnipeg Model using the Systematic Systems Analysis (SSA)[45] approach that JMD originally developed, that the three authors have used for a multitude of reviews,[46] and that JMD and CS teach and mentor to individuals and organizations. Using the Winnipeg Model and its associated SAFER Matrix[©47] helps ensure all parts of the healthcare system – patients and their family, personnel, equipment and environment, the organization, and regulatory agencies – are considered in the analysis, as well as in recommendations for improvement. This is what is meant by a systems analysis. The Winnipeg Model has therefore avoided the problem identified with many other models used in accident investigation, with their focus "almost exclusively on the potential for human error at the sharp end of systems operation", failing to consider "other levels of the system, including supervisory, managerial, regulatory and government levels".[48]

The approach is also systematic, meaning that it is methodical, contributing to ensuring important things are not missed. The Winnipeg Model considers the complexity of healthcare, helping us to understand how the components of the system dynamically interact and contribute to an outcome. This systems approach differs from other commonly used approaches, such as Root Cause Analysis, that were derived from industry and are linear in nature. As Professor Sidney Dekker, of the School of Humanities, Languages and Social Sciences at Griffith University, Brisbane, said so precisely, "What you call the 'root cause' is simply where you stop looking any further".[49]

Thus, when reviewing what happened to a patient, we refer to investigating within the context of system factors, meaning the review should uncover as much information as possible about the five system components. Additionally, we need to understand the decisions and actions of other personnel, to integrate how all these factors could have influenced the patient's outcome. Using a systems approach such as this, to frame and describe what happened to a patient, acknowledges that healthcare delivery is complex. The approach also shifts the spotlight from one or a few healthcare providers, onto the entire healthcare system. Since we find it is often challenging, if not impossible, to know 'what caused what' directly, regardless of how proximal or how tightly coupled a specific action of a healthcare provider might appear to be to a patient's outcome, this approach uses the language of contributing factors. Because the terms cause and blame are often closely associated, we believe that by eliminating the use of the former term, the likelihood of inappropriately defaulting to blaming an individual is reduced.

To make improvements to care, we need to understand how the entire system contributed. At one end of the spectrum, harm can sometimes be almost entirely related to the patients' own factors – their age, underlying disease(s), medications, and overall frailty, to name a few. Patients could have also contributed to the event with decisions they made and actions they took or did not take. (Stating this is not intended to blame the patient but to recognize the contribution of each component that went into the event leading to harm.) At the other end of the spectrum, the four remaining groups of factors might have predominated, and provided such overwhelming factors that those of the patient represented a negligible contribution. In general, though, in the majority of situations in which patients are harmed, we find there is usually some contribution from each of the five factors, although the proportion of each contribution varies widely.

The philosophy of SSA encompasses five main points. First, investigations are conducted, if appropriate, in accordance with applicable legislation that relates to healthcare evidence gathered to improve the *quality of care* of medical, hospital, or related transportation care. For places with this legislation, information gathered in the course of an investigation conducted under the legislation cannot be used in the course of a legal action. Second, investigations do not review the performance of specific providers or patients, with all individuals de-identified from the beginning, to reduce positive or negative bias. Third, there is no search for errors or violations and no judgments, including that of negligence, are passed on any individual's decisions and actions, nor on avoidability or preventability of the outcome. Fourth, investigations do not result in any disciplinary actions against anyone involved and review of individuals' performance is conducted separately and independently. Fifth, the purpose of the investigation is to produce practical recommendations aimed at the system level deficiencies discovered during the course of the review and not aimed at any individuals.

SSA has three main phases, conducted by a few trained investigators, and excluding any of the staff who provided the care, to ensure objectivity. In Phase 1, information is collected by gathering details from the patient's healthcare record, talking first with the patient and/or family, to learn what happened to them and seek their input on which changes should be made with respect to the care received. This is followed by interviewing others directly and indirectly involved in the event, using the Cognitive Interview technique.[50] Where possible, information is acquired from multiple other sources. From this information, a Timeline is developed.

In Phase 2, answers to three questions are sought. What happened to the patient? How did it happen? Why did it happen? These three questions align with Donabedian's Outcome, Process, and Structure, respectively. Collected information is then analyzed for system deficiencies in each of the five components of the system, using the SAFER Matrix™, the analytical tool of this Phase.[47]

Phase 3 is that of recommending improvements. System deficiencies identified in Phase 2 are linked to future improvements at the system level, recognizing the dynamic interconnectedness of all the system factors. Recommendations are devised to explicitly describe the improvements and required actions.

Person Oriented Reviews

Incident Decision Tree

Based on work that Reason did on his "decision tree for discriminating the culpability of an unsafe act",[51] Sandra Meadows and Karen Baker, both with a background in Human Resources, and Jeremy Butler, an aviation Human Factors expert and a Non-Executive Director of the UK's National Patient Safety Agency (NPSA), developed the Incident Decision Tree (IDT) for the NPSA and then NHS England.[52] The aim of the IDT was to define where the line lay between the acceptable and unacceptable behaviors to which Reason had referred.[51] Meadows and her colleagues set up the IDT with a series of structured questions. These were to help managers decide if suspension of a healthcare provider was essential or if alternatives might be possible and feasible.

Users of the IDT were encouraged to first consider if the harm was deliberate, before considering if the individual being assessed could have been affected by substance abuse or an underlying medical condition. The third part of the assessment questioned if an individual had taken an unacceptable risk, which can be an extremely difficult question to answer, when temporally and geographically removed from the context of the actions. Should there have been affirmative responses to any of those questions, the IDT process recommended a user consider various options, some of which had a disciplinary tone. In each case, the individual being assessed was encouraged to consult a union representative. Although this approach helped to describe what unacceptable behavior looked like, it did not address what the actual repercussions might be, or if they would be influenced by the severity of patient harm.

For a healthcare worker though, the bigger concern with the IDT was the order of the questions, which made it appear as though the person being assessed was presumed guilty of a punishable action until shown to be innocent. (We appreciate that the IDT was developed in the UK shortly after Dr. Harold Shipman, the serial killer, was apprehended (in 1998), tried, and found guilty. We understand the enormous effect his crimes had on the country and the medical and judicial systems.) A variation on the UK IDT, published by the Institute for Healthcare Improvement, followed the same logic of first looking for problems with the individual.[53] Neither approach included a review of other system components, or the effect any system factors could have had on the individual's decisions and actions, or directly on the patient's outcome, before reaching a decision about culpability.

More recently, the NHS has updated the IDT to the "Just Culture Guide", the aim of which is to support "consistent, constructive and fair evaluation". The guide is not intended to be used routinely, rather, when an investigation brings a suspicion that the individual requires support or intervention to work safely. The first question is a *deliberate harm test*, which is then followed by a *health test* to determine if there are concerns about the worker's mental or physical health or substance use. From there the guide moves the manager (investigator) on to a *substitution test*, followed by a *foresight test*. Finally, the manager is cued to determine if there were any mitigating circumstances. In addition, an investigator is instructed to assess "one action (or failure to act)" at a time, using the guide and repeating the process if there are multiple actions to be assessed. While there are obvious improvements of this version[54] over the previous one, the guide still starts with the question of intent to harm, with a health check coming later in the process. We also have concerns with the picking apart of an event, looking at the details of discrete actions or inactions. First, when we provide care, we often do not think of each separate step but of a collection or bundle of things that must be done or not done. Second, judging individual steps in a sequence could potentially sway the review one way or the other, because of the ever-present problems of faulty, overwritten memories and all-too active hindsight bias. Therefore if discrete actions are looked at, this should be done within the context of system factors, including preceding and subsequent actions of the individual and other players.

Systematic Individual Assessment

In contrast to these and other methods, our preferred approach is that of Systematic Individual Assessment (SIA), which the three authors developed.[55] Similar to SSA, SIA also employs the Winnipeg Model to ensure the system is taken into context when assessing an individual's decisions and actions. This is important when being just. Healthcare systems, which include regulators, need to commit to healthcare workers that the system and relevant factors will be considered before any decisions are made about discipline.

Additionally, it is important to ensure the individuals under review are actually responsible for their actions, before determining if they should be held accountable. The IDT approach did "not seek to diminish health care professionals' individual accountability". Rather, use of the tool was to help managers "consider systems and organizational issues in the management of error".[52]

There is a clear distinction, though, between responsibility and accountability. For an individual to *have* responsibility means that the person is deemed able to complete the task to a certain level of performance, that is, to carry out the actions and behaviors required. For an individual to *be* accountable, the individual is required to ensure that the task is actually completed as required and that the results of the task match those desired. Lastly, accountability cannot be assigned to an individual with no responsibility, thus requiring consideration and determination of responsibility before that of accountability. With that distinction made, we now move to the process of conducting a Systematic Individual Assessment (SIA).

With SIA, the first task is to check on the individual's well-being, and if necessary, connect them with help before a formal assessment is even started. The assessor needs to determine if the individual is psychologically well enough to safely continue providing care for patients and to proceed with a formal assessment. If they are not well enough, both a return to work and the assessment should be postponed until the individual can be helped and has improved.

In an SIA there are three fundamental decisions to be made. Each decision is preceded by a step of collecting, organizing, or analyzing relevant information. Decision One asks if the assessment should proceed. Again, information is collected from the chart, interviews, and other sources, and organized into a chronology of events. This provides the lens through which an assessor can view the decisions and actions of the individual. If the information suggests an individual may have been impaired in any way, either as the result of a medical condition or the use of a prescribed drug or a prohibited substance, then an SIA is not the recommended approach. In this situation, a human resources specialist and/or the individual's professional regulatory body should be engaged.

The other question to address at this point is whether or not the individual's peers would likely have behaved similarly or not. Should the answer not be clear, then what is known as Johnston's Substitution test can be used,[56] which preferably involves at least two or more peers. This potentially gives an assessor a range of opinions about the tasks carried out, decisions made, and actions undertaken. Peers should have training and experience similar to the individual being assessed, as well as no obvious biases (such as a personal connection with the individual or patient), and not know about the case. (The latter might require peers to be coached to not consider the patient's outcome in their responses.) Additionally, peers should be given the same information the individual had, as well as the context of the situation, including system factors known at the time. The assessor asks peers a series of questions, including the usual way of doing things for the tasks and the specific workplace (which could vary), and the range of acceptable actions, including the context of the care delivered. Next, peers are asked for their opinions of the individual's decisions and actions. Questions should be open-ended and not leading, with peers coached as to there being no right answer, but told only what the individual did and how. The assessor is trying to determine if peers would have behaved any differently. Would the peers condone "work-as-imagined" or would they choose "work-as-done"?[57] If the answer were to be "work-as-done", then discipline should not be considered and no further assessment undertaken. If the answer is or possibly is "work-as-imagined", then the assessor moves forward to the next decision.

If peers would have behaved differently, then Decision Two is approached by asking if the individual's actions or inactions were unintentional, and/or if errors (in the form of slips, lapses, or mistakes) were made. In a Just Culture, individuals are not punished for making errors, nor is the degree of harm suffered by the patient taken into consideration.

Decision Three determines whether or not what the individual did was 'acceptable'. This step is undertaken if the actions or inactions were deliberate and deviated from acceptable ways of delivering care, thus meeting the broad definition of noncompliance (violations). This step is also undertaken in situations where an assessor is unsure about the proper classification of the actions/inactions.

To make the decision if actions were acceptable or unacceptable, two elements must be considered. The *first element* is the individual's motivation(s) underlying their decisions. The Dalai Lama once said that actions should not ultimately be measured by their success or failure, but by the motivation behind them.[58] Insight into an individual's motivations can be gained through interviews of those who were involved in the events, including the patient and any family members present. We need to understand if there are good reasons to believe that what the individual did had a reasonable chance of benefiting the patient(s). A follow-up question is who or what was more likely to benefit from the individual's actions or inactions. Sometimes an individual may be motivated by wanting to influence another part of the system, for example, to cut corners to gain efficiencies and more quickly move on to the next task (or next patient). If the answer was not the patient, and that it was for the benefit of the individual, then the individual's motivation was misplaced.

Next, an assessor considers the *second element* – the influence that system factors possibly had on the individual. This is not a quantitative evaluation based on the number of factors but rather a judgment of the forces affecting the individual at the time. Additionally, before reaching a final decision about whether or not actions were acceptable, an assessor should consider the four biases potentially influencing an individual's assessments and review the findings. These should be challenged and conclusions possibly adjusted, employing debiasing strategies.

For Hindsight Bias, the assessor should counsel interviewees to put aside (as much as possible) any knowledge they had of the outcome. The assessor should purposely think about what information the individual had when making decisions and undertaking actions, and how quickly events might have unfolded. Thus, the assessor should try to estimate how much pressure the individual was under to process information, make decisions, and possibly take actions rapidly, while recognizing the individual 'did not know what was coming'.

Combating the Illusion of Free Will requires the assessor to revisit conclusions about an individual's actions and decisions. The assessor should consider the possibility of being influenced by the belief that people can choose to be perfect or not.

With the Fundamental Attribution Error, an assessor can self-question if at any point during the assessment process they had been influenced by believing the individual did or did not do something – because of an underlying personality trait or character defect.

To overcome the Symmetry Bias, an assessor can review the assessment and substitute the patient's actual outcome with one in which the patient did not suffer any harm. After reflection, the assessor should self-challenge to see if the same conclusions would be reached.

At the end of the assessment, if the actions or inactions are found to be unacceptable, then the manager completing the assessment should evaluate the range of disciplinary options. These options should be titrated to the seriousness of the misguided motivations and not to the seriousness of the patient's outcome. In situations where actions or inactions were deemed to have been errors or acceptable noncompliance, there may be an indication for nonpunitive restorative actions. These represent an approach to protect and/or enhance an individual's future performance. Examples include treatment for a physical or psychological health condition; further physical, psychological or cognitive assessment; coaching, education, or training; or modification of the individual's job or practice in a temporary or permanent way, involving changing the scope, amount, timing (hours or shifts) or location of work, and assigned responsibilities. As the name implies, these responses are not considered punitive and are intended to assist the individual. It is important that it be made clear to the individual that it was the performance that was judged – and not the individual – and that the performance could be improved.[59] It is also important that organizations proactively determine and be clear about the difference between nonpunitive restorative actions and disciplinary actions, for which there is a well-recognized range.

When the Line Has Been Crossed

To further the pursuit of a Just Culture, healthcare systems must proactively communicate an approach such as this to their personnel and then be seen to be following the approach. The healthcare system, however, also involves regulators. There is little comfort to healthcare professionals if the organization, for which they work or with whom they have an appointment, follows one assessment philosophy while their professional regulator takes a different approach. One of the ways to help healthcare providers start to heal psychologically is to be able to assure them of the alignment of assessment approaches between organizations and regulators. This requires a commitment to cooperation that unfortunately is uncommon in most jurisdictions. Also required is a review of actions determined to cross the line – by both organizations and regulators – and what should next be done with the individual. Organizations and regulators that are able to do this are to be saluted, as this cooperation is a critical part of the quest for a Just Culture, and therefore a safety culture.

Restorative Justice

With such a commitment to cooperation, organizations and regulators could then work together to codevelop and institute what is termed *restorative justice*. This is a concept that originated, at least in English-speaking countries, in New Zealand and has spread from there to Australia, Canada, the United Kingdom, and the United States of America. In general terms, restorative justice "seeks voluntary participation in its processes, focuses on both victims and offenders in a conflict, and includes the 'community at large' as an important stakeholder in the effort to restore social harmony".[60] Restorative justice is half of a pair of legal concepts – retributive justice being the other half. In contrast to the social and reparative focus on the victim and offender of the latter, retributive justice refers to the "repair of justice through unilateral imposition of punishment", that is "proportional to the severity of the wrongdoing".[61] (This is the legal equivalent of the idea of the historic eye for an eye.)

In 2008, Wenzel and colleagues emphasized the importance in restorative justice of healing the hurt, of the victims, of the offenders to rebuild their "moral and social selves" and of the communities to mend "social relationships".[61] A decade later, Sydney Dekker and Hugh Breakey, at Griffith University, Australia, considered the intersection of Just Culture and both retributive and restorative justice in healthcare. They considered certain Just Culture approaches to be retributive,[62] providing answers to questions such as "Which rule has been broken?", "Who did it?", and "How bad is the infraction, and so what do they deserve?" They contrasted this approach with three restorative questions: "Who has been hurt?", "What are their needs?", and "Whose obligation is it to meet those needs?"[63]

We suggest that these concepts, in concert with those of Wenzel and colleagues,[61] are reflective of our philosophy in dealing with patients and families, and personnel after a patient has been harmed. Similarly, the principles underlying both the SSA and SIA methodologies and dealing with individuals whose actions have crossed the line (excluding those with intent to harm) as well as our broadened view of a Just Culture, which we introduce in Chapter 8, all support this more humane and moral way of providing better and safer healthcare.

Comparing Healthcare with Other Industries

Further inspiration for a more restorative approach can be seen if we compare the above approach to how other domains, in particular aviation, review the actions and behaviors of individuals who have crossed the line. We see three main differences – in rules versus guidelines, substance use, and intention of actions.

Rules Versus Guidelines

Responses to breaking rules are perhaps the most contentious. Industries other than healthcare, such as nuclear power, aviation, shipping, and rail, are highly regulated and rule-bound, as are all the branches of the armed forces. There are two distinct reasons for individuals in those industries to follow the rules. First, following them is considered the mark of a professional, who among other criteria, displays high levels of technical proficiency compounded by precise following and application of rules. Second, violations of rules can result in injuries and loss of life to those who break them, as well as to any associated individuals. Punishment and sometimes criminal charges may follow.

In contrast, healthcare probably appears completely unregulated, although this is a gross oversimplification. True, there are "fewer explicit rules than [in] other high-hazard industries".[64] However, there are many regulations, such as those for licensing or the issuing of practice permits to doctors, nurses, pharmacists, respiratory therapists, and various types of technicians. Hospitals have many policies and rules that govern staffing, the running of the clinical areas (such as operating rooms and laboratories), and the non-clinical departments (kitchens and where equipment is cleaned and disinfected equipment). Certain types of equipment, such as those used in radiation therapy for cancer patients, are subject to international regulations. What is missing in healthcare, however, is the high degree of specification applying to exactly how procedures are carried out, and which is found in other domains.

Healthcare does have standards, policies, and specific procedures, some with highly detailed protocols. But there are also guidelines, which is where perhaps, the largest difference lies. Guidelines were well-defined in a 1990 report edited by Drs. Marilyn Field and Kathleen Lohr of the US Institute of Medicine, as "systematically developed statements to assist practitioners and patients make decisions about appropriate health care for specific circumstances".[65]

Guidelines are part of Evidence-Based Medicine,[66] the basic idea of which is to translate new clinical evidence from Randomized Controlled Trials in clinical research into statements that can guide improvements in healthcare. The initial format was to include statements about care and evidence underpinning the statements. Current statements now include what the Cochrane Centre calls "Plain Language Summaries" (PLS), which use language, structure, and content standardized to facilitate readers' comprehension, as well as translation into other languages.[67]

At first there was resistance to guidelines, with some clinicians protesting they did not wish to practice *cookie cutter medicine.* The curious point, however, was that while standards required adherence, guidelines only suggested ('guided') what clinicians should do. Guidelines were descriptive and not prescriptive. Hospitals liked guidelines, as their use tended to decrease variability in patient care and sometimes decreased complications, improving outcomes. All this was happening in the 1990s, when Reason was writing about the Just Culture and violations and when, in North America at least, there was a crisis in malpractice coverage, with soaring premium rates. For some practitioners, especially in the specialties of neurosurgery and obstetrics, premiums were beyond their ability to pay, leading to loss of practitioners from healthcare. The addition of more and more detailed standards, as well as increasing use and development of guidelines, helped to bend the curve of the insurance costs downward, but of course this was not cause and effect, with many other contributing factors at play. Thus, the push to introduce more guidelines continued, despite the fact that these were still not rules.

While Clinical Practice Guidelines (CPGs) are meant to help guide clinical decision-making about the care to be provided *to* a patient, they are also intended to help clinicians and their patients work *together* through a process of shared decision-making. Doctors therefore have "flexibility and room for clinical judgement", which also makes it "difficult to state unequivocally that a violation has occurred".[64] This situation contrasts greatly with that on the flight deck. Aviation does not really have anything similar to CPGs. Additionally, once airborne, the Captain is in charge and certain rules apply to all the airplane's crew, which they (almost always) follow. Thus, there is an innate and large difference between the highly detailed procedural rules of aviation and other industries, and the detail-poor, judgment-rich guidelines of healthcare.

Substance Use

The first difference between our thinking and Reason's Culpability Decision Tree is how individuals with alcohol or drug dependencies are dealt with. Reason considered certain actions to be "egregious", with his examples including both sabotage and substance abuse. While we agree with including sabotage in a list of appalling actions that clearly crosses the line, we think including "substance abuse"[51] is less clear. However, we appreciate there are differing points of view about this concept, which depend on whether one works in aviation, industry, or healthcare.

In aviation and other industries, being under the influence of drugs or alcohol is explicitly prohibited by policies or regulations. For example, in Canada in 2019, the possession of small amounts of marijuana for personal use was decreed to no longer be a criminal act. Because of the Cannabis Act, Transport Canada changed its requirements about all personnel needing to be fit for duty. As a result, those working in aviation must not be under the influence of *any* substance that could impair the individual's abilities, because of the effect on aviation safety. The oil and gas industry is similar. Organizations set their own policies around alcohol and drug use, and many companies perform random testing of employees. In the event of an accident, it is common practice to run tests to determine if employees had alcohol or drugs in their bodies.

In contrast, substance use by healthcare providers is treated quite differently, depending on the country in which the individuals work. In Canada, the UK, New Zealand, and Australia, substance use (Substance Use Disorder or SUD) and alcohol use (Alcohol Use Disorder or AUD) are generally considered medical conditions. Although not condoned, these are initially treated as SUD or AUD. The individual using drugs or alcohol is provided with resources and referred for medical help, often coupled with a mandatory leave of absence and treatment. A review by Human Resources may be carried out. Programs are available through the regulatory bodies for most types of healthcare professionals, such as doctors, nurses, and pharmacists. Programs often include monitored return-to-work sessions and restrictions on scope of practice. Punitive and/or criminal charges are considered only in extremely rare situations, for example, if a substance abuser refuses to participate in restrictions on care, monitoring, or practice restrictions or is deliberately deceitful and uncooperative, despite treatment efforts. Of course, not punishing individuals who use substances does not apply to those who steal or otherwise divert anesthetic agents, sedatives, narcotics, and other medications from healthcare, for misuse by others.

The situation is not quite so clear in the USA, with its much larger population and more fragmented regulatory forces (at federal, state, territorial, local, and tribal levels). Substance use has been considered a crime for many decades and is treated as such, rather than as a chronic disease, as shown by the War on Drugs, passage of the Controlled Substances Act and establishment of the DEA – the Drug Enforcement Administration. Unfortunately, legislation or policies requiring punishment of healthcare substance users can make it difficult for those affected (or even their friends and family) to ask for help. As a result, substance use, and its possible effect on patients, will remain a hidden problem and an important system factor. However, in the past decade or so, opinion has been shifting and substance use is now becoming seen and treated more often in ways similar to that described in the countries listed above.

Intention of Actions

The third major difference concerns intentions when breaking rules. As described earlier in this chapter, understanding intentions is important when reviewing individuals. We think that intentions are formulated twice. The first is when the individual decides if any rules should be broken and the second when the individual then determines their intentions toward the outcome for the patient. Thus, when considering both intentions, with errors there is neither intention to break rules nor to create harm as an outcome. With violations, any intention to break one or more rules depends on the type of violation.

With what we call Structure-driven noncompliance (Reason's "situational violations") there is neither intention to break the rules nor to harm and indeed, Reason termed these "non-malevolent infringements" and "non-malevolent acts".[68] With both Process-driven ("routine") and Outcome-driven ("optimizing") violations, individuals intended to break the rules and also set their intentions for the outcome. While these intentions are for the good of the patient with Process-driven violations, once an individual has crossed the line to making Outcome-driven violations, then it may be difficult to determine from the individual what his or her true intentions were. Did the individuals choose their actions with their own well-being or desires as their primary concern, or did they put their patient first? When asked, many healthcare providers would say, "Of course, my primary concern was for my patient", even if it did not appear to be so. For example, the care provider who goes on break, and therefore delays administering a required and important dose of antibiotics, clearly does not have the patient's best interests at heart. Determining intention might be even harder with individuals found to have committed sabotage. For example, in 2000 Dr. Harold Shipman, a British primary care practitioner, was found guilty of murdering 15 of his patients, although he might actually have killed 250 patients. Despite the forensic evidence against him, he continued to deny his guilt until the day he died in jail by suicide. These are cases where clear agreement is required between organizations and regulators, including when to refer matters to the police.

In summary, systems thinking is an important concept in Just Culture. When healthcare providers are involved in events in which patients are actually or nearly harmed, a systematic review of the system should be undertaken. Additionally, an assessment of the individual's actions may be required. Healthcare organizations and regulators should use a common set of precepts to guide such assessments. This would help to engender healthcare professionals' trust that if they are involved in such an event, they will be treated fairly and similarly by both their organization and their regulator. Once established, the precepts should be openly communicated and discussed proactively and then (importantly) seen to be followed after an event, so as to establish the required trust. The precepts that a healthcare professional should expect are that any questionable actions will be assessed within the context of system factors, which will be understood by conducting a thorough, systemic, and systematic review of what happened. An assessor's possible biases should be considered and checked before any decisions are reached. Individuals under assessment will be treated with respect – they will not be named and shamed, and they will be offered support. Finally, the healthcare providers who had responsibility for the tasks under question will be expected to accept appropriate accountability for their action(s) or inaction(s). In the next chapter, we will complete the story of the potassium chloride events in the Calgary Health Region and the changes that were made as a result.

References

1. Tuer D. It is vital we learn from these mistakes. *Calgary Herald*. 2004 Mar 24;A3 (col. 4).
2. Olsen T. Hospital tragedies boost CHR critics. *Calgary Herald: Inside Politics*. 2004 Mar 19;A6 (col. 5).
3. Ferguson E. Grits seek independent investigation. Klein feels internal probe sufficient. *Calgary Herald: Tragic Error at Foothills*. 2004 Mar 19;A4 (col. 1).
4. Toneguzzi M. Two patients dead in tragic error at Foothills Hospital. *Calgary Herald*. 2004 Mar 19;A1(col. 6) & A4(col. 3).
5. Ward J, Mark M. Mar not interested in looking for blame. *The Calgary Sun*. 2004 Mar 19;5.
6. Richards G. Prowse made people "feel good". *Calgary Herald: Foothills Tragedy*. 2004 Mar 20;A4 (col. 6).
7. Toneguzzi M. Pharmacy inquiry results to be public. *Calgary Herald: City & Region*. 2004 Mar 25;B1 (col. 1).
8. Braid D. CHR's disclosure a hopeful sign. *Calgary Herald: Foothills Tragedy*. 2004 Mar 20;5 (col. 1).
9. Braid D. Pharmacy staff to answer for deaths. *Calgary Herald: Exclusive*. 2004 Mar 21;A1 (col. 1).
10. Toneguzzi M. National expert will investigate mix-ups. Health region vows to learn from fatal mistakes. *Calgary Herald*. 2004 Mar 24;A1 (col. 6) & A3 (col. 1).
11. Robson R, Salsman B, McMenemy J. External patient safety review. *Calgary Health Region*. 2004.
12. Keep it arm's-length. *Calgary Herald: Opinion*. 2004 Mar 25;A18 (col. 1).
13. Hall A, Fagen R. Definitions of system. In: von Bertalanffy L, Rapoport A, editors. *General Systems*. Ann Arbor: University of Michigan Press; 1956:18–28.
14. Marchal J. On the concept of a system. *Philos Sci*. 1975;42:448–68.
15. Rowe H. *Signals and Noise in Communication Systems*. London: D. Van Nostrand Co. Ltd.; 1966.
16. Meadows D. *Thinking in Systems. A Primer*. London: Earthscan; 2009.
17. Perrow C. *Normal Accidents: Living with High-Risk Technologies*. New York: Basic Books; 1984.
18. McCarthy IP, Rakotobe-Joel T, Frizelle G. Complex systems theory: Implications and promises for manufacturing organisations. *Int J Manuf Technol Manag*. 2000;2:559–79.

19. Holland JT. Complex adaptive systems. *Daedalus*. 1992;121(1):17–30.
20. Chuang S, Howley P. Systems thinking in healthcare: From theory to implementation. *Focus Syst Theory Res*. 2019;115–30.
21. Glassman RB. Persistence and loose coupling in living systems. *Behav Sci*. 1973 Mar;18(2):83–98.
22. Weick KE. Educational organizations as loosely coupled systems. *Adm Sci Q*. 1976 Mar;21(1):1–19.
23. Read GJ, Shorrock S, Walker GH, Salmon PM. State of science: Evolving perspectives on 'human error'. *Ergonomics*. 2021 Sep 2;64(9):1091–1114.
24. Senge P. *The Fifth Discipline*. New York: Doubleday; 1990.
25. *Evidence Scan: Complex, Adaptive Systems*. London: The Health Foundation; 2010 Aug. [cited 2022 Feb 9]. Accessed from: https://www.health.org.uk/publications/complex-adaptive-systems
26. Ryan AJ. What is a systems approach. *J Theor Sci*. 2008; arXiv preprint arXiv: 0809.1698.
27. Digby J. *Operations Research and Systems Analysis at RAND, 1948–1967*. The RAND C. Santa Monica: The RAND Corporation; 1989.
28. Hitch C. An appreciation of systems analysis. *J Oper Res Soc Am*. 1955 Nov;3(4): 466–81.
29. Precoda N. Air weapons systems analysis. *Oper Res*. 1956 Dec;4(6):684–98.
30. Deniston O, Rosenstock I, Van Getting V. Evaluation of program effectiveness. *Public Health Rep*. 1968;83(4):323–35.
31. Bower JL. Systems analysis for social decisions. *Oper Res*. 1969 Dec;17(6):927–40.
32. Box G, Draper N. *Empirical Model-Building and Response Surfaces*. New York: Wiley; 1987.
33. Sterman JD. All models are wrong: Reflections on becoming a systems scientist. *Syst Dyn Rev*. 2002;18(4):501–31.
34. Sinclair M. The Report of the Manitoba Pediatric Cardiac Surgery Inquest: An inquiry into twelve deaths at the Winnipeg Health Sciences Centre in 1994. Winnipeg, Manitoba; 1994. [cited 2022 Feb 9]. Accessed from: http://www.pediatriccardiacinquest.mb.ca/pdf/pcir_intro.pdf
35. Donabedian A. Evaluating the quality of medical care. Part 2. *Milbank Mem Fund Q*. 1966 Dec;44(3(suppl)):166–206.
36. Reason J. The contribution of latent human failures to the breakdown of complex systems. *Philos Trans R Soc London B, Biol Sci*. 1990 Apr 12;327(1241):457–84.
37. Eagle CJ, Davies JM, Reason J. Accident analysis of large-scale technological disasters applied to an anaesthetic complication. *Can J Anaesth*. 1992 Feb;39(2):118–22.
38. Moshansky VP. *Commission of Inquiry into the Air Ontario Crash at Dryden. Final Report*. Ottawa: Ministry of Supply and Services; 1992.
39. Helmreich RL. Human factors aspects of the air Ontario crash at Dryden, Ontario: Analysis and recommendations to the Commission of Inquiry into the Air Ontario crash at Dryden, Ontario. In: Moshansky VP, editor. *Commission of Inquiry into the Air Ontario Crash at Dryden. Final Report*. Ottawa: Ministry of Supply and Services; 1992.
40. Davies J. Application of the Winnipeg model to obstetric and neonatal audit. *Top Health Inf*. 2000;20(4):12–22.

41. Vincent CA. Analysis of clinical incidents: A window on the system not a search for root causes. *Qual Saf Health Care.* 2004 Aug 1;13(4):242–3.

42. Rasmussen J. Risk management in a dynamic society: A modelling problem. *Saf Sci.* 1997 Nov;27(2–3):183–214.

43. Vincent C, Carthey J, Macrae C, Amalberti R. Safety analysis over time: Seven major changes to adverse event investigation. *Implement Sci.* 2017 Dec 28;12(1). Doi: 10.1186/s13012-017-0695-4.

44. Macrae C, Stewart K. Can we import improvements from industry to healthcare? *BMJ.* 2019;364:11039.

45. Davies JM, Lange IR. Investigating adverse outcomes in obstetrics. *J Obstet Gynaecol Canada.* 2003 Jun;25(6):505–15.

46. Duchscherer C, Davies J. Systematic systems analysis: A practical approach to patient safety reviews. Calgary, Alberta: Health Quality Council of Alberta; 2012. [cited 2022 Feb 9]. Accessed from: https://hqca.ca/health-care-provider-resources/systematic-systems-analysis/

47. Davies J. Report on the Pediatric Cardiac Surgery Program. Winnipeg Children's Hospital. Pediatric Cardiac Surgery Inquest. Winnipeg, Manitoba; 1998.

48. Dallat C, Salmon PM, Goode N. Risky systems versus risky people: To what extent do risk assessment methods consider the systems approach to accident causation? A review of the literature. *Saf Sci.* 2019 Nov;119:266–79.

49. Dekker S. *The Field Guide to Understanding Human Error.* Aldershot: Ashgate Publishing Limited; 2014.

50. Edward Geiselman R, Fisher RP. The cognitive interview: An innovative technique for questioning witnesses of crime. *J Police Crim Psychol.* 1988 Oct;4(2): 2–5.

51. Reason J. *Managing the Risks of Organizational Accidents.* Aldershot: Ashgate Publisher; 1997.

52. Meadows S, Baker K, Butler J. The incident decision tree: Guidelines for action following patient safety incidents. In: Henriksen K, Battles J, Marks E, Lewin D, editors. *Advances in Patient Safety: From Research to Implementation.* Rockville: Agency for Healthcare Research and Quality (US); 2005. [Cited 2022 Feb 9]. Available from: https://www.ncbi.nlm.nih.gov/books/NBK20586/

53. Frankel A, Haraden C, Federico F, Lenoci-Edwards J. A framework for safe, reliable, and effective care. White Paper. Cambridge, MA: Institute for Healthcare Improvement and Safe & Reliable Healthcare; 2017. [Cited 2021 2022 Feb 9]. Available from: http://www.ihi.org/resources/Pages/IHIWhitePapers/Framework-Safe-Reliable-Effective-Care.aspx

54. A Just Culture Guide. National Patient Safety Agency's Incident Decision Tree. NHS England and NHS Improvement. NHS 0932 JC Guide A3. [Cited 2021 2022 Feb 9]. Available from: https://www.england.nhs.uk/wp-content/uploads/2021/02/NHS_0932_JC_Poster_A3.pdf

55. Flemons W, Davies J, Steinke C. Systematic Individual Assessment (SIA). Unpublished; 2021.

56. Johnston AN. Organizational factors in human factors accident investigation. *Proceedings of Sixth International Symposium on Aviation Psychology*, Columbus, OH, 1991:668–73.

57. Hollnagel E. Resilience engineering and the systemic view of safety at work: Why work-as-done is not the same as work-as-imagined. Bericht zum 58. Kongress der Gesellschaft für Arbeitswissenschaft vom 22 bis 24 Februar 2012. Dortmund: GfA-Press:19–24.

58. Goldstein J. *Mindfulness. A Practical Guide to Awakening.* Boulder: Sounds True; 2013:102.

59. Fuller R. Behaviour analysis and aviation safety. In: McDonald N, Johnston N, Fuller R, editors. *Aviation Psychology in Practice.* Aldershot: Ashgate Publishing Ltd.; 1994.

60. Chiste KB. Origins of modern restorative justice: Five examples from the English-speaking world. *UBC Law Rev* [Internet]. 2013;46(1):33–80. [cited 2022 Feb 9]. Available from: https://heinonline.org/HOL/LandingPage?handle=hein.journals/ubclr46&div=6&id=&page=

61. Wenzel M, Okimoto TG, Feather NT, Platow MJ. Retributive and restorative justice. *Law Hum Behav.* 2008;32(5):375–89.

62. Marx D. Patient safety and the "just culture": A primer for health care executives. Columbia Univ. 2001.

63. Dekker SWA, Breakey H. 'Just culture:' Improving safety by achieving substantive, procedural and restorative justice. *Saf Sci.* 2016 Jun;85:187–93.

64. Amalberti R, Vincent C, Auroy Y, de Saint Maurice G. Violations and migrations in health care: A framework for understanding and management. *Qual Health Care.* 2006 Dec;15(suppl 1):i66–77.

65. Field M, Lohr K. *Clinical Practice Guidelines: Directions for a New Program.* Washington, D.C.: National Academies Press; 1990.

66. Cochrane A. Sickness in Salonica: My first, worst, and most successful clinical trial. *BMJ.* 1984;289:22–9.

67. Plain language summaries of health evidence. Our Evidence. Cochrane. Trusted Evidence. Informed Decisions. Better Health. Cochrane Policy Institute. [cited 2022 Feb 9]. Available from: https://www.cochrane.org/evidence

68. Reason J. *Human Error.* Cambridge: Cambridge University Press; 1990.

Chapter 7

"Get Something Positive Out of This Tragedy."[1]

When the two patients died as a result of the potassium chloride mix-up, regional executives, a number of middle and frontline managers, and many healthcare providers were violently awoken from their delusion of acceptable care. The lethal events were characterized by some as catastrophic failures of a healthcare system. Additionally, the prospect of being in the crosshairs of politicians, the prolonged glare of media, and the intensity of public scrutiny for an undetermined period of time was not something any of the Region's executives wanted. The only thing worse would have been to have another catastrophic failure and to go through similar events a second time.

No one had wished to be on the front page of the local newspaper, especially not for what seemed like days on end. The Region had held its first press conference announcing the deaths of the two patients on Thursday, March 18th. Because the announcement was made in the afternoon, none of the newspapers that day were able to print anything about it. However, the next day, to those in the Region what felt like a media onslaught began. The coverage, almost all of it negative, continued for days on the papers' front pages or the front pages of their City sections. Columnists and editorialists provided their perspectives, which were unflattering and often directly to the point. These perspectives were rightly seen to reflect the reactions of the public – those whom the Region served.

Saturday, March 28th was Day 10 of the coverage. Although the title of the article on the front page did not seem negative, "Calgary isn't only city battling ER crunch",[2] readers from the Region were mentally braced for the cutting

DOI: 10.4324/9781003185307-8

words that might follow. On this day, however, the media's opinions seemed less critical. Overcrowding in the city's emergency rooms, while recognized as problematic, was not unique to Calgary, and the city's population had grown more than 10% in the previous four years.

The same day's paper also carried a reminder to its readership, describing the importance of what the Region had done when it informed external organizations that something bad had happened. In "Hospital deaths produce ripples across the country", the columnist described some of the responses from the Director of Pharmacy's email, sent out immediately once details of the mix-up were known. He'd written to other hospitals producing their own CRRT and related products. Responses of some centers were included. These ranged from feeling "heartsick for the families and professionals" and "double-checking (their) work as a result", to being "concerned" and meeting to discuss the problem, to having dealt with the problem a few years previously.[3]

Two days later there was finally some truly good news on the front page. The provincial government announced $82 million for healthcare facilities, of which $70 million was to go to the FMC to expand the emergency department, trauma services and ICU, and ten additional (staffed) beds for patients, with another twelve in 2005. (The Region had asked for 300 new beds.) A five-story addition to the FMC would be completed by then, with new ORs and special diagnostic imaging services. Two other city hospitals were to receive $7 million for expansion. Additionally, more money was allocated for the purchase of land in the southernmost part of Calgary for a fourth adult hospital. Jack was quoted as saying they were "comfortable" that the government understood their "priorities".[4]

All was then quiet on the media front until April 3rd, when an article appeared describing the External Review Team members, who had started their work two days previously. The team leader was an emergency room doctor and head of patient safety for another provincial health region. The two other members of the review team were a pharmacist and medication safety consultant, and an aviation accident human factors specialist. The lead was quoted as saying that an event such as the one in Calgary would shake the "confidence and trust the community places in the healthcare system", adding "No review or learning can undo the two recent deaths". He agreed with the Region's Board Chair, saying "any solace" they could give the two families would be in the team's "actions" in providing "concrete steps" and suggesting "improvements" to minimize such events in the future. He commented favorably on the Region's "openness" and "unfettered access to people and information". The team expected to release their report to the public by June. Importantly, he added he would not make "further public comment"[5] until then, using the approach employed at the time by aviation accident investigators.

The reporting of good news seemed to continue. One article, entitled, "Delectable delights for hospital patients" described a "revamped wellness menu" for patients. This new menu was apparently the start of trying to alter the image hospital food had conveyed in the past to patients, their families, and the public. Changes were based on research carried out in the Region from talking with and surveying patients. A patient service coordinator from one of the hospitals also commented that she and her colleagues saw "patients as partners in their wellness".[6]

A few days later, the Region's new integrated electronic diagnostic imaging system was highlighted. The "largest in Canada" at that time, the system stored patients' CT scans, X-rays, and reports digitally. The system was projected to save doctors hours of time in tracking down films. Doctors could also look at images with colleagues in different locations, immediately after the images had been created. The Region planned to institute the same system in its eight rural hospitals over the next year or two.[7]

Even an announcement that the Region would cut "80 positions" was seemingly greeted with equanimity. Admittedly, the announcement from the Region was metered by a projected cost saving of $11.1 million dollars. The decisions resulted from a review of administrative costs started the previous autumn. Recommendations included "criteria" for the "appropriate use of catering".[8] Although only a handful of meetings qualified for catering, for example, evening meetings that included volunteer patient and family advisors, the Region was determined to be careful about everything, including its budget.

However, the Region's Chief Operating Officer (COO) was appropriately cautious about the front pages. As a result, not long after the two patients died, he sent a directive to his VPs of Clinical Operations. He requested a list of issues or scenarios that could lead to the next serious or fatal event. The goal was to fix it before an event happened.

This initiative was announced on Day 35. Under the headline of "CHR safety review approved. Task group asked to identify patient hazards", the article described the aim of the review as essentially finding hazards that had not been previously identified. WF was interviewed and commented the Region had "always seen a need for patient safety" but it was vital to ensure an "atmosphere where staff feel comfortable to come forward and report concerns without the threat of repercussions". This atmosphere had previously been lacking in the Region. The Safety Task Group was a small working group, mandated by Jack and composed of senior clinical and operational leaders, led by the WF and the academic safety advisor. The Safety Task Group's review was to include looking at the Region's safety data, interviewing individuals, and also checking publications, including other organizations' safety reports. Jack considered "continued learning and open dialogue" to be important. He wanted an initial report from the Safety Task Group by May 31st, with a final report to include results of all reviews of the two deaths and a plan for safety for the Region.[9]

Thus, in the middle of managing the crisis, the Safety Task Group found itself taking a crash course in what was known as proactive safety management – looking for hazards before they could harm. The Region did not have a safety information system that might reveal where hazards existed in the system, or which ones were most likely to lead to harm.

The Safety Task Group then had to identify the mitigation strategies needed to manage the potential for harm that each hazard posed. Once the list had been created, the more challenging task was to develop an approach to prioritize dealing with each of the hazards. Which one or ones should be tackled first? Which could wait? This meant understanding each of the hazards more fully and evaluating their mitigation strategies. Those involved were committed to the tasks and believed in the concepts, but recognized how much work lay ahead.

What the COO received in response to his directive represented the best attempt by experienced administrators, senior clinicians, and the Safety Task Group. The reports highlighted the issues worrying these individuals. For some, items on their lists were those keeping them awake at night – and their lists were long. The COO needed to continue to be wary of the unseen hazards and of their grave potential for another tragedy that would then hit the headlines.

The headlines remained quiet about the Region for some time, but on June 10th, the media silence was broken. The front page of the City section read "Credibility is on trial", announcing "Calgary Health Region: Superbug Deaths" and "Authority insists it is open and honest". Comments by an opposition party politician about there being a "pattern of denial" were met with those from a Regional spokeswoman stating the Region had made "every effort to be accountable". However, the daughters of a woman, who died from "bowel complications" after in-hospital treatment for pneumonia, stated her hospital roommate had likely died of the same *Clostridium difficile* infection.[10] The CMO and the Medical Director of Infection Control and Prevention were interviewed and stated the current "upsurge" in cases was "not serious, not fatal and well under control".[11] Their position, however, was complicated by an article ("published online") on June 4th, 2004, in the *Canadian Medical Association Journal (CMAJ)* of a "CMAJ investigation", which described the problem in Calgary.[12,13] This story was then picked up by one of the national newspapers. News of deaths in Montreal and Calgary ran under that newspaper's succinct headline, "Virus kills dozens".[14] The CMO, when given the information, appeared "deeply embarrassed", stating he had not done "enough due diligence" when initially asked about the *C. diff* problem. He also promised, that if he found cases that appeared to be related to *C. difficile*, then he would "undertake to let the public know about it".[11]

One of these newspaper articles also rekindled the COO's concern about hazards and media exposure. The columnist commented that the Region was "going through an agonizing process" to determine what and how to inform the public,[11] but the headlines continued. On June 11th, the headlines shifted to the main front page, informing the public of a "Medical mix-up blamed in death".[15] This time the death was not in the Region but elsewhere in the province, with a healthy man given the wrong painkiller after an accident. Again the link was made to the potassium and sodium chloride mix-up, but the *C. difficile* investigation was also mentioned. This was the topic again on June 12th, as a local columnist stated that there had been two deaths from *C. difficile* in the Region, one in February and one in April. He also described the Region as having an illness, with "information blockage being the main symptom". Although the Region had a method to follow infectious disease cases, "top officials" were unaware of either death. The death of the patient in April had yet to be entered into the system, while the death of the patient in February was not entered "because it began in the community, not in hospital". The Region acknowledged there was a possibility that other patients could have died from *C. difficile*. The columnist added the "information illness" was "all too evident" and he hoped that the changes to top management, announced on the City front page would "start to cure it".[16]

Those headlining pages were indeed about a major change in the Region's Executive that would not take place until the September Labour Day weekend. The CMO was transitioning to the position of "Advisor to the President", with Jack commenting that the CMO had provided "leadership and vision". His replacement was not announced. The Senior VP responsible for Capital Planning and Development was retiring[17] and, in an article three days later, was laudably described as "Calgary's master builder".[18] His position was to be filled by the previous COO, who would also look after "People and Learning, and Strategic Business Alliances as Executive Vice-President". Additionally, the medically qualified CIO was elevated to a new position as "Executive Vice-President and Chief Clinical Officer" (CCO). In that role he would look after the "operational and Executive Medical Directors, and the Offices of the Chief Medical Officer, Chief Information Officer and Chief Nursing Officer".[17] The changes had been planned for months and were not connected with the deaths related either to potassium chloride or *C. difficile*.[19]

The headlines continued the next day when Jack was again interviewed, with "Health boss vows to improve" and "...they'll learn from mistakes" catching readers' eyes. The gist of the article was that the Region was truly committed to changing how it operated, including being "committed to telling the public" about everything that was going on. Jack asked the media, the public in general, and patients and their families to ask questions and to raise concerns. "Let's not be afraid of anything that can improve healthcare". He also expressed his concern the families of the two patients who died of *C. difficile* had not been told exactly what the medical problem was. Jack went on to describe the disclosure policy, one of the four new policies, stating it would provide descriptions of what patients and families and the public would be told. He also said the prompt response of the CMO and Head of Infection Prevention and Control to the reporter's questions was an attempt to assist the media and be as open as possible. He suggested that, on review of the situation, they should preferably have taken time to ensure they had all the facts before speaking with reporters.[19]

Jack also spoke out for the integrity of the Region's workforce, expressing his concern and dismay about the attitude the media took against the Region, in comparison to the other health regions in the province. "When a person dies in Red Deer after a medical mistake", then the newspaper described this as an "accident", Jack said. However, with our potassium chloride related deaths, the "first headline said we were killing people". He commented that this type of reporting was very hard on everyone who worked in the Region, and who were "being bounced around by these stories – thousands of ethical, dedicated people, whose only goal (was) to help people".[19]

And with that interview, the Region's front page position was over for the next two weeks.

The reappearance was triggered by the newspaper having obtained copies of previous reports about the need for a Central Pharmacy, a week before the anticipated release of the External Review Report. Cited as "exclusive" to the newspaper, again there were headlines, with "Health Region hoped to cut errors". The Central Pharmacy was described as being at the heart of the potassium-related deaths, despite having been touted two years previously when it opened as designed to "save money and possibly lives".[20]

The following day on June 27th, WF, as Chair of the Safety Task Group, was quoted in the newspaper as anticipating that they were "counting on" the External Review Report for recommendations "to make the system safer". His group had already put together some concepts the Region should be examining, and they were hoping the report would be "very open and frank". An opposition politician was also interviewed, stating "A well-done report properly acted on will help everybody".[21]

The External Review Report was actually released at a time when the province, as well as the country, was focused elsewhere. On Monday, June 28th, a federal election returned a landslide victory for the Liberal party, except in Alberta, where the results were solidly conservative. This matched the provincial government. The newspaper headlines the next day read, "Canada tilts left … but Alberta sticks to the right".[22]

On Wednesday June 30th, with headlines taken up by the election results, a more subdued headline offered readers the news of "Human error, flawed system led to drug mix-up deaths". The front-page portion of the article described the report as offering 66 recommendations.[23] In total, $2 million was to be spent by the Region on upgrades to acute care pharmacy facilities, where safety-related problems had also been found.[24]

A second article appeared on the front page of the paper's second section. There, the large headline, "Fatal flaws admitted" sat beneath a description of the error as being easy to make. The error was similar to "reaching for salt at the table and applying pepper to the food, but with far more deadlier consequences". The report detailed both human errors and a system in which there were a number of "hidden or latent weaknesses or system design failures".[1]

Responses to the Report from the Region's Board and Executive were highlighted. The Board's Chair likened the report to a "road map" leading to a positive outcome of the tragedy. The organization was "accountable" to learn from the tragedy and become a "better organization". Jack mentioned that the Region already had a "number of initiatives to try to minimize such an event from happening again".[1]

The report also uncovered a missing "central issue". This was a policy describing how staff involved in "healthcare system failures" would be dealt with by the administration.[1]

Fortunately, changes to the bricks and mortar of the Region were not the only improvements, with a never before recommendation made for a safety-related change at the Executive level of the Region. WF told the press a "framework for patient safety" would be established. This was to include a Vice-President level position for an individual who would be both responsible and accountable to the CEO. Each of the Region's five portfolios would have a "clinical safety committee", reporting to a region-wide safety body. The Region's already-established Safety Task Group was assigned another important task, that of reviewing the External Review Report's recommendations and conveying that review to the Region's Board in the autumn.[24] The Safety Task Group would then take over the work, overseeing the massive changes to be made, as well as reviewing the Region's approach to patient safety and developing recommendations to improve the approach.

At the Press Conference held to discuss the External Review, WF had cautioned those present that there was "no guarantee" against another mix-up. His words recalled what the Region's Board Chair had sagely advised after the reports of the initial investigations into the two deaths. "As much as I would like to promise that mistakes will never happen again, I cannot. We are dealing here with the frailties of human judgment and human activity. However, we must do everything possible to make our system safe and as much as possible take the frailties of human error out of the system".[25]

The Region knew all too well that promising patients and families a problem had been *prevented* and would *never* recur was a very poor idea. Experience in the Region and elsewhere had shown that after a bad outcome, most patients and/or families asked what was going to be done to *prevent* the same thing from happening to someone else. Such promises, made to a patient, a family, and the public were found to be hollow statements if what had been promised had not been carried out, or if there were to be another, similar event. Should either occur, then any trust that had been restored after the event was lost, probably not to be regained.

That had indeed happened in Calgary. Two days after the first Press Conference in March, a newspaper article described a mix-up between potassium and heparin (a blood thinner) made in 2000. A written statement dated June 28, 2000, from the previously named "Calgary Regional Health Authority" said: "It is our belief that issues surrounding the similar labeling of the heparin and potassium will in fact be changed so that incidents such as this will be averted in the future. We want you to rest assured that we do respect the serious regard of this incident and that we will continue to make every effort to mandate the changes necessary in the future".[26]

A family member of one of the previous mix-ups made a statement to the press, describing her heartbreak to learn of more victims, as well as her shock and frustration. She and her mother had been "promised" the same action would not be repeated and that it would be prevented. The families of two other victims of problems in the Region also gave comments, despite their situations not relating to potassium. What they said also reflected their dismay, frustration, and lack of confidence in the Region and the care provided.[27] They had lost trust in the Region.

Thus, at the June Press Conference, WF had also described two additional safety steps that were being made. First, in the Central Pharmacy, the revised system was undergoing trials to proactively find other problems created by the changes themselves. Despite looking, not seeing everything "in front of us" was part of "being human". Other recommendations were to be subject to "feasibility studies" before any implementation.[28]

By the end of July, there was little doubt that big changes would be made. Three months earlier, the Board Chair had committed to ensuring that the Region had the "best practices in place". He added, "Nothing less will do. We owe those families who have suffered a loss this certainty".[25] The transformation was underway.

The Region's Patient Safety Strategy

For some individuals and organizations, safety is a non-event, that is the absence of an accident, or in the case of healthcare, the absence of harm. Some might say this was because of good fortune. However, as much as humans want to blame or give credit to luck, we dispute using it to explain an outcome.

At the most superficial level, invoking luck is to take the defeatist approach that 'stuff happens', that if something happens it is random and simply a matter of luck – good or bad. Secondly, this line of thinking implies accidents and bad outcomes for patients cannot be predicted. We know both these concepts to be false and misleading. When something bad happens it is because of a number of factors in the system that came together to produce that outcome. When something bad does not happen, this could be because an organization purposefully designed its care delivery system to reduce the likelihood of failure.

For patients requiring CRRT in critical care areas, the Region had been compounding the needed dialysate solution for the previous ten years without apparent problems. But there was no way for the Region to know with certainty if there had been close calls. It was possible that errors had been caught before the dialysis solution had even been prepared. Although the Region had a rudimentary, paper-based, incident reporting system, the systematic analysis of errors, close calls, themes, or trends was not something that was often, if ever, done.

The Region had been relatively innovative in creating a Quality Improvement and Health Information portfolio (QIHI) in 2000. (Before this, some departments and programs had been carrying out various activities related to safety and quality, some for decades. However, such activities were not widespread in the organization.) Having this organizational portfolio was intended to provide resources to many of the larger departments and programs to facilitate their engagement in quality improvement efforts. At that time, emphasis was on quality improvement, with few resources and activities focused specifically on patient safety.

The early 2000s was a time of increasing financial strain. The health system had seen tremendous cuts during the mid-1990s, made by a conservative government wanting to right-size the health care budget. For Calgary, this meant two hospitals were decommissioned. With Calgary's substantial population growth over several years following this time, the Region was struggling to provide healthcare services to a larger population, with fewer hospital beds and a reduced budget.

In 2003, financial cuts were made in many departments across the Region. In the case of QIHI, this meant a budget reduction of 17% in that year. Other departments were making cuts over a three-year period. Pharmacy was one of the departments under financial constraints and tough decisions were made. This meant that the Region underinvested in recruiting clinical pharmacists, at a time when there was emerging evidence that having pharmacists work directly with complex care units, such as Critical Care and Internal Medicine, resulted in fewer medication-related adverse events.

In 2004, triggered by the news of the two potassium-related deaths, former patients came forward with their stories of having had potassium chloride instead of sodium chloride mistakenly flushed into their IV lines. But the Region had no easy way to go back and learn if the events had been reported, how many similar events had been reported or investigated, or what, if any, changes had been made to reduce the probability of events like that recurring. Furthermore, the Region had not even been able to recognize the earlier anecdotal events as symptoms of problems deeper in the system. Had it done so, the Region could have made system-wide changes in the way concentrated potassium chloride was handled in its pharmacies or on its nursing units.

Following the death of Kathleen Prowse, many individuals were working hard at several levels in the organization, determined to understand "What?" happened, "How?", and "Why?". The Region's leaders made decisions to look at the detailed issues related to CRRT preparation in their Central Pharmacy. The Pharmacy Department conducted a near-immediate event analysis of the CRRT mix-up, which allowed them to make several changes rapidly to reduce the likelihood of recurrence.

Even more importantly, the Region's leadership was prepared to use the tragedy as an opportunity to take a broad look at what should be done differently, to make care safer across the Region, and not just for certain medications. A more systematic internal review was conducted by the Region's Critical Incident Review Committee to uncover other issues that the Region might need to address. External reviews were initiated and a Safety Task Group was set up. Perhaps some in the Region sensed that it had passed its "tipping point".[29] Others, possibly, recalled the words of the Judge who had presided over the Fatality Inquiry in 2003, when he had castigated the Region for its attitude. The judge had said "A system under siege or in crisis requires dramatic change, not incremental change".[10,30]

The External Review Team released its findings and its 66 recommendations to the Region and to the media in June 2004. The HQCA released its report with 23 recommendations at about the same time. The Region's internal Safety Task Group report was released three months later and contained an additional 41 recommendations. A review of the three reports showed nine overlapping recommendations, leaving a total of 121 unique recommendations for the Region to consider. The Executive team and the Board accepted all 121.

Although the dialysate deaths were linked to bottles of 250 mL of potassium chloride located only in the Central Pharmacy, both the external review and HQCA reports recommended sweeping changes to the storage and handling of potassium chloride intended for single patient use on nursing units. The 10 mL vials of concentrated potassium chloride that were ubiquitous on nursing units were removed and replaced with patient-specific, premixed bags from pharmacy. Exceptions were made for critical care areas, where it was considered essential to patients' lives to have concentrated potassium chloride at hand. There, vials were to be stored in special, locked cabinets with a process requiring double sign-out by two nurses. All the other recommendations in the reports, specific to the storage and handling of concentrated potassium chloride in each of the city's hospital-based pharmacies, had already been implemented.

What also followed these reports was a period of intensive planning, implementation of changes, tracking of progress, and regular reporting to the Executive and to the Board. Although the more immediate and pragmatic recommendations were focused on dealing with concentrated potassium chloride and other high hazard medications, changes far beyond pharmacy and medication safety resulted, with improvements to pharmacy infrastructure, pharmacy human resources, and pharmacy information systems.

Both the External Review Team's report and the Region's Safety Task Group report laid out a mandate for structural and cultural changes to the Region, which would help to instill patient safety as a core value woven into the fabric of care. To many, what emerged from the Region's Leadership and Board meetings was bold and unprecedented. The announcement, when it came, was for a multi-year and multi-million dollar rollout of a strategy, the goal of which was to change the attitudes and behaviors of the Board of Directors, the CEO, the Regions' Executives, the Clinical Operations' executives, their directors, hundreds of frontline managers, over 22,000 frontline staff and more than 1,000 physicians.

The leaders of Canada's largest integrated healthcare region, while under the lens of media scrutiny, rapidly needed to learn about organizational safety. During that time, many other healthcare institutions were still trying to work out the precise meaning and the scope of what *safety for patients* entailed. In contrast, the Region was unfortunately dealing with a tangible example of what could occur if safety was found to be lacking in one small corner of the organization. WF, the new CCO, and Jack coauthored a description of the strategy, which was published in a Canadian healthcare journal,[31] slightly more than eighteen months after the two deaths. The coauthors also acknowledged that patient safety could include "occupational safety, environmental safety, physical plant and equipment safety, and business risk management" in addition to "clinical safety".[31] However, the Safety Task Group had decided, after much debate, that their patient safety strategy would focus on the latter component, the "day-to-day practices" that directly affected patients.[31] Considering the magnitude of even that task for the Region, and the extent of its approach to safety in early 2004, this decision would be the right one.

The Region's safety strategy for patients encompassed what was learned from a large number of sources. These included the External Review Report, the writings of Reason,[32] other safety literature from healthcare and safety-critical domains, the Institute of Medicine reports,[33,34] and the experience of other leading organizations. Written sources of information were combined with the wisdom of the Safety Task Group.

The new strategy had four cornerstones: Organizational Structure, Resources, Culture, and Leadership and Accountability. These supported the everyday, ongoing work of *safety management*, facilitated and driven by new policies and procedures. Also, to ensure that the new movement gained traction and established some momentum, a focus on communication and education was essential.

Organizational Structure

After the tragic deaths, having a functional organizational structure to support patient safety was seen as being important. The previously existing QIHI portfolio was expanded and renamed to specifically include safety – Quality, Safety and Health Information (QSHI). This portfolio was headed by a new VP position, thus showing that safety and quality had a specific voice at the senior leadership table.

As well, the Region implemented a hierarchical network of clinical safety committees (CSCs) across three structural levels that reflected the organizational structure – the Clinical Executive, the Clinical Portfolios, and Departmental and/or major programs and services. The result was approximately twenty CSCs at the department/program/service level reporting to five clinical portfolio CSCs, which then reported to the highest-level safety committee – the Regional CSC.

At a practical level, the CSCs had two objectives. They were mandated to fix what they could within their span of control, and if an issue was bigger than what the committee could manage because of accountability or funding, they were to move the issue up a level. This meant leveraging the hierarchical structure of the CSCs. The committees' terms of reference also included accountability to their corresponding level of leadership and to the safety committee above them in the hierarchy. This was another new way of doing things, through the establishment of direct connections between safety committees and decision-making leaders. This structure ensured that, at each organizational level, a CSC had direct access to the leaders at that level.

The previously existing Regional Critical Incident Review Committee (CIRC) had its reporting structure changed from the Medical Advisory Board to the Regional CSC. CIRC membership had originally been only physicians, because of legislative requirements that had changed in the past. Subsequently, other types of care providers could be members and not just guests. Changing the reporting structure also helped move the CIRC from the days when hospital administration and physicians functioned quite separately to one where committees functionally reflected the patients' care team.

Resources

In the aftermath of the two deaths and the heightened focus to make patients safer, the Region invested in three major areas, those of pharmacy, patient safety, and a new reporting system. In addition, the Regional leadership accepted a recommendation to establish a several million-dollar patient safety contingency fund. This contingency fund could be drawn on to make timely, safety improvements that would address threats from newly identified hazards. Before this, funding requests had to wait for annual budget planning and approval.[31] Now, a nimble and flexible approach was taken, with decisions about accessing the safety fund made by the Region's operational executives, the CCO, portfolio VPs, and EMDs, based on a recommendation from one of the CSCs.

Pharmacy

Recommendations from the reports of the three reviews addressed several important pharmacy issues. Pharmacy staffing was increased, with the creation of several clinical pharmacy specialist positions for specific patient care areas. The pharmacy facilities at two hospitals were renovated and expanded, and mixing of all non-commercial intravenous solutions was centralized. Pharmacists' access to workstations and electronic references was improved, and technology was upgraded to electronically connect rural hospitals' pharmacies with their urban partners.

Patient Safety

Several new positions were created within the new QSHI portfolio. There were six clinical safety leaders, one for each clinical portfolio and one for support services; an additional analyst position for the new reporting system; a human factors expert; and a new manager. A position for an educational specialist was also added. The main focus of the clinical safety leaders (CSLs) was to support the new safety committees in their portfolios, which they did by reviewing safety learning reports and facilitating safety reviews. The human factors expert initially focused much of his time on redesigning medication storage on nursing units and in other clinical areas. Eventually his focus broadened beyond medication-related safety issues as he engaged with more Regional teams, to include projects ranging from a urinary catheter removal evaluation, to the use of simulated modeling for planning, design, and operations of healthcare facilities.[35] Eventually, an additional human factors expert was hired, to assist with equipment-related issues and to conduct human factors assessments as part of the procurement process.[36]

Reporting System

To identify best practices and the requirements for an electronic system to support those practices, a comprehensive review of safety reporting systems was carried out, including those used in aviation as well as in healthcare. (Some of the important functionality that was built into the system was described in Chapter 4.) The basis was narrative reporting, where staff simply told their story, with the form having a minimum number of mandatory fields. Reporters could also leave suggestions for possible solutions to the problem being reported. A comprehensive medication list was provided by pharmacy, which allowed standardization of reporting of medication problems and easier analysis. A feedback mechanism was built in to provide feedback to the reporter that the report had been received, as well as a query function that could tell the reporter about the status of the report.

The system was set up to facilitate the logging, classification, analysis, and tracking of reports, as well as the lessons generated from them. All these functions had been almost non-existent with the old, paper-based system, which had a 30-day average turnaround time between a report being completed and then received in an office. There it might languish in a drawer or be compiled with others and sent to a manager to be dealt with. The incidents were poorly defined, and there was no guarantee that serious events would be appropriately investigated, or that findings or recommendations would be stored in an information system or acted upon to make changes. In contrast, the new reporting system also allowed for the customization of classification schemes. The CSLs could review and triage reports for their portfolio, and clinical managers were able to review de-identified reports, as well as data summaries of events and hazards from their areas. Having clinical managers with their specific safety knowledge review these reports facilitated their being able to extract the pertinent safety messages for their staff. This "safety intelligence"[37] was fundamental to demonstrating safety problems and issues to staff, and how changes would be made to enhance patient care. Safety reviews were also documented in the system, and recommendations from reviews could be tracked until they had been completed.[38]

Culture

Soon after the work began to answer the question about how to make care in the Region safer, the Safety Task Group decided to examine the issue of culture. In 2003, the National Quality Forum had released its recommended "Thirty Safe Practices for Better Healthcare". At the top of the list was "Create a healthcare culture of safety".[39] The Region evaluated the feasibility of putting into operation Reason's definition of a safety culture, with its four interdependent components. One of those components was for an organization to be flexible. That is, during crises, an organization should be capable of shifting decision-making power from the top of the bureaucracy to "task experts on the spot".[32] While in non-healthcare industries this shift might require a change in mindset, in healthcare this is the de facto way of looking after patients. Clinical experts are in the driver's seat.

Thus, for the Safety Task Group, the focus of its work on culture was on the other three components, hence a new reporting system to support an informed culture. The safety reporting system was to be supplied with stories of hazards sent in by a willing workforce, thus supporting a reporting culture. In theory, the workers then trusted that the organization would not blame or punish them for reporting errors, all the while understanding where the Region had drawn the line "between acceptable and unacceptable behaviour".[32]

However, the Region did not have such a line. Furthermore, whatever guide managers, human resource specialists, and department heads used to decide about discipline, following events in which patients were nearly or actually harmed, was opaque to frontline workers, including physicians.

When we think about the outcome of accidents or other untoward events, what makes healthcare organizations unique in comparison to industrial organizations is the patient. This differentiation applies to any comparison we can make, including application of the basics of safety theory. Thus, when patients suffer harm there is another aspect of culture that must be developed – the proper, humanistic response to them and their families. This was not part of the Region's culture when Kathleen Prowse suffered serious harm following her hip replacement surgery. The Region did not have a disclosure policy nor did it have a policy that justified informing others about serious events in which patients were harmed. Therefore, following Kathleen's death, the Safety Task Group set about creating a suite of safety policies and procedures.

Four new polices, each with an associated procedure, were developed. They were Reporting Safety Hazards and Patient Harm, Just and Trusting Culture,

Disclosing Harm to Patients, and Informing Principal Partners and Stakeholders about Safety Issues. The policies were developed by separate Working Groups, which shared some members. Apart from the concepts, some of the discussions at the Working Groups focused on the wording of the policies, adopting definitions from the Canadian Patient Safety Dictionary.[40] The policies were rightly considered vehicles of communication of the Region's values and principles, and thus, every word was carefully considered.

Reporting Safety Hazards and Harm to Patients

Reporting was defined as "communication between healthcare providers and the Region".[31] The policy stressed the importance of having its healthcare providers report – anything – that worried them or that had occurred. The Region committed to ensuring the confidentiality of the reporter when requested. In situations where patients had been minimally or moderately harmed, reporting was *encouraged*, but the Region *required* reporting in all cases of severe (including fatal) harm. According to the policy, which stated the Region's desire and gave its organizational blessing, everyone, from personnel (at all levels) to patients, families, volunteers, and even visitors, was to be encouraged to report safety hazards, although the final product included only reporting by personnel.

When this policy was created there was intense discussion about mandatory versus voluntary reporting. If reporting were to be deemed mandatory, the discussion focused on the possibility of sanctions when individuals did not report. But then, if there were to be no sanctions, could the system really be mandatory? This type of discussion could be seen to contradict attempts at establishing a Just Culture, where the intent was to move away from discipline for anything except the most egregious actions, such as intentional harm. The Region chose to have a voluntary reporting system. Conversations such as these were necessary to institute and cement trust among all the different players.[41]

Just and Trusting Culture

The Working Group for this policy recognized the importance of learning about safety hazards and events in which patients were harmed or nearly harmed, as well as committing to ensuring that healthcare providers would not be disciplined if they made errors. Group members also followed Reason's thinking about taking a *just approach*. One individual also came up with the idea of adding the phrase "and trusting". This addition accomplished two things. First, it helped show the difference between industry and healthcare. Second, the policy then encompassed both the Region's being just and the providers being able to trust the Region as an outcome[42] of its commitment to and ongoing demonstration to being just.

To effect this, the Region committed to two related types of safety evaluations. The first used JMD's Health System Safety Analysis method (or HSSA), with its human factors focus on understanding system-related contributing factors,[43] that evolved into the SSA methodology described in Chapter 6. The second method was that of Administrative Reviews, conducted in situations where an evaluation of an individual healthcare provider's performance was required. These reviews evaluated the appropriateness of the Region's policies, standards, or guidelines in situations where workers were in noncompliance with established policies, standards, or guidelines. This evaluation then allowed the Region to understand the circumstances that led to the noncompliant action(s) before a decision was made on how to respond to the individual being evaluated.

Disclosing Harm to Patients

This policy committed the Region and its providers to acknowledge to a patient and family about any harm that a patient suffered, provide an apology, and disclose factual information about how the harm occurred. (The policy was put in place well before it was the thing to do or mandated by the (then) CCHSA, now Accreditation Canada.) In the case of a close call, the healthcare provider had discretion to decide about disclosure, with the focus of the decision being based on what was in the best interests of the patient and not those of the care provider.

Informing Principal Partners and Stakeholders About Safety Issues

The fourth policy recognized the Region's duty to communicate to its stakeholders about findings that could represent a hazard, either in the Region or elsewhere. Part of the thinking behind the policy reflected the Region's responsibility for public health. The policy also recognized its duty to inform, to uphold the principles of transparency and maintenance of trust when safety issues occurred, including events in which patients had been seriously harmed.

Leadership and Accountability

The fourth component of the Region's Patient Safety Strategy was leadership and accountability. Culture change requires leadership, and it starts at the top. Accountability for safety needed to be explicit.

To demonstrate this, additional changes were made in the Region, including incorporating patient safety into each member of the Executive's individual accountability agreement. All the Executives were required to attend a primer on the basics of safety and quality. Attendance was close to 100%. At the level of the Region's governance, the Board of Directors' Quality and Safety Committee received regular reports on current patient safety issues and the progress being made in implementing the Region's patient safety strategy.

Safety Management – Developing a Continuous Improvement Ethos

As mentioned previously, quite soon after the two deaths, the COO asked the VPs and EMDs for a proactive identification of hazards that could trigger the next tragedy, as well as strategies that would mitigate the possibility of harm resulting from the hazards. The focused search for hazards became part of the Region's safety strategy, that of Safety Management. This was not quite a Safety Management System (SMS), as a comprehensive SMS addresses governance, policies and procedures, safety performance measurement and monitoring, and safety communication.[44,45] An SMS also enables the sharing of lessons learned so that all organizations can become safer, by making use of this knowledge transfer activity. In 2004, the Safety Management Cycle represented a good start towards one.

The Safety Management Cycle was a continuous improvement cycle with three components, akin to Reason's concept of a learning culture. The first component focused on *managing hazards*: identifying them, analyzing them (including prioritization), and developing recommendations/plans for mitigating risk. The second component was *system improvement*, which included developing solution ideas, testing ideas, and implementing the best one(s). The final component was *measurement and safety information*, referring to the monitoring of improvements and acquiring new information from reports, analyses of close calls or patient harm events, and safety information from other organizations. Because it was envisioned to be a cycle, monitoring of safety information then flowed back into the first component to illustrate how data and information should drive the identification and analysis of hazards.

One barrier to healthcare more widely adopting aviation's safety management concept is healthcare's complexity. Healthcare does not have an easily defined scope of business and does not fly a limited type and number of aircraft. For example, the Tenth Edition of the International Classification of Diseases has over 69,000 diagnostic codes and in excess of 70,000 procedure codes. These are only the diagnoses and procedures that have been recognized and classified. Despite such differences between the two domains, principles of proactive management can and should be adopted in healthcare.

Starting in 2004, the source of the information for the Safety Management Cycle came from the frontlines. Modeled after a concept learned from Children's

Hospital and Clinics of Minnesota, inpatient unit-based Safety Action Teams (SATs) were started by the Region. The Region had sent some safety team members to visit these Minnesota facilities to learn about their safety activities and their reporting systems. The visitors were impressed with the concept of the SATs and how frontline staff were empowered to make changes that improved safety.[46] When the safety team returned to the Region, they recommended SATs be established, which they were. The SATs were not led by managers but by those who did the work of providing and supporting care at the bedside. They had a simple three-part mandate – to identify hazards, to fix problems they could fix, and to tell somebody about the problems they could not fix. Again, the new way was to have those who interacted with hazards to identify them and do what they could to mitigate their effects at a local level.[47] At the time, these SATs were not only novel but also considered an advancement over the old ways of doing things.

If a problem was identified, then great efforts were made to see what could be done to improve the situation, if the problem could not be eradicated. For example, there was a focus on ensuring that nurses had a quiet space in which they could prepare medications before taking them to a patient's room. Doing this while not being disturbed – by other nurses, patients, their families, or the general hubbub of a busy nursing unit – was not always possible and yet has been shown to be enormously important in reducing errors while preparing and dispensing medications.[48] Anyone who had anything to do with the renovation of these units was actively involved, including the pharmacy staff, the nurses, the newly hired human factors expert, the facilities planning and management staff, and the construction teams. On one unit, a previously under-used linen room was quickly and successfully converted, providing the required but previously 'not available' space.

As time and further studies have shown us, some of these local level mitigations, while adaptive when implemented, can have the potential to "impede the development of longer term solutions".[49] This was found in Calgary, where many local level fixes were implemented by the SATs, but there was no mechanism to translate this locally helpful work into necessary changes in the larger system.[47]

Although larger, system-wide changes did not occur as a direct result of the SATs, structural changes did occur in many facilities through the Region's capital planning team. Many renovations were undertaken, removing parts of institutions from the "rust belt of healthcare" as the CMO described the work.

Exciting developments happened beyond renovating existing facilities, with the free-standing Alberta Children's Hospital (ACH)[35] opening in September 2006. The VP of Planning and Facilities Management and his team had adopted the concepts of "Evidence-Based Design", with its emphasis, for example, on single occupancy patients' rooms, as well as the business case of spending more now for safety to save future costs of treating problems.[50] Although there were concerns from the province's regulators in charge of costs, the Regional planners moved forward, building tomorrow's facilities today, rather than yesterday's today. The design of the ACH set a new standard in family-centered care, with the design team eliciting and using input from those for whom the facility was being built – children and their families, as well as care providers. This was a great change from simply taking adults' opinions of what children might like. For example, the window's bottom sills were lowered so that children could see out – at their insistence. The children were correct. Almost two decades before the ACH opened, a study had showed that patients who had a view of a "natural scene", rather than that of a "brick building wall", made a faster recovery after gallbladder surgery.[51]

A new addition to the Foothills Medical Centre, the McCaig Tower, which opened in 2010, made use of human factors-based simulation techniques to improve the design of the trauma operating room.[52,53] As well, the South Health Campus, the design of which was started after the two deaths, made even more use of human factors-based simulation to assist with the building design. The results of four human factors studies saved the Region a considerable sum of money (estimated at $1.7 million CAD in 2016), as well as minimizing or avoiding "40 or 50 years of inconvenience",[54] as design changes were made before concrete was poured. Also included in these facilities was greater emphasis on various safety-enhancing factors, including more single patient rooms, increased working space and light, and flexibility for future needs. The latter was largely based on building large single rooms fully equipped with two sets of oxygen and other outlets, should a sudden need to increase capacity arise, for example, should a pandemic erupt.

Beyond significant infrastructure changes, a curriculum for safety education and training was developed and taught, with the educational content purposefully designed to target different groups within the organization.[55] For example, there were sessions called "Leading the Way" that were provided to the leadership. Courses on general patient safety concepts were made available to all staff and physicians, and a course was designed specifically for individuals who were identified to be ambassadors for patient safety in their clinical area.

Patients and families were an integral part of all of this work, and the Region's Safety Management Cycle. Individuals who had suffered harm or family members of patients who had been harmed became partners in the organization's transformation. A committee of these dedicated individuals was established, with a formal reporting relationship through the VP of QSHI to the CCO (by his decision). Members met monthly to discuss patient safety and issues about patients' experiences. Many of them assisted with education and training, by either co-presenting or attending sessions where they would share their stories. These sessions played an invaluable part in the transformation of the Region.

Although the descriptions above include a large list of work in progress and accomplishments in the Region, even more was achieved. Much of this was to do with the fact there was a new atmosphere of excitement, energy, and enthusiasm for the new ways of doing things. These emotions had emerged from those that had suddenly appeared in March 2004, when the news of the deaths of the two patients reverberated around the Region. A wave of anxiety and concern erupted, to be replaced, once all the potentially lethal bags of CRRT had been found, with a sense of urgent determination to get to the bottom of the problems. The release of the External Review Team's Report was met with welcome relief, as though a long-feared diagnosis had been discounted and a more benign but equally important, long-term condition replaced it. There was a new sense of urgency to make improvements to safety. Thus the fear and negativity that originally resulted from the potassium tragedy was replaced was optimism, enthusiasm, and a *let's get it done* mentality.

And big changes did result. These included physical additions and renovations to buildings and nursing units. They also involved the creation of new guiding policies and procedures on safety, education sessions describing the reasoning behind the changes and what staff could do to make patients safer, and partnering with patients and families in different ways. All these changes were designed to ensure the success of the strategy for integrating safety within a large healthcare system.

In this chapter, we have described the changes the Region underwent after the Region's leaders released their strategy for transformation. These changes started with the Region developing its Patient Safety Strategy, and the resulting changes in organizational structure, allocation of resources, focused attention on fostering a culture of safety, and a clear recognition of the role of leadership to achieve this.

References

1. Toneguzzi M. Fatal flaws admitted, human errors, system blamed for drug mix-up. *Calgary Herald: City & Region*. 2004 Jun 30;B1 (col. 6) & B3 (col. 1).
2. Toneguzzi M. Calgary isn't only city battling ER crunch. *Calgary Herald*. 2004 Mar 28;A1 (col. 2)–A5.
3. Gray D. Hospital patient deaths produce ripples across the country. *Calgary Herald: City & Region*. 2004 Mar 28;A11 (col. 1) & A12 (col. 3).
4. Dohy L, Canton M. Communities split over new schools. Education health receive boost. *Calgary Herald*. 2004 Mar 30;A1 (col. 6)–A10 (col. 4).

5. Toneguzzi M. Foothills death review begins. *Calgary Herald: City & Region.* 2004 Apr 3;B1 (col. 1)–B4 (col. 3).

6. Toneguzzi M. Delectable delights for hospital patients. CHR cooks up revamped "wellness" menu. *Calgary Herald: City & Region.* 2004 Apr 4;A10 (col. 1)–A11 (col. 5).

7. Toneguzzi M. Medical images go online. *Calgary Herald: City & Region.* 2004 Apr 8;B7 (col. 1).

8. Toneguzzi M. Health region cuts 80 positions, saves $111 million. *Calgary Herald: City & Region.* 2004 Apr 15;B4 (col. 4).

9. Toneguzzi M. CHR safety review approved. *Calgary Herald: City & Region.* 2004 Apr 22;B22 (col. 1).

10. Ferguson G. "Credibility is on trial," Calgary Health Region: Superbug deaths. Authority insists it is "open and honest". *Calgary Herald: City & Region.* 2004 Jun 10;B1 (col. 2)–B4 (col. 1).

11. Braid D. "Credibility is on trial", Calgary Health Region: Superbug deaths, not even top doctor knew what happened. *Calgary Herald: City & Region.* 2004 Jun 10;B1 (col. 5)–B4 (col. 3).

12. Eggertson L. Hospitals battling outbreaks of *C. difficile. Can Med Assoc J.* 2004 Jul 6;171(1):19–21.

13. Eggertson L. Quebec strikes committee on *Clostridium difficile. Can Med Assoc J.* 2004 Jul 20;171(2):123.

14. Headline: Virus kills dozens. Globe & Mail. 2004 Jun 4.

15. Richards G, Poole E. Medical mix-up blamed in death, man died after wrong drug administered. *Calgary Herald.* 2004 Jun 11;A1 (col. 1)–A6 (col. 1).

16. Braid D. Information block afflicts health region. *Calgary Herald: City & Region.* 2004 Jun 12;B2 (col. 1).

17. Toneguzzi M. Health region shuffles deck. *Calgary Herald: City & Region.* 2004 Jun 12;B1 (col. 1)–B2 (col. 3).

18. Braid D. Calgary's master builder. *Calgary Herald: City & Region.* 2004 Jun 15;B2(col. 4).

19. Braid D. Pharmacy staff to answer for deaths. Health region boss Jack Davis vows those responsible will be held accountable. *Calgary Herald: Exclusive.* 2004 Mar 21;A1 (col. 1).

20. Toneguzzi M. Health region hoped to cut errors. 2004 Jun 26;A1(col. 5)–A8 (col. 1).

21. Toneguzzi M. Pharmacy check policy debated. *Calgary Herald.* 2004 Jun 27;A11 (col. 3)–A15 (col. 4).

22. Canada tilts left…but Alberta sticks to the right. *Calgary Herald.* 2004 Jun 29;A1.

23. Human error, flawed system led to drug mix-up deaths. *Calgary Herald.* 2004 Jun 30;A1–B1.

24. Toneguzzi M. Pharmacy prescribed $2-million upgrade. *Calgary Herald: City & Region.* 2004 Jul 2;B1 (col. 5) & B2 (col. 1).

25. Tuer D. It is vital we learn from these mistakes. *Calgary Herald.* 2004 Mar 24;A3 (col. 4).

26. Deadly mix-up happened before. *The Calgary Sun.* 2004 Mar 20;1.

27. Slobodian L. Medical mix-up occurred before. *Calgary Herald*. 2004 Mar 20;A1 (col. 1) & A5 (col. 5).

28. Richards G. Pharmacy too lax, says relative. *Calgary Herald: City & Region*. 2004 Jul 1;B1 (col. 5) & B4 (col. 1).

29. Gladwell M. *The Tipping Point: How Little Things Can Make a Big Difference*. New York: Little, Brown & Company; 2000.

30. Delong M. Report to the Minister of Justice and Attorney General in the matter of a public inquiry into the death of Vincenzo Dominic Motta pursuant to the Fatality Inquiries Act [Internet]. Calgary; 2003 Apr [cited 2022 Feb 9]. Available from: https://open.alberta.ca/dataset/af9117da-e5c5-4360-a19e-242d011d76a1

31. Flemons W, Eagle C, Davis J. Developing a comprehensive patient safety strategy for an integrated Canadian healthcare region. *Healthcare Q*. 2005 Oct 15;8(Special Number):122–7.

32. Reason J. *Managing the Risks of Organizational Accidents*. Aldershot: Ashgate Publisher; 1997.

33. Kohn L, Corrigan JM, Donaldson MS (eds.). *To Err is Human: Building a Safer Health System*. Washington, D.C.: National Academies Press; 2000.

34. Institute of Medicine (US). *Crossing the Quality Chasm: A New Health System for the 21st Century*. Institute of Medicine (US) Committee on Quality of Health Care in America. Washington, D.C.: National Academies Press; 2001.

35. Chisholm S, Shultz J, Caird J, Lord J, Boiteau P, Davies J. Identification of intensive care unit (ICU) system integration conflicts: Evaluation of two mock-up rooms using patient simulation. *Proc Hum Factors Ergon Soc Annu Meet*. 2008 Sep 1;52(12): 798–802.

36. Davies J, Caird J, Chisholm S. Trying before buying: Human factors evaluations of new medical technology. In: Anca J, editor. *Multimodal Safety Management and Human Factors. Crossing the Borders of Medical, Aviation, Road and Rail Industries*. 1st ed. Aldershot: Ashgate Publishing Limited; 2007. pp. 316–323.

37. Fruhen LS, Mearns KJ, Flin R, Kirwan B. Safety intelligence: An exploration of senior managers' characteristics. *Appl Ergon*. 2014 Jul;45(4):967–75.

38. Davies J, Duchscherer C, McRae G. A new reporting system: Was the patient harmed or nearly harmed? In: Anca J, editor. *Multimodal Safety Management and Human Factors. Crossing the Borders of Medical, Aviation, Road and Rail Industries*. Aldershot: Ashgate Publishing Limited; 2007. pp. 61–71.

39. Thirty safe practices for better healthcare [Internet]. Washington, D.C.; 2003 [cited 2022 Feb 9]. Available from: https://psnet.ahrq.gov/issue/safe-practices-better-healthcare-2006-update

40. Davies J, Herbert P, Hoffman C. The Canadian patient safety dictionary [Internet]. Ottawa: The Royal College of Physicians and Surgeons of Canada; 2003 [cited 2022 Feb 9]. Available from: https://www.ottawahospital.on.ca/en/documents/2017/01/patient_safety_dictionary_e.pdf/

41. Newell S, Swan J. Trust and inter-organizational networking. *Hum Relations*. 2000 Oct 1;53(10):1287–328.

42. Grandori A, Soda G. Inter-firm networks: Antecedents, mechanisms and forms. *Organization Studies*. 1995 Mar 30;16(2):183–214.

43. Davies JM, Lange IR. Investigating adverse outcomes in obstetrics. *J Obstet Gynaecol Canada.* 2003 Jun;25(6):505–15.
44. Toff N. Human factors in anaesthesia: Lessons from aviation. *Br J Anaesth.* 2010 Jul;105(1):21–5.
45. Davies J, Delaney G. Can the aviation industry be useful in teaching oncology about safety? *Clin Oncol.* 2017 Oct;29(10):505–15.
46. Morath J, Turnbull J. *To Do No Harm: Ensuring Patient Safety in Health Care Organizations.* San Francisco: Jossey-Bass Inc.; 2005.
47. Duchscherer C. Improving safety management at the sharp end: A plan for integrating safety action teams in the Calgary Health Region [dissertation]. Victoria, BC: University of Victoria; 2008. [cited 2022 Feb 9]. Available from: https://dspace.library.uvic.ca/bitstream/handle/1828/1537/duchscherer_carmella.pdf?sequence=1&isAllowed=y
48. Chaudhury H, Mahmood A, Valente M. The effect of environmental design on reducing nursing errors and increasing efficiency in acute care settings. *Environ Behav.* 2009 Nov 5;41(6):755–86.
49. Amalberti R, Vincent C. Managing risk in hazardous conditions: Improvisation is not enough. *BMJ Qual Saf.* 2020 Jan;29(1):60–3.
50. Berry L, Parker D, Coile R, Hamilton D, O'Neill D, Sadler B. The business case for better buildings. *Front Health Serv Manage.* 2004;21(1):3–24.
51. Ulrich RS. View through a window may influence recovery from surgery. *Science.* 1984;224:420–1.
52. Biesbroek S, Shultz J, Kirkpatrick A, Korbeek J. Human factors evaluation of an interventional trauma operating room mock-up. *2012 Symposium on Human Factors and Ergonomics in Health Care*, Baltimore, MD: Human Factors and Ergonomics Society Inc.; 2012. pp. 38–73.
53. Kirkpatrick AW, Vis C, Dubé M, Biesbroek S, Ball CG, Laberge J, et al. The evolution of a purpose designed hybrid trauma operating room from the trauma service perspective: The RAPTOR (resuscitation with angiography percutaneous treatments and operative resuscitations). *Injury.* 2014 Sep;45(9):1413–21.
54. Health Quality Council of Alberta. Simulation-based mock-up evaluation: Framework [Internet]. Calgary, AB; 2016 [cited 2022 Feb 9]. Available from: https://hqca.ca/wp-content/uploads/2018/05/HQCA_SME_Framework_062217S.pdf
55. Flemons W, Davies J, Wight D, Mikkelsen A, Harvie M. Patient safety principles. Definitions, descriptions and rationale. Blueprint Project. Transforming Patient Safety Education in Alberta [Internet]. Calgary, AB; 2010 [cited 2022 Feb 9]. Available from: https://hqca.ca/wp-content/uploads/2018/05/BP_Principles_062210.pdf

Chapter 8

"A Major Shake-Up."[1]

Soon after Jack had learned about Kathleen Prowse's death, he'd had no hesitation in notifying the Chair of the Region's Board and the Deputy Minister of Health and Wellness, and as previously described, the resourceful CMO had directly notified the Minister of Health and Wellness. Confirmation was received the Minister had informed the Premier. So all the people who needed to know, knew, and were supportive from the start with the direction the Region planned to go in managing the crisis.

Of course, not all the province's politicians felt the same way. The Leader of the Opposition said Jack needed to be removed, on the basis that he had not heeded warnings about understaffing and overworking of those in hospital pharmacies. He added that the Region's management needed a "major shake-up", being "run too much like a patronage playground for the premier", with the consequence of "another tragedy".[1] Ironically, these comments were to foreshadow events that were to come in a few years and which were to change everything and affect everyone in the Region.

In 2004, the Minister of Health and Wellness had anticipated the positive contribution of a new program that would help healthcare safety in Calgary. This was a Region-wide electronic Patient Care Information System (PCIS), linking different healthcare professionals, and importantly having all the Region's hospitals on the same system. The aim was to help practitioners in viewing and updating their patients' health-related information, such as medications, allergies, and laboratory results.[2] Led by the CIO, PCIS was a Calgary-specific initiative – perhaps the first one in the country where all the acute care facilities in a large urban center could use the same information system to access patient

DOI: 10.4324/9781003185307-9

information. This development also came at a time when specific concepts, such as computer order entry, were considered vital to improving patient safety.[3]

Release of the External Review Team's report validated and added impetus to the changes already started and planned. As promised, the Region had neither vetted nor approved the report before it was sent to the media. Indeed, most of the senior Executives had not seen the report until the day before the Press Conference.

The External Review Team report did not lay blame. One reporter quoted the CEO of the Pharmacists Association of Alberta, who expressed his positive reaction,[4] but another reporter denounced the lack of blame. His headline read "Incompetence of pharmacy staff clear". He took exception to part of the report's statement that there was no evidence of "incompetence, carelessness or willful violation of rules or standards". He questioned why "administering a lethal poison after a series of blunders" was not "incompetence", if not on the part of the workers, then at the level of the administrators.[5]

Similarly, there were differences between the families of patients who had received incorrectly mixed CRRT. Another of Kathleen Prowse's daughters released a statement on behalf of the family. They had been included in the External Review and were "grateful". They also expressed their sympathy to the Central Pharmacy workers, recognizing not all problems could be avoided. They added their hearts went out "to all of those who were involved in this unfortunate tragedy".[6] However, the family members of the first dialysate victim were split on blame. A brother stated that blaming the system was not equal to "people doing their jobs properly". It was "people" who did the wrong things. Another family member was clear the family didn't want to blame one individual but expressed anger at the Pharmacy. Although they weren't asking for "somebody's head on a platter" they were frustrated with the Pharmacy, described as "too lackadaisical, especially with poisonous chemicals".[7]

Much work was obviously necessary and much followed, resulting in large numbers of changes throughout the Region. These involved diverse areas, many different aspects of care, and even how those in the Region thought about care. There was still the palpable sense of urgency to make things better, with new teams forming and the usual pace of work accelerating, although not so rapidly as in the first few hours and days after the deaths. But not all the changes were welcomed by everyone. There were still some holdouts to the old ways of doing things. Others were frustrated by either the changes or the lack of them. However, discussions continued, as did the changes. Some of these had come from the 121 recommendations from the reviews of the fatal events. Others had been triggered by two conferences, and what did and did not happen there.

In 2004, the Region's culture was intertwined with those of the other eight healthcare regions, the government ministry (Alberta Health and Wellness) and the Office of the Minister of Health. When the Region decided to increase its transparency with its patients, families, and the public, it didn't have a lot of dance partners to choose from in the province. This was brought into sharp focus during planning for the Fourth Canadian Healthcare Safety Symposium held in Edmonton, Alberta, the province's capital, in October 2004.

The first three Canadian Healthcare Safety conferences took place in Halifax, Nova Scotia. They were initiated in 2001 by Dr. Pat Croskerry, who was a PhD psychologist before entering medical school and becoming an emergency room physician. Croskerry had an interest in human error and how it applied to diagnosing patients. In 2001, he decided to host a meeting in Halifax, focusing that interest in "Frontline Approaches in Clinical Practice". He invited an impressive list of national and international speakers, all of whom appeared. The conference went so well that Croskerry agreed to host a similar meeting for the next two years, with JMD who had spoken at "Halifax One", enthusiastically volunteering to help him with planning and organization. After two increasingly successful years but limited, local logistical support, Croskerry decided that 2003 would be the last meeting in Halifax.

Understanding the value of the symposium and the following it had developed, JMD offered to move the conference out west. To do this, she needed to convince healthcare leaders in Alberta to provide funding and support. The Calgary Health Region, Capital Health (the Edmonton-based region), the HQCA, and the College of Physicians and Surgeons of Alberta quickly agreed to work together under her leadership. The symposium would be held in Edmonton in the fall of 2004 and in Calgary in 2005. As the Region's representative, WF joined the planning group, as did the CMO. Funding was secured for professional meeting organizers, to support the volunteer planning group. As Co-Chair of the Symposia, JMD purposely kept the Halifax name for the Series, to ensure the meetings' origins were not forgotten and because previous attendees had attached themselves to the name, often asking for updates of the *next* Halifax.

As it turned out, Halifax 4 in Edmonton would be held seven months after the two deaths in Calgary. Members of the planning committee were determined to give voice to patients and families who had suffered harm in their healthcare journeys. In part, this was an acknowledgment that healthcare needed to be more open with the patients and the public it served. Another important part was that healthcare leaders needed to learn and to admit that patients were hurt far more often than anyone had previously understood, thus recognizing the concept that a problem cannot be properly addressed until its existence is acknowledged. Thus, for this part of the program, the committee decided to ask for participation by the family of a patient whose death had been partly related to their healthcare in Alberta, although not in either Calgary or Edmonton. The family agreed to share their experience firsthand at the conference. A group of respected, senior healthcare leaders from across Canada and the United States had also agreed to be part of the session.

This was likely to be the first time in Canada that a patient's family would be provided with a public platform to share their story, in front of a large number of national and international healthcare professionals and leaders. (In fact, this was attempted at Halifax 3 but was met with extremely strong opposition on the day, from local healthcare officials.) Three weeks before the start of the Edmonton conference, concerns were raised in the planning committee about how well a Public Forum would be accepted. A message from an unnamed, senior health-care bureaucrat in Alberta had been received, advising that the session could not proceed as planned. Committee members were told the patient's family could not appear live on stage. The representative bureaucrat did not want a patient's family speaking publicly, unscripted, and with invited media in the audience because it all might go badly. The program was changed to include a video of an American family's tragedy, a local media person was not to be involved and the event would no longer be televised. Obviously, changing attitudes and culture was not going to be easy.

Several months later the same planning group reconvened to start work on Halifax 5, which would be held in Calgary. The members were undeterred from their experience in Edmonton and wanted to try again. A similar session was planned for the evening before the conference started, in the ballroom of a downtown Calgary hotel. Admission was free. All Halifax 5 conference attendees were invited to this preconference Public Forum, as were healthcare workers, the general public – and the media. Jack was approached to get his support for a session with patients' stories. The hope was that if there was once again strong pressure from senior government bureaucrats, he could intervene to keep the session from being cancelled.

Jack required no convincing – he willingly signed on to help. The committee had learned from different sources about several possible families in Calgary and the surrounding area, and who had had challenging experiences with their healthcare journeys. A decision was made to interview five of them, with each family consenting to tell their stories on video. The families were also invited to the session and to participate in the discussions – if they chose to. Kathleen Petty, a well-known television and radio journalist accepted an invitation to chair the session. Jack volunteered to introduce the evening's event and, after the videos were shown, to be part of a panel to discuss the stories. This would include taking questions from the audience. As it turned out, before the conference started, Jack was needed to intervene to counter potential interference from senior government officials. He was successful, and there were no last minute cease and desist orders as there had previously been.

On the evening, the hotel's ballroom was pushed to capacity, with hundreds in attendance and almost all the overflow chairs filled. The stories were powerful. Two of the stories involved children who had died. In another video, a couple recounted endless weeks of watching their premature newborn living through complications in the neonatal ICU and not receiving the information they were desperately seeking. Two parents told of their experience in the pediatric oncology unit where there were several fumbles, at times poor communication, and at least two errors with medications that could have been fatal but fortunately were not. Ironically, the patient's father was a safety expert for a national railway and very familiar with Reason's industrial safety theories and the characteristics of safe systems.

Many attendees were shocked that a healthcare system would be so open, could share these stories in such a public way with the media present, and could have the CEO and several other executives there in the audience and taking questions. The conference and these actions all continued to deliver the same message, which had emerged at the news conference about the potassium-related deaths eighteen months previously. The Region was fulfilling its commitment toward being more transparent.

The Symposium's planning committee was finally successful in being able to deliver what they knew was essential – to have stories told by the patients and families involved, and an open discussion about the imperfections and problems in healthcare. Committee members understood that problems couldn't be solved until those seeking care and working in the system were prepared to and given permission to admit and to discuss them. But again, not everyone in the Region was on board with this new direction and approach.

This mixed response mirrored the media's reaction the following day, in particular, the local newspaper spotlight, which once more was on the Region. Although the potassium-related deaths had occurred some nineteen months previously and neither of the two families was ready to share its experiences with the public, the top headline for the front page of the city section was again in full capital letters: "MEDICAL MIX-UP". This was followed by "Inquiry unnecessary: CHR boss". In response to the reporter's question, Jack had "denied the need" for a Fatality Inquiry, stating the Region had already investigated all possibilities. (In fact, the Chief Medical Examiner had decided not to refer the two cases to the province's Attorney General and that meant a Fatality Inquiry would not be held.)

The article went on to state that two days earlier there had been a call for a "formal examination of the medical mistake that killed her mother". That call came from Deb Prowse, who had given an interview to the newspaper, as her first public statement since her mother had died. In her opinion, the External Review Report "didn't go far enough". What was missing for Deb were the "circumstances"[8] that led up to the dialysate mix-up and her mother's death. What Deb was referring to, but not detailed in the article, were the events related to her mother's postoperative complications after hip surgery, when she had suffered life-threatening bleeding. There had been no apology, disclosure, or support and Deb was still extremely distressed. However, Deb had attended the Public Forum and being there was perhaps for her the start of a positive change, although in her mind, the jury was still out on this question. There was still much the Region had to do to regain her trust.

Newspaper coverage after the first full day of the conference again pushed the Region onto the front pages of the newspapers,[9] with descriptions of two of the families and their stories. An unnamed Regional official stated it was "always difficult to determine whether the medical mistakes caused or contributed to such deaths". However, WF clarified that he and his colleagues would not look and then say a "single error" was the cause of a "similar problem".

The final day's newspaper coverage was slightly more positive. That reporter summarized the meeting as showing "patient safety (was) improving, but further advances (were) dependent on officials being more transparent when problems (arose)". She quoted the then CEO of the Canadian Patient Safety Institute (CPSI), Philip Hassen, who applauded the Region for its openness. As a former executive in Calgary hospitals, Hassen was sanguine of the dangers of healthcare and stated that everyone should be "concerned but not frightened". He added the comment that the entire Canadian healthcare system required work. The reporter ended her article noting the symposium would be held the next year in Vancouver.[10]

The Symposium also attracted a very favorable review in a book about partnerships between patients and families and healthcare organizations. The Series had earned a national and international reputation for "helping to create an awareness of patient safety issues and bring new knowledge of safety theories and practices to health-care leaders, clinicians, and planners". Jack's statement at the Public Forum was quoted. "Patient safety is something everyone, including patients and their families, must work together to address". Two specific themes were identified, the "need for improved communication" and the avoidance of "finger-pointing when safety issues (were) identified". While there were differences of opinion as to the importance of what had been done in contrast to what still remained to be done in Calgary, there was unanimity for the need for continued collaboration between patients and families and their providers to "achieve its goal of creating a 'culture of caring'".[11]

Despite some of the positive publicity, the public session and the overall media coverage made many in the organization uncomfortable and confirmed in their minds they did not agree with this new approach. However, many welcomed the change, including Deb Prowse. Perhaps she had had to see and to hear for herself that the Region was actually serious about transforming how it worked with its patients and families. For Deb, there was less doubt left after this event and her attendance at Halifax 5 was one of the factors that helped her change her attitude toward the Region.

Several weeks after the Halifax 5 conference, four of the five families who had shared their stories felt they could now trust the Region enough to work with it. They wanted to create a Patient and Family Advisory Committee. Several others also came forward. By this time Deb was starting to feel ready to take a chance with the Region and she then volunteered to join the others on an advisory committee. She started to participate in discussions and teaching in the Region, adding her voice to those who wished to change hearts and minds. This was the start of her long-term commitment to patient safety.

Other individuals also underwent changes – in their beliefs, their thinking, and their actions. Of all those involved in this story, apart from Deb, one other person should be mentioned. That was Jack Davis, the CEO, who, from the start believed in doing the right thing, although to some observers, he perhaps wasn't always sure what that looked like. He was also open to the concept of doing things differently, despite facing strong disagreement and even censure, from both within the Region and external to it. Perhaps it was because of listening to and participating in the discussions with his safety-oriented Executives and safety advisors. Perhaps it was because of the walk in the snow he took with the lead of the External Review Team that helped clarify his thinking. They had met at Jack's house and, it being a spring day in Calgary, went outside to enjoy the fresh air and to discuss what was to be done. We don't know exactly what was said but Jack continued doing the right things to advance and support all those working in safety and quality. He became personally involved in safety and quality activities. For as long as he was the CEO of the Region, he attended conferences, gave presentations, and contributed to publications.

Two individuals who remained steadfast in their support were the Chair of the Region's Board and the Minister of Health and Wellness. In countries like Canada with socialized healthcare systems, the distance can be very short between these two positions, with the latter holding ultimate accountability for what happens in the healthcare system. Neither the Chair, a successful business-man, nor the Minister, a lawyer, had a background in healthcare. Both, however, had been in position for some years and, during that time, had gained insight into healthcare safety and quality. The Board Chair was immediately supportive when Jack had informed him of the deaths and the Region's plans. The Minister, in the face of intense political pressure, stated his similar position and never wavered. He commented both publicly and in private what he knew to be true about healthcare systems. "There is human frailty in every process – and we need to factor that when designing how we provide care". He also had a deep understanding of people, saying, "Naming and blaming does not bring back the dead. That is not a constructive exercise". In 2004, the Region needed to have two insightful leaders like this to facilitate it moving forward with its plan for transformational change.

In the 2008 book *High Performing Healthcare Systems*, Professor Ross Baker, of the Institute of Health Policy, Management, and Evaluation, at the University of Toronto, and colleagues reviewed in detail five international[12] and two Canadian systems. Their goal was to understand which particular strategies and investments had been made that made these systems stand out compared to peers. The purpose of the book was to shed light on important initiatives so that other centers might learn from them. Calgary was one of the two Canadian case studies Baker chose for his book *High Performing Healthcare Systems*. Many of the Region's initiatives mentioned in the book were quality and safety initiatives[13] that had been achieved since the potassium-related deaths and could be tied back to that event.

This unbiased look at the Region by external experts validated the decision made in 2004 to use the tragedy to help transform the Region's culture and the delivery of healthcare in Calgary. In the introductory chapter, the authors commented that some successful examples might also be "islands of excellence in a sea of mediocrity".[13] With the benefit of hindsight, those who were familiar with the advancements in patient safety made by the Region over a few short years are left to wonder whether or not the funders of healthcare organizations, which in countries like Canada means governments, pay much if any attention to publications like this.

For the Region, a politician's somewhat prescient call in 2004 for a "major shake-up"[1] of the Region in fact came about four years after the comment was made. On April 16, 2008, the provincial government, with its new Premier and new Minister of Health and Wellness, announced the launch of an "aggressive action plan to make public health system more efficient and ensure equitable access to services". In addition, there was to be a "new model for health authority governance within two months". A timeline of further announcements, over the following three, six, and nine months, was promised.[14] The next news release came sooner than expected. One month later, the Minister described the plan to create one provincial board for the province, merging the nine health boards and those of Alberta Mental Health and Alberta Cancer, as well as the Alberta Alcohol and Drug Abuse Commission. Reporting directly to the Minister, the "superboard" would be responsible for health services delivery for the province. The timing of the merger would depend on "region contracts, bylaws, union agreements and management structures" having been dealt with.[15]

The media responded in Edmonton by quoting the Minister who wanted "equitable" care in Alberta. While a laudable goal, he did not cite data but said that other Members of the Legislative Assembly had brought him "instances of where one side of the road in one of the regions deliver[ed] services different from people who live[d] on the other side of the road".[16]

The response of the knowledgeable and experienced, national health journalist, André Picard, provided more insight. Although the change appeared "mundane and bureaucratic", Picard stated it stripped the "regions of the power to shape services to local needs". Importantly, the change muzzled the "public voice in healthcare". The Region was described as being "light years ahead of the rest of the country on patient safety" and had a model for "healthcare delivery for the next generation" through the Medical Ward of the 21st Century,[17] which opened earlier that week.[18] (W21C was a joint venture between the Region and the University of Calgary, with its state-of-the-art Medical Unit at FMC.[19]) Other special programs noted by Picard were chronic disease management and "alternative payment plans" instead of paying doctors a standard fee for each service. Any "failings of regions" were in general related to a "lack of provincial leadership". Picard concluded by stating that "What matter[ed] was not structural change but the vision". He suggested the Premier's government should describe how the changes would "promote innovation, improve access, and bolster the quality of care", instead of offering "empty rhetoric" and a "power grab".[17]

Jack's response was documented in his blog. He started by thanking the Board Chair and all the Board members for their "dedication and hard work", their support and for ensuring the Region had "good governance". He then went on to welcome the new board, complimenting the new Chairman as an "outstanding individual" who would do a "great job leading this new provincial board". He also welcomed the new interim provincial CEO, with whom he had previously worked, stating he was looking forward to working with both of them. Jack's message then changed as he addressed the workforce, stating he wanted to be "very, very clear, though, that it's business as usual for the Calgary Health Region". The work done by every member of the staff was "critical and [had] to carry on each and every day". He encouraged everyone "to stay focused on our core business which [was] providing the very, very best health care we can to the citizens that we serve". He considered everyone in the Region to be part of "one large team" and that each one was "very, very important to the job that we do on a daily basis". After some comments about issues that needed to be addressed around "capacity and funding in the Region" and wanting to put them before the new board, Jack concluded by "thanking each and every one for the tremendous job [done] each and every day". He also indicated his ongoing personal support, as well as the support of the Executive team to all in the Region.[20]

Thus, the Region continued with its business as usual, trying to provide good care and work at ongoing changes and developments. Then, on Saturday, June 21st, the headlines read "Top health bosses face axe" and "Health minister says jobs will likely be cut in July". The Minister was quoted as saying "there [would] likely be people working in senior administration today who will not be there in the future". He was criticized for this by an opposition Member of the Legislative Assembly, who considered the "uncertainty" created by the announcement. He questioned how much could be accomplished "by dropping a bombshell like that and waiting two or three weeks for the other shoe to drop". However, the new Board had "seconded senior employees from all the regional health authorities to help build the new administrative structure".[21] Two of these individuals were to come from the soon-to-be-former Region. They were the medically qualified Executive VP and CCO, who would become the "interim COO for urban centres", and the Region's CFO, who was to hold the same position in the new organization.[22]

On Tuesday, July 8, 2008, the Minister relieved all the Boards and CEOs of their duties.[23] Before leaving the building, Jack had thanked the Region's employees and physicians, posting a message on the Region's website. "During my time as Chief Executive Officer, it has been both a privilege and a pleasure to have worked with you".[22]

Jack was interviewed for the last time by the senior local columnist, who had often been one of Jack's and the Region's strongest critics. The columnist described Jack as "walk[ing] the executive plank" that day. The article started with Jack's admission that he "virtually offered himself for firing", telling the Chair of the new board not to delay and the "longer you have ambiguity about who's in charge, that's bad for a health system" as large as the Region was. He also commented he knew he wouldn't be involved in the future with the new organization and wasn't worried. The situation of being fired wasn't about him, but "about health care". He also agreed generally about centralization, with some aspects of the organization benefiting from a provincial approach, that wasn't possible when dealing with the different regions. For example, there was a problem with having "nine regions competing for health care providers". The article closed with Jack admitting he would miss all those with whom he worked and the "immense respect" he had for them. The columnist noted that "after nearly 38 years in and out of government", just briefly, "one of Alberta's shrewdest bureaucratic warhorses was choked up".[24] Alberta Health Services (AHS), a province-wide health region, and its new CEO and Board, was now in charge. The former Calgary Health Region was incorporated into AHS as the Calgary Zone.

The Journey Never Ends

Safety is a journey, not a destination. If we want our healthcare systems to be safer, we can take a tactical approach by choosing to implement any number of published leading practices. These practices might involve changes in processes for care, or changes in the structural elements that support those processes. In addition, organizations or groups of providers could choose to develop a strategic plan that addresses attitudes and behaviors. Taken together, these concepts come under the overarching concept of culture, which earlier in this book we described as "the way we do things around here".[25]

Purposely trying to change an organization's culture, how we do things here, is a large undertaking. First, we cannot literally change the culture. There is no button, labeled "Push Here", to do so. What we can do is help individuals learn to do things differently and help them to understand why the new approach should be helpful. From this, we hope to also see a change in attitudes and behaviors, which generally equates to a change in culture. Second, any attempts to make these changes must be supported from the top of the organizational structure where change is planned. Support could come from the level of a unit or group of healthcare providers, a program, a department, or an entire healthcare organization. In the case of the former Region, it was the latter.

Our initial efforts were directed at shifting attitudes about safety by discussing the safety culture constructs proposed by Reason,[26] as discussed in earlier chapters. To change behaviors, the Region invested in fundamental alterations to its reporting system. Dedicated positions were established to manage information, increasing its availability to trigger and foster opportunities for system improvements. The Region adopted a Just Culture policy, which declared the Region's commitment to not punish anyone for making errors. The Region also committed to a systematic analysis of adverse events so as to better identify and understand system problems and issues. An infrastructure was built to support continuous improvements when safety issues (or system deficiencies) were uncovered, including a system for communicating important safety information. And as previously described, the Region's Executive team committed to a sizeable safety contingency fund to make necessary fixes relatively quickly without having to wait for the annual budget cycle. This new infrastructure made it easier, faster, and more efficient to make needed adjustments in the myriad units, programs, and departments that made up the Region. Presentations and educational courses specific to patient safety were developed and taught to all levels of the organization, from executive and senior leaders down to those providing support and direct care to patients. All these features, together with consistent messages about safety and careful attention to language, were tools that were used to shift attitudes and behaviors.

What we discovered through four years of carrying out this purposeful work was first, how important it was to make and communicate big decisions that influenced culture. Second, we came to realize that the real cultural change we all sought had not been previously described. We believe that this is best described as a Just Culture, but using a broader interpretation of its meaning compared with how Reason initially described the term.[26] In this chapter, we explore what an expanded definition of Just Culture looks and feels like.

Making Changes

To commit to change requires us to admit that the status quo is no longer tenable. As described in Chapter 4, giving up on old ways of thinking and adopting "double-loop learning"[27,28] requires humility and the ability to undertake a different approach when making (important) decisions. Having the Region make substantial changes meant change had to start with the CEO.

And it did. When Jack freely admitted in front of many different groups that he had not had his eye as squarely on patient safety as he should have, his reasoning was straightforward and believable. Not having been a frontline care provider himself, he assumed that as long as the Region had highly trained, competent healthcare professionals, which he was convinced was the case, the Region's patients would be safe. Soon after the two deaths, Jack then admitted he had been wrong. His strategy was not enough. He also acknowledged that leading while sitting in a corporate office was not sufficient. The Region's leaders had to be visibly engaged with frontline providers and their managers. Jack vowed to change his perspective and to support changes in the way the Region actually functioned.

Underlying these concepts of leadership was the larger issue of how the Region had previously chosen to deal with tragedies. The Region had not listened to stakeholders. The Region also lacked a "safety imagination",[29,30] vitally necessary when reviewing information about hazards[31] and hazardous situations. Additionally, the Region had a deep-seated historical reluctance to share safety-related information, doing so sometimes internally, but rarely externally. Those were the old ways, and the Region made three major changes in its direction involving leaders' roles, transparency, and blame and accountability. These three changes were indispensable to moving the organization toward a state of readiness to work with and not just for patients and their families.

Having Leaders Actively Engaged

When organizational leaders, such as Jack and his executives, as well as the Board of Directors, made decisions, they either sent out statements about these decisions or let them speak for themselves. Senior, middle and frontline managers, healthcare providers, patients and their families, and the public consciously or unconsciously endeavored to learn what messages were being sent. Were the leaders' decisions congruent with what they said or had been saying? Most of us can recognize when leaders are true to their words. But should leaders become hypocritical or adopt veiled sincerity, then any progress toward improvements in a culture will be stifled if not destroyed.

Thus, when Jack and the Board Chair committed to learn from the potassium chloride tragedy, to conduct business differently, and to focus on a strategy for patient safety, many were watching to see if these statements were anything other than platitudes. Both individuals remained true to their words. The Board Chair built accountability for safety into the Board, with its members overseeing the Region's Patient Safety Task Group. Jack made investments in infrastructure. As described in Chapter 7, these were enormously important. Without changing the structure of the system, any changes in process, in how things are done, will be dependent on individuals hoping to remember a new way of doing things, all the while continuing to use workarounds that are still required by the old and flawed structure.

Jack also made investments of his own time. When asked, he attended the very first patient safety officer course that the Institute for Healthcare Improvement (IHI) offered in June 2004. At the time, WF was in the then-evolving role of the lead for patient safety in the Region and he had enrolled in the eight-day course. Applications for the course were only accepted if the organization's CEO committed to attending the last two days. Although Jack was not a big fan of conferences or multi-day commitments outside Calgary, he traveled to Cambridge, Massachusetts. There he met some of the world's top patient safety leadership change agents. These included Don Berwick, Jim Conway, Allan Frankel, Michael Leonard, and Julie Morath, to name just a few. That year, Jack would attend the IHI's National Forum. The following summer he hosted Berwick at a specially called meeting of Canadian Healthcare CEOs, held in Alberta's Rocky Mountains, learning and comparing notes on patient safety issues. In 2006, Jack joined a group of academics from the University of Calgary, including the Dean of the Faculty of Medicine and JMD, and presented a talk on the transformation of the Region at a multi-modal safety conference in Melbourne, Australia.[32]

Within the Region, Jack mandated that Safety Walk Rounds[33] were to be implemented across the Region, with all members of the Executive Management Team, operational VPs, and EMDs participating. He and the Region's other executives quite literally walked the talk, signaling the new attitude. Safety was everyone's concern, everyone's business. On one occasion, when visiting a nursing unit that was short of staff that day, Jack volunteered to make beds, if that would help until additional staff could arrive. The offer was not lost on the staff.

Executives, other senior leaders, and physician leaders were also heavily engaged, with some leaders taking training on specific aspects of safety and quality. When the Region finally acquired a course on disclosure, other leaders learned how to disclose harm to patients and families, and some even became instructors of these disclosure courses. Changes were made also to department and site leadership committees to incorporate patient safety into their terms of reference.

In their article on leadership for safety, Professor Rhona Flin, an Organizational Psychologist at the Industrial Psychology Research Centre, University of Aberdeen, and her recently qualified PhD student, Dr. Stephen Yule, described how leaders could "demonstrate their commitment to safety". Although Flin and Yule were describing senior managers, their criteria also apply to Jack and the Executive team. First on the list was "developing and providing resources for a comprehensive safety programme", which Jack had announced, funded, and ensured that it reported directly to him. "Concern for people" was evident from the day the executives had been informed of the deaths and the problems in the Central Pharmacy. While we have not given explicit examples of "encouraging participatory styles in middle managers and supervisors", the educational safety sessions included this aspect, as well as "being clear and consistent in their support for safety", which leaders from Jack down embraced. Jack, in particular, displayed "transformational behaviors",[34] as he frequently spoke about putting aside personal wishes, and doing things and making changes for the greater good, which are the essence of safety in healthcare.

Being Transparent with Patients, Families and Other Stakeholders

In 2004 the Region, like most healthcare organizations in Canada, did not have a good record of being transparent with the public it served or the patients it had treated when things did not go well. As previously mentioned, having struggled through previous Fatality Inquiries ordered by the province's Justice Minister and Solicitor General, the Region's image was seen by many as tarnished. When the Region decided to inform the public through the media about the two tragic deaths, the Board, the Executive, and Senior leaders knew the initial reception would be negative. They also knew that disclosing to the families in a forthright way could be challenging. They were correct on both points. However, those involved in the Region imagined a future where things would be done differently. Perhaps they also believed that this tragedy could be a catalyst to transform the Region to one of their imaginations.

Similarly, telling patient stories publicly at Halifax 5 was felt by some to be a big gamble. No Canadian healthcare CEO up to that point, and very few afterward, had demonstrated the courage to do so. However, Jack showed that working with patients and families who had endured tragedies of various magnitudes was not as frightening as many in healthcare believed. Such interactions need not be considered taboo. When channels of communication remain open, individuals not only listen with their ears but they hear with their hearts and minds, and everyone sees we are all working on a common goal to make things better for future patients. Our barriers start to fall away and we realize that the situation does not need to be *us versus them*.

The push for greater transparency with stakeholders had to address conversations with patients and families in general and specifically in situations where care had not gone according to plan and patients had suffered harm. As described above, in 2004, the Region and indeed few healthcare organizations in North America or elsewhere in the world had a disclosure policy or procedures for guiding these necessary conversations. This was uncomfortable territory. Most healthcare administrators, providers, and malpractice insurers still believed sharing information with patients and families was not good policy. Furthermore, apologies were out of the question as being too risky and inviting lawsuits.

When the Region's Patient Safety Task Group developed its disclosure policy and procedures, there was a long, challenging approval process. However, after a year of development and presentations to various committees and groups in the Region, the documents were presented to the Region's Executive Management Team. The Region's General Counsel attended the meeting and provided his opinion – against proceeding with implementing the disclosure policy. As he explained, philosophically he was not personally against the concept. However, as Legal Counsel he had been in discussion with the Region's insurer and their lawyers. His opinion was that they did not yet support it. As a result, he believed the insurer would likely refuse to pay any claims should it believe that voluntary disclosure had contributed to legal success for the patient. From a risk management perspective, the argument was compelling. But that argument would be successful only if the definition of risk management was limited to the Region's financial and legal interests, as it historically had been, in the Region and in many other organizations. After some further discussion, Jack again made a decision. He declared that the Executive would support the disclosure policy and not wait for their insurer to catch up with the times. As he later explained, "I have been waiting to get out from underneath the insurer and this may be the time and the reason to do it". This was a defining moment, when the Region's senior lawyer had *a* vote at the table, not *the* vote at the table. This decision was also, for those who were there, visible evidence of Jack's leadership and commitment to the safety and well-being of the Region's patients and families.

Shifting Attitudes About Blame and Accountability

As important as top leaders are for supporting and guiding changes in attitudes and the way that business is conducted, followership is equally if not more important. And this importance has not been as recognized as it should be.[35] Followership does not mean being the veritable yes-person all the time. Strong followers help leaders become better by appropriately challenging them when necessary, especially about interpretations of values and principles. The decision to be more transparent was shaped by people close to Jack to whom he listened, when the decision was made to hold the news conference about the two potassium-related deaths.

However, the more challenging decision for the Region to make, that initially exposed a strong difference of opinion, between some Regional Executives and followers, concerned the issue of accountability. When something tragic happens and the errant actions of one or more individuals appear tightly coupled with the outcome, then accountability is often seen as synonymous with punishment. Jack was quoted by a well-known newspaper columnist, two days after the news conference announcing the two deaths, that he was an "absolute believer in a very high level of accountability for those in healthcare".[36] And by accountability, Jack meant some form of discipline or punishment.

However, as we have previously recounted, several of the followers, who themselves were leaders of large clinical portfolios, had a fundamentally different opinion about accountability. In particular, the Vice-President in charge of the clinical portfolio overseeing all pharmacy services, put her job on the line. She was firmly against making a decision about the fate of the pharmacy technicians before the facts were fully explained as to what happened, how and why, through a proper investigation. When the facts were assembled and demonstrated that there were several error-provoking conditions in play, the focus shifted from disciplining these individuals to correcting the flawed system in which they worked. This was one of the examples that paved the way for approval of a Just and Trusting Culture policy some months later. Among other things, the policy acknowledged that the Region would not discipline healthcare workers, including physicians, for making errors – regardless of the patient's outcome. At the time the Region was thought to be unique among other healthcare organizations, in Canada or internationally, in adopting and following such a policy.

Just Culture: Broadly Speaking

In 1997, Reason provided a description of a Just Culture and justified why it was a fundamental part of a Safety Culture. He wrote that a Just Culture represented the feeling in an organization where workers were encouraged to provide essential safety-related information, and to do so willingly because there was trust. By this, we interpreted his meaning as the workers trusting they would not be punished for most actions taken, even if those actions contributed to an accident. Importantly though, he also said it would be "clear about where the line must be drawn between acceptable and unacceptable behaviour".[26]

In the aftermath of the tragic, potassium-related deaths in 2004, we agreed with Reason's philosophy and initiated work on defining the line. We started with a Just Culture policy that stated healthcare providers would not be punished for making errors. Our work since, and particularly over the last several years, has led to our belief that the concept of a Just Culture is broader than this. Indeed, it became increasingly obvious based on our experiences that the concept of Just Culture should be expanded so it encompasses all or most areas of patient safety about which we are passionate. However, we have also recognized the need to keep the concept focused.

To that end we have taken Reason's concept that related specifically to frontline workers and broadened it to include doing the right things for all those involved in an adverse event. We believe this expanded interpretation of a Just Culture is predicated on using a broader definition of just, as "consonant with principles of moral right or of equity; righteous; equitable; fair".[37] This more encompassing vision speaks to the fair, equitable, and morally right treatment of the people who work for and with the organization, and as well as the patients and their families who depend on it.

Culture as a concept is challenging to describe, let alone change or put into action. Our Just Culture recipe includes ingredients both for healthcare providers, and for patients and families. For healthcare providers the recipe includes knowing where the line has been drawn, a fair assessment of the decisions and actions that possibly contributed to an adverse event, and being provided with the necessary support in the aftermath of an adverse event, to allow for healing. For patients and family members, the ingredients include information, an apology, and support, all of which are required to meet their needs when an adverse event occurs. All these concepts have been discussed in previous chapters but we felt it important to show their connections under the banner of a broadened definition of Just Culture in healthcare. The final ingredient, paying attention to language, acknowledges the power that some patient safety terms have when misused and because, simply put, words matter.

Before we summarize these ingredients we would like to highlight three important points. First, this approach is not a panacea for patient safety. Rather, it is a piece of the larger concept of patient safety. We appreciate the start of any discussion of patient safety is recognition of our striving for the Hippocratic ideal of do no harm, which we interpret to include both physical and psychological harm. To support this interpretation requires us to include Reason's idea of an informed and learning organization. This type of organization responds appropriately to events and reports of harm, and also to close calls, errors, and noncompliant acts. The organization also routinely works proactively and pre-dictively, seeking to mitigate the probability of harm from hazards and hazard-ous situations as much as possible. Rather than not forgetting to be afraid, which was included in Reason's definition of a safety culture, and which could interfere with assessment, decision-making, and taking action, we suggest that everyone in the organization "value and encourage 'intelligent wariness'".[32] Second, achiev-ing a desired change in culture that is not paralleled with structural changes will have little effect. To quote Perrow's warning in this regard, "Changing the culture of an organization to correct its ways has become a mantra... where con-cerns with culture, rather than structure and power, dominate".[38]

Culture is the reflection of what people believe and think, how they behave, and why they act in certain ways, and each of these concepts is influenced in part by the individuals' structural environment where they work.[39] In essence, the structure (or form) of an organization enables and supports their thinking and actions. Indeed, Agnew and colleagues described that both management commitment and adequate staffing (structural issues) were "predictors" of "all safety outcome measures". Changing the structure, such as "addressing staff def-icits",[40] can also drive changes in process (or function). Third, both healthcare providers, and patients and families need to be treated with respect and require empathy when adverse events occur. This is the starting point for our view of a Just Culture.

Healthcare Providers

To do the morally right thing for healthcare providers means, first, they have been told about and understand the line distinguishing between acceptable and unacceptable actions before and not after an adverse event occurs. Having high-lighted why humans are prone to errors and the fact that outcomes of these actions are unintentional, errors clearly fall on the side of the line where disci-pline is not considered. Just as clearly, on the other side of the line are actions representing willful intent to harm or intent to act with blatant disregard for a high likelihood of a poor outcome. We would submit that the term 'blamewor-thy' be used only for these types of actions and, as such, discipline is expected. More challenging to assess are those actions characterized as noncompliant but with either structural problems in the system or group norms driving them, because there can be many different factors behind them.

Second, organizations striving for a Just Culture must commit to work-ers undergoing a fair assessment where the context and the system factors are considered. The only way system factors can be understood is to commit to a comprehensive, system-focused analysis using a methodology such as SSA. We also described how biases contribute to the flawed decision-making that under-lies not only many adverse events but also to unfair assessments of an individu-al's actions. Therefore, we believe part of an organization's commitment to their healthcare providers is that it will strive to understand, expose, and mitigate bias in the assessment of actions following the occurrence of an adverse event.

Third, an organization with a Just Culture supports its healthcare providers when they may have unwittingly contributed to an adverse event because pro-viders, like patients and families, can often be profoundly affected emotionally. The details of these supports were previously described but we emphasize that it is important to provide the opportunity to recover and heal. We also recognize that in some cases, healthcare leaders can be deeply affected by a serious adverse event and therefore will need and benefit from similar types of support. Such was the case in the Region where the Pharmacy Technicians, as well as several leaders, were very distressed by the two potassium-related patient deaths. Along these lines, in the spirit of helping providers and leaders to heal following an adverse event, an organization should do everything it can to avoid blaming people. Blame should not be part of an organization's day-to-day lexicon because of how it adds to the negativity of the situation, undermining what is actually required, and that is compassion.

Patients and Families

First and understandably, patients and families have a great need to understand what happened, as well as how and why it happened. Provision of this informa-tion, referred to as disclosure, should be based on a complete understanding of the system's breakdowns after a thorough analysis using SSA or another system-based method, rather than using a person-focused approach. Gathering and analyzing this information takes time, so the expectations of patients and fami-lies should be understood and effectively managed. The system-focused analysis is also important for developing a plan or set of recommendations for system improvement to reduce the likelihood other patients will be similarly harmed in the future. It is important to share this with the patient and their family, as most of them want to see that something positive comes out of their negative experience. Second, patients and families need and deserve an appropriate apol-ogy. The apology should address not only regret and remorse for the harm suf-fered, but also specifically acknowledge the system deficiencies, including errors and noncompliant actions that contributed to the patients' harm. The disclosure conversation(s) and the apology will be more effective and meaningful if patients and families experienced an empathetic connection with the healthcare provid-ers and leaders who were involved with the events that lead to harm.

Establishing this type of connection requires these individual(s) to have skill-fully used empathetic listening to develop understanding. Empathy provides the foundation for demonstrating respect for patients and families, as does offering them support. Like healthcare providers, patients and families often need sup-port to help them cope with the aftermath of the adverse event. This may or may not include financial support or compensation.

Language

Culture is influenced by what words are used, how they are used and understood or misused and misunderstood. We have already highlighted why blame is a particularly loaded term and is best avoided. We have also discussed 'medical error'. Although ubiquitous in the medical literature and among providers, the term is rarely used by patients and members of the public. In fact, the concept of 'medical error' refers to what providers did or did not do and is therefore not oriented toward patients. Additionally, the idea that 'medical error' *causes* (or even equals) patients' harm is counterproductive. Errors represent things done or not done, that is, they are actions or inactions. The tasks undertaken in medicine or in healthcare in general, such as preparing medications and making decisions, are no different to preparations and decisions made at home. Nor do errors rep-resent the outcome of the actions for the patient. This is where the confusion lies – in automatically linking specific erroneous actions to outcomes, and with that, sometimes dreadful outcomes for patients. In actuality, the link between actions and outcomes is seldom clear in healthcare. We must put error[41] – and not 'medical error' – into the proper context of human nature, human factors science, system models, and what is known about complex adaptive systems.

One other term is that of "unsafe acts". The term was first used by Sidney Williams in the 1930s when he was writing about automobile accidents.[42] The description was increasingly employed from the 1950s onward but became more well-known after being taken up by Reason. In 1990, he described three types of "unsafe acts" – errors, violations, and sabotage – and also sometimes referred to them as "active failures".[43] Understanding these three types of actions, and how they differ, is very important in the context of Just Culture, specifically in the assessment of individuals. However, if we were to use a term then we prefer the term "safety significant acts" as proposed by David McNair, an aviation accident investigator at the Transportation Safety Board of Canada, because of the inher-ent hindsight bias in the term 'unsafe'. As McNair explained, some of the actions to which "unsafe acts" has been applied in accident investigation were actually those considered "normal or expected". Additionally, not all actions contribute to a negative outcome and some "positive safety acts" might have reduced the "consequences of an occurrence".[44]

We must all understand the language used in healthcare and its influence, and be careful with our words and the terms we use. This is particularly important in the conversations we have with patients and families when a patient has suffered harm. Importantly, we need to ensure the words used in healthcare do not contribute further to harm. We can do this by changing what we teach in healthcare classrooms, as well as use in our patients' rooms and in hallways. Doing so will increase the probability of our consciously moving past blame to a mindset of inquiry and compassion.

Using this expanded concept of Just Culture and applying it to how healthcare providers as well as patients are treated, we hope will make healthcare better for everyone. This includes patients and families, healthcare providers, and administrators and leaders of healthcare organizations – if we focus on healing in every sense of the word. Healing is only possible when we act with compassion, expressing our concerns for others' sufferings and being empathetic. All might require time to recover from the event. But after that interval, having everyone working together to make care safer, in the name of the patients, the families, and the providers, can be healing for everyone involved.

Thus, in synthesizing this broad discussion of Just Culture we propose the following expanded yet concise definition of the term. "For those receiving and providing healthcare, a Just Culture has a clearly defined line between acceptable and unacceptable actions, and fosters an atmosphere of trust, respect, and fairness, requires information sharing, and promotes support and healing, especially when someone is harmed".

Just Culture: Future Direction

We have made the point that the Just Culture needs to address issues that affect both healthcare providers and patients so opportunities for healing can be realized. We have also stressed that the focus of the attention after most adverse events should not be about blame. Still, there will be cases where, after a proper investigation and taking into account biases, the conclusion will be reached that one or more healthcare providers did cross the line and discipline is indicated.

In these situations, but where there was not willful intent to harm, the final piece of the Just Culture should be restorative, rather than retributive, justice. Such an approach also supports the goal of healing. For this to manifest though, healthcare organizations and regulators need to be in agreement. There is little comfort to healthcare professionals if the organization, for which they work or with whom they have an appointment, follows one assessment philosophy while their professional regulator takes a different approach. One of the ways to help healthcare providers start to heal psychologically is to be able to assure them of the alignment of assessment approaches between organizations and regulators. This requires a commitment to cooperation that, unfortunately, is uncommon in most jurisdictions. Organizations and regulators that are able to do this are to be saluted, as this cooperation is a critical part of the quest for a Just Culture, and therefore a safety culture. With such a commitment to cooperation, these organizations could also then work together to codevelop and institute restorative justice.

An Opportunity Not Lost

One option the Region had for managing the two deaths would have been simply to fix the labeling and storage of concentrated potassium chloride, as well as the process for compounding dialysis solutions in the Region's Central Pharmacy, and stop there. This would have taken a few days or weeks at most and someone could have let the families know the problems had been fixed and that this issue would likely never happen again. Odds are, they probably would have been right. Perhaps the technicians involved could have been warned to be more careful and then disciplined, or even dismissed. Political masters would have been reassured, the media need not have been involved and the Region could have returned to the everyday business of delivering healthcare.

However, several leaders in the Region recognized that breakdowns like this were not as isolated as they wanted to believe they were. Interestingly, a short Editorial piece in one of the local newspapers in March on Day 7 had questioned "if the system [was] vulnerable to mishaps, in the way a poorly designed on-ramp encourages road accidents?"[45] The Region did indeed have many Vulnerable System Syndrome characteristics, and there was a growing consensus among the leaders that the response to this tragedy, and for the safety of patients in general, had to be addressed in a different way.

Doing things differently would not have been possible without the willingness of the Executive, led by Jack, to alter their attitudes and thinking about how to respond to tragedy. The Clinical Operational Executives, Vice-Presidents, and their dyad partners – the Executive Medical Directors – were instrumental in this evolution. Executives are accountable to a Board of Directors and therefore it was telling that the Board, and in particular the Board Chair, supported this transformational change. Both the Region's Board Chair and its CEO, supported by the Minister of Health and Wellness, held a steady hand on the Region's direction. Their actions as leaders allowed the lessons learned to be translated into organizational change, which in turn, made healing possible for many of the players in this story. And in thinking about these individuals, as well as others who led at lower levels in the Region, we are reminded of the words of Walter Lippmann a Pulitzer Prize–winning journalist. We have paraphrased what he said about Franklin D. Roosevelt, thinking it a fitting description. "The final test of leaders is that they leave behind them in others the conviction and the will to carry on".[46]

Another leader, who could speak of the necessity of organizational transformation, came from outside the Region. In 2005, at Halifax 5 held in Calgary that year, Jim Conway was one of the speakers. At the time he was a Senior Fellow at the Institute for Healthcare Improvement (IHI), and he gave an interview about what he had learned when he was the former COO of the Dana Farber Cancer Institute (DFCI) in Boston. Conway had helped steer the DFCI through its own tragic event in 1994, when two patients were mistakenly given a four-fold overdose of chemotherapy. One patient, Betsy Lehman, was the healthcare columnist for the Boston Globe and the mother of three small children. Her death was as shocking and tragic as the death of the two Calgary patients were to the Region. Based on his experience in helping to change the culture of an iconic institution, Conway said this about healthcare tragedies. "The fact that we in our organizations have suffering, harm, death, tragedy, near misses – there is nothing about that, that discriminates us from any other hospital in the country or the world. Those events happen everywhere. What absolutely will discriminate us is those organizations who have the ability to take the suffering, the tragedy, the harm and the misery, and use those, in the name of the patient and the family and the staff, as extraordinary levers to take an organization to a very different place. The organizations that do that are absolutely discriminating themselves from most other organizations and they should be applauded".[47]

This profound statement highlights an important lesson from the Region's potassium chloride story. We owe our patients, their families, and those healthcare providers involved, a promise that we will not lose the valuable lessons learned. Nor will we forget those who suffered. Remembering helps to recreate losses into something positive. Emotionally, it would have been easier not to recount the same story over and over again – but that would have allowed the story to have been forgotten. Healthcare systems, as Conway said, would do well to remember their patients' stories and to continue to tell them.[32,48] These stories can also help other organizations, so they can learn how to deal with their specific problems and to change their practices. Furthermore, an organization's people must understand why they are constantly changing things. The answer to that is to get better, to get safer. It is for this very reason that it was important to the three of us to tell this story.

Our story is now over but the journey has not ended. We hope those who wish to do things differently – more safely, better, and in a kinder way, will find some of what we have described to be helpful. We also hope that together we will all be able to work in and receive care from a healthcare system in which these principles, of being truly just and fair to all, are part of the system's organizational and regulatory DNA, reflecting our values, beliefs, our wishes. We think these are the right things to do and the right way to do them.

References

1. Ward J, Mark M. Mar not interested in looking for blame. *The Calgary Sun*. 2004 Mar 19;5.
2. Toneguzzi M. Stop health-care blame game. *Calgary Herald*. 2004 Mar 27;A1 (col. 1) & A16 (col. 2).
3. Farbstein K, Clough J. Improving medication safety across a multihospital system. *Jt Comm J Qual Improv*. 2001 Mar;27(3):123–37.
4. Toneguzzi M. Fatal flaws admitted, human errors, system blamed for drug mix-up. *Calgary Herald: City & Region*. 2004 Jun 30;B1 (col. 6) & B3 (col. 1).
5. Braid D. Incompetence of pharmacy staff clear. *Calgary Herald*. 2004 Jun 30;B1 (col. 2)–B2 (col. 5).
6. Richards G. The Robson report on deadly drug mix-up, Family praises pharmacy mea culpa. *Calgary Herald: City & Region*. 2004 Jun 30;B2 (col. 1).
7. Richards G. Pharmacy too lax, says relative. *Calgary Herald: City & Region*. 2004 Jul 1;B1 (col. 5) & B4 (col. 1).
8. Lang M. Medical mix-up, Inquiry unnecessary: CHR boss Davis says fatal errors already investigated. *Calgary Herald: City & Region*. 2005 Oct 21;B1 (col. 1).
9. Lang M. New deaths revealed under Calgary Health Region care, Teen's grieving family wants answers. *Calgary Herald*. 2005 Oct 22;A1 (col. 1)–A6 (col. 1).
10. Knapp S. Treatment errors, hospital safety relies on openness, officials vow to learn from mistakes. *Calgary Herald: City & Region*. 2005 Oct 23;A11 (col. 5).
11. Johnson B, Abraham M, Conway J, Simmons L, Sodomka P, Schlucter J, et al. Partnering with patients and families to design a patient and family centered health care system: recommendations and promising practices. Chapter 9. Partnerships within Quality Improvement and Patient Safety Organizations. Page 116. 2008. Institute for Family-Centered Care 7900 Wisconsin Avenue, Suite 405 Bethesda, MD 20814 and in collaboration with Institute for Healthcare Improvement 20 University Road, 7th Floor Cambridge, MA 02138. Bethesda, MD; Apr.
12. Baker G, MacIntosh-Murray A, Porcellato C, Dionne L, Stelmacovich K, Born K. Learning from High-Performing Systems: Quality by Design. In: *Chapter 1 in High Performing Healthcare Systems: Delivering Quality by Design*. Toronto: Longwoods Publishing; 2008. pp. 11–26. [cited 2022 Feb 9]. Available from: https://www.longwoods.com/content/20133/books+/chapter-1-introduction.-learning-from-high-performing-systems-quality-by-design
13. Baker G, MacIntosh-Murray A, Porcellato C, Dionne L, Stelmacovich K, Born K. Learning from high-performing systems: Quality by design. Chapter 7: Calgary Health Region – Calgary, Alberta. In: *High-Performing Systems: Quality by Design*. Toronto: Longwoods Publishing; 2008. pp. 221–44. [cited 2022 Feb 9]. Available from: https://www.longwoods.com/content/20150/books+/chapter-7-calgary-health-region-calgary-alberta

14. Government of Alberta. Government launches aggressive action plan to make public health system more efficient and ensure equitable access to services. New model for health authority governance within two months. News Release. Alberta; 2008.
15. Government of Alberta. One provincial board to govern Alberta's health system. News Release; 2008 May.
16. Markusoff J, Mclean A. Tories create health superboard. Stelmach plan will see single body rule nine regions. *Edmonton J.* 2008 May 16: A1–A2.
17. Picard A. Regionalization: A step back for Alberta Healthcare? Alberta Health Services Board: New Governance Model' centralization. *The Globe and Mail.* 2008 May 22;L5. https://www.theglobeandmail.com/life/health-and-fitness/centralization-a-step-back-for-alberta-health-care/article719842/
18. Toneguzzi M. Ward of the future opens at Foothills. *Calgary Herald: City & Region.* 2004 May 1;B6 (col. 4).
19. W21C Research and Innovation Centre. W21C, Our Story [Internet]. W21C. [cited 2022 Feb 9]. Available from: https://www.w21c.org/about/
20. Davis J. Message from Jack Davis. Former CEO, Calgary Health Region. 2008 May 16.
21. Lang M. Top health bosses face axe. *Calgary Herald: City & Region.* 2008 Jun 21;B1 (col. 1)–B4 (col. 1).
22. Lang M. Eight health bosses sacked, Two CHR officials appointed to senior posts. *Calgary Herald: Top City News.* 2008 Jul 9;A3 (col. 1).
23. Lang M, Braid D. Health bosses face axe today. *Calgary Herald.* 2008 Jul 8;A1 (col. 5).
24. Braid D. Health boss "encouraged" firing. *Calgary Herald: Top News.* 2008 Jul 8;A5 (col. 1).
25. Deal T, Kennedy A. *Organization Cultures: The Rites and Rituals of Organization Life.* Reading: Addison Wesley; 1982.
26. Reason J. *Managing the Risks of Organizational Accidents.* Aldershot: Ashgate Publisher; 1997.
27. Argyris C, Schön D. *Theory in Practice. Increasing Professional Effectiveness.* San Francisco: Jossey-Bass; 1974.
28. Argyris C, Schön D. *Organizational Learning: A Theory of Action Perspective.* Reading: Addison Wesley; 1978.
29. Ramsden J. Shall safety be improved? *Flight International.* 1984 Nov 17:1328–31.
30. Pidgeon N, O'Leary M. Man-made disasters: Why technology and organizations (sometimes) fail. *Saf Sci.* 2000 Feb;34(1–3):15–30.
31. Pidgeon N, O'Leary M. Organizational safety culture: Implications for aviation practice. In: Johnston N, McDonald N, Fuller R, editors. *Aviation Psychology in Practice.* Aldershot: Ashgate Publishing Ltd; 1997:21–43.
32. Davis J, Davies J, Flemons W. The Calgary health region: Transforming the management of safety. In: Anca J, editor. *Multimodal Safety Management and Human Factors: Cross the Borders of Medical, Aviation, Road and Rail Industries.* Aldershot: Ashgate; 2007. pp. 31–40.
33. Frankel A, Graydon-Baker E, Neppl C, Simmonds T, Gustafson M, Gandhi TK. Patient Safety Leadership WalkRounds™. *Jt Comm J Qual Saf.* 2003 Jan;29(1):16–26.

34. Flin R, Yule S. Leadership for safety: Industrial experience. *Qual Saf Health Care.* 2004 Dec 1;13(suppl_2).
35. Oc B, Bashshur MR. Followership, leadership and social influence. *Leadersh Q.* 2013 Dec;24(6):919–34.
36. Braid D. Pharmacy staff to answer for deaths. Health region boss Jack Davis vows those responsible will be held accountable. *Calgary Herald: Exclusive.* 2004 Mar 21;A1 (col. 1).
37. *OED Online.* Just, adj [Internet]. Oxford: Oxford University Press; 2021 [cited 2022 Feb 9]. Available from: https://www.oed.com/
38. Perrow C. *The Next Catastrophe.* Princeton: Princeton University Press; 2007.
39. Donabedian A. Evaluating the quality of medical care. Part 2. *Milbank Mem Fund Q.* 1966 Dec;44(3(suppl)):166–206.
40. Agnew C, Flin R, Mearns K. Patient safety climate and worker safety behaviours in acute hospitals in Scotland. *J Safety Res.* 2013 Jun;45:95–101.
41. Read GJ, Shorrock S, Walker GH, Salmon PM. State of science: Evolving perspectives on 'human error'. *Ergonomics.* 2021 Sep 2;64(9):1091–114.
42. Williams S. The causes of automobile accidents. *Am Bar Assoc Sect Insur Neglig Compens Law Proc.* 1935:55–9.
43. Reason J. *Human Error.* Cambridge: Cambridge University Press; 1990.
44. McNair D. Unsafe or safety-significant acts? In: Anca Jr J, editor. *Multimodal Safety Management and Human Factors: Crossing the Borders of Medical, Aviation, Road and Rail Industries.* Aldershot: Ashgate Publisher; 2007:17–30.
45. Keep it arm's-length. *Calgary Herald: Opinion.* 2004 Mar 25;A18 (col. 1).
46. Lippman W. Roosevelt has gone. *New York Herald Tribune.* 1945 Apr 14.
47. Conway J. Personal communication (Video interview at Halifax 5). *Canada: The Fifth Canadian Healthcare Safety Symposium*; 2005.
48. Musson D, Helmreich R. Team training and resource management in health care: Current Issues and future directions. *Harvard Heath Policy.* 2004;5(1):25–35.

Afterword 1

Jack Davis MSc
Former CEO and President, Calgary Health Region

The nearly two decades, which have gone by since the tragic events related to the deaths of two patients under the care of the Calgary Health Region in 2004, have not dulled the memory of my experience and what I learned from these events, both in the immediate aftermath and over the next few years.

Before I became the CEO and President of the Region, I was the Deputy Minister for Alberta's (then-named) Department of Health. Before the deaths, what I knew from my experience in government and in running a health authority was that a major challenge for all of those working in healthcare and for patients and their families is there are many risks involved in delivering care. Many of the interventions available in healthcare come with the possibility of significant harm to our patients. Safety must be an integral part of every healthcare system!

When a tragedy occurs, there is usually a search for an explanation and, in almost all cases, the explanation helps families achieve closure. When the explanation turns from deaths related to natural causes to those contributed to by the actions of the healthcare providers, such as their errors, and by factors and deficiencies in the rest of the system, the tragedy can escalate into a crisis of confidence. This crisis often focuses on the healthcare providers, sometimes on the larger healthcare system, and occasionally on the people in positions of authority leading and managing the system. Add to this the fact that healthcare is always under close scrutiny by the media, tragic events often lead to front-page stories calling for extreme measures to be taken to punish those who are responsible.

These crises can escalate quickly and there is no time to hesitate. But the actions taken cannot be impulsive. Leaders need to find and strike a balance between maintaining public confidence while ensuring demonstrations of corrective action and accountability. Transparency is essential.

Most importantly, patients and families are owed a demonstration that the healthcare system in question takes full responsibility for the factors contributing to the tragedy. In 2004, we were very fortunate the families involved were not asking for the healthcare providers to be fired or for criminal investigations. The families wanted the Region to accept responsibility and get on with initiating corrective actions of the problems in the system. They wanted the comfort of knowing the deaths of their loved ones would not be in vain and that the Region would ensure that no one else died in similar circumstances in the future.

I also knew that in the midst of a crisis it is important to seek advice from capable and trusted individuals. While being pressured and also while considering taking punitive action against those involved, the advice I received was not to act too quickly and to take the time to properly assess the situation. We could have moved more quickly but we were choosing to do the right things for the right reasons. We not only investigated the event on our own but we engaged a qualified and independent group to review the entire situation. We made it clear to the media the event would be truly independently reviewed and that there would be a full and transparent report released to the public on the day it became available to the Region.

I also received exceptional advice about leadership, culture change, and system improvement strategies from the Region's patient safety team. As an organization, the Region had not been targeting specific investments in leadership or resources for improving safety for its patients. What emerged as we worked through our review processes was the realization there was a weakness in the organizational culture in the Region. At worst, this culture reflected the fear our providers and staff had in safety reporting and talking about errors and processes they believed needed to be improved. This problem started at the top of the organization where patient safety was not prioritized to the extent necessary. Clearly, accountability for this rested squarely with me as the CEO.

The impact of the tragedy focused me on giving patient safety the highest of priorities. This meant making a fundamental shift in what we did and how we did things – a shift in our safety culture. We needed to move to a *just and trusting culture*, where bringing forward errors and recommendations for how to improve anything in the system was highly valued.

Changing culture is always a challenge. In this case though, patient safety was so embedded in the values of our healthcare providers and everyone else working in the Region that when they saw the refocused leadership at the Executive level, there was enthusiasm and energy for doing what needed to be done. We made changes that many individuals in the organization, as well as patients and families, were heavily involved in. Everybody had a part.

I reorganized our Executive and allocated significant resources to patient safety. We worked with other similarly affected families, our providers and staff, and all others who wanted to take on the challenge of improving patient safety.

The Region became involved with national and international efforts dealing with similar patient safety issues. We realized that we were not alone in pursuing the highest standards and outcomes possible for our patients. You don't want these events, but if they happen, it allows an organization's leadership to see their true values and beliefs and how aligned they are as a group.

Looking back, if I could coach myself in the CEO role back in 2004 with what I learned subsequently it would be this:

1. Know your principles and follow them. You don't have to make it really complicated. Do the right thing and other things fall into place.
2. Trust must be established long before the crisis happens. But trust works both ways: I have to trust and I have to be trusted.
3. You don't have the luxury of pausing to ponder for long – move quickly, but thoughtfully, with the advice of the people you trust. Once you make a decision to act – then act. Leaders need to be seen making decisions.
4. You can't let the lawyers call all the shots. They have *an* opinion, not *the* opinion.
5. There will always be those who think badly of you. And if this is expressed in the media, check tomorrow. Media moves on quickly to cover the next bad thing.
6. And always do your best to look after the needs of the patients and families.

Afterword 2

Deborah E Prowse QC

I'm Deb Prowse and I am Kathleen Prowse's youngest daughter. Mum's story could have ended as just another statistic of patient safety – but for the commitment of many people who were dedicated to promoting and supporting what was known as the safety culture. For approximately a year after Mum died, I was occupied winding up her estate and every task I undertook reminded me of the loss our family had suffered and my anger toward the healthcare system that had killed her.

The year following Mum's death, Calgary was the host site of a Public Forum as part of the Halifax Series of Safety Symposia, named after the city where the series was started in 2001. Jack Davis, the Calgary Health Region's CEO, agreed to make families' stories of harm the focus of the Public Forum. He had made the commitment after Mum died to listen to patients' and families' stories and now he wanted to fulfill that commitment by ensuring the stories would be told publicly. Just a few months before the conference was to start, I was contacted and asked if I wanted to participate. Unfortunately, the invitation came when I was at a very angry stage in my grief and I had little trust in the healthcare system at that time.

Upon receiving the invitation, I sought out the guidance of one of my wise friends, an executive coach. She was very busy and the only time she could see me was at one of her son's basketball games. I jumped at the chance to talk with her. We sat in a hallway of a school one evening and she asked me one of the hardest questions I had ever been asked. She said, "What do you want your message to be?" I was dumbstruck. Over the next hour we mapped out what was truly important to me, finding a way to honor my Mum's death by helping others so they would not have to go through a similar situation. It was easy to land on this message as Mum had raised me with the saying, "If you are tired, discouraged, or sick, do something for somebody quick". And I needed to do something. From the moment we had this conversation, I felt empowered to make the decisions about what I really wanted and that anger would not serve me – ever. So, when I was invited to at least attend the Public Forum, I agreed. And attending that was truly life changing for me.

The woman who was my Health Region liaison arranged that I would go to the Public Forum in the company of her husband. She later became a friend, confidante, supporter, and advocate for me. (I have always maintained that her husband was there to make sure I didn't hurt anyone, given the anger I had been feeling.) At the Public Forum I listened, sometimes painfully, sometimes tearfully, to the stories of people who were just like me, others who had suffered harm or who were survivors of patients who had not lived through their healthcare experience. I was oddly comforted by knowing I was not alone. At the end of the evening, at the reception, Jack Davis was speaking with Jim Conway, Executive Vice President and Chief Operating Officer of the Dana-Farber Cancer Institute (DFCI) in Boston. Jim had come up to Calgary to attend the Safety Symposium and I heard him say, "So now that you have listened to the stories, what are you going to do with all of these patients and family members?" Jack thoughtfully responded, "We are going to bring them together into a safety council and keep listening". I felt an incredible fluttering in my heart because I knew I was going to be part of that next step.

Within months, I volunteered to be a founding member of the Calgary Health Region Patient Family Safety Council. We did not come together to wallow in our stories. We all came with a wish to make changes in the healthcare system so the circumstances that brought us together did not happen again, so the failures to rescue, the delayed or wrong diagnoses, the medication close calls, and the falls and subsequent cover-ups would not happen again. While there was initial trepidation and distrust that we would actually be allowed to make a difference, we were an incredibly supported and empowered group. We had the support of the CEO and the Vice-President and COO. There were system champions among us to open the doors for us in a system that was not really ready to welcome the Patient Family presence and our voices. I think we underestimated, or never really considered, the fear we were all experiencing as we started to work together on patient safety issues.

Within another year we were being invited to participate as partners with the Canadian Patient Safety Institute (CPSI) at the next international Halifax Series Symposium, with speakers such as Sir Liam Donaldson from the WHO. I don't think anyone at that time was prepared, in any trauma-informed way, for how difficult it was going to be, to bring dozens of people together who had suffered harm and were at differing stages of grief and anger. This was a very difficult experience, but I think the Calgary group left there feeling absolutely committed to continuing to reach out – beyond all borders – to promote our new tag line of "Every patient safe"/"La sécurité pour tous les patients". This statement became the vision of Patients for Patients Safety Canada, the national group we formed in partnership with the CPSI.

I continued to look for events to which I could take the stories I was hearing and to use them to get the attention of the policy makers and decision makers to make a difference related to patient safety. The last group of which I was a founding member was our provincial group at the Health Quality Council of Alberta, where I co-chaired the Patient/Family Safety Advisory Panel. Through this work, I was invited to sit at many tables of discussion and policy determination, and one of the things I heard repeated so often was that having patients involved in the discussions changed things for the better.

In 2009, as a result of my profile in advocacy and the networked connections I had made, I was invited to co-chair the Minister's Advisory Council on Health. I was honored to be able to travel around Alberta and hear the stories of Albertans about their healthcare experiences. This work lasted almost two years and resulted in the introduction of a new Alberta Health Act. It became very clear to me during this time that the patient's perspective of their health care experience was a crucial factor in patient safety and also needed to be captured for quality improvement. Later, when I was selected to be the first, permanent Health Advocate for the province, my primary focus was to gather information from patients and family members and ensure we were listening for every opportunity to learn, and then take the learning to where it could be used in making changes. All my staff were mediation-trained, so we took a very restorative approach to the stories of complaints and concerns we heard and we constantly shared the learning from everything we heard.

I have told my Mum's story many, many times over the last seventeen years, sometimes to small local groups and sometimes to larger national and international groups. I would become very excited and exhilarated each time I received an invitation to speak or to participate by sharing her story or any of the hundreds I have heard since 2004. But my bucket list dream invitation was to speak at an ISQua (International Society for Quality in Health Care) conference, where I felt there would be an audience that had a global commitment to patient safety and quality improvement. This dream came true in July 2021. I spoke about the disclosure process after harm and the need for patients and family members to hear the acknowledgment that something bad had happened, the genuine apology for what happened and the harm done, and the actions to ensure it did not happen again. These things are what I have heard hundreds of patients and family members beg and cry for and demand over the years I have been listening to stories. These are the things we need – to move from harm to healing.

After Mum died, the family had several meetings with 'the suits' of the organization. But for me there was something, or perhaps more importantly, someone missing from these conversations and that was those individuals who were most involved in what had happened to Mum. About two years after Mum died, the Region's Liaison for our council, the same woman who had invited and protected me when I attended the Halifax Forum, opened the door for me to meet the Director of the Central Pharmacy where the dialysate mix-up had been made. We met one afternoon in a nondescript room, and sat and cried together for hours. We realized that both of us had been on a journey of grief, shame, and fear. But, we had been kept apart from each other by a healthcare system that did not yet understand the importance of a restorative approach to healing after harm. Bringing us together made healing so much easier.

The Director and I spent several years speaking publicly together about each of our perspectives of living through what had happened, and we drew strength from each other as we spoke about moving from harm to healing together. I was so privileged to have been able to work with him up until his death a few years ago. And I was even more privileged to work on presenting the message of "We are in this together when adverse events occur". Two years after I met the Director, at the end of an emotional presentation to a group of leaders and providers in the Calgary Health Region, I looked up and there stood a woman crying in front of me. I immediately apologized for making her cry. She apologized – for being the pharmacy technician who made the dialysate of potassium chloride instead of sodium chloride. We held each other for a long time and then the Director facilitated another meeting where I could meet her in a different setting, together with her husband. This was an incredibly moving meeting, which I'm hopeful helped her as much as it did me in moving forwards.

I recently read a book on the final stage of grief being "finding meaning" and everything I have done over the last seventeen years, in being a patient safety advocate, made sense. I might have started out to make myself feel better. Since that start, though, my driving force has been to minimize the possibility of others having to go through adverse events without the support they deserve. We all deserve and need a system that values the people who work in it and the patients and family members who depend on it. To me, this is what a Just Culture represents and supports.

Index

Printed in the United States
by Baker & Taylor Publisher Services